OXFORD POLITICAL THEORY

Series editors: Will Kymlicka, David Miller, and Alan Ryan

THE CIVIC MINIMUM

OXFORD POLITICAL THEORY

Oxford Political Theory presents the best new work in contemporary political theory. It is intended to be broad in scope, including original contributions to political philosophy, and also work in applied political theory. The series contains works of outstanding quality with no restriction as to approach or subject matter.

THE CIVIC MINIMUM

ON THE RIGHTS AND OBLIGATIONS OF ECONOMIC CITIZENSHIP

STUART WHITE

OXFORD

UNIVERSITY PRESS

OXFORD
UNIVERSITY PRESS

Great Clarendon Street, Oxford OX2 6DP

Oxford University Press is a department of the University of Oxford.
It furthers the University's objective of excellence in research, scholarship,
and education by publishing worldwide in

Oxford New York

Auckland Bangkok Buenos Aires Cape Town Chennai
Dar es Salaam Delhi Hong Kong Istanbul Karachi Kolkata
Kuala Lumpur Madrid Melbourne Mexico City Mumbai Nairobi
São Paulo Shanghai Taipei Tokyo Toronto

Oxford is a registered trade mark of Oxford University Press
in the UK and in certain other countries

Published in the United States
by Oxford University Press Inc., New York

British Library Cataloguing in Publication Data

Data available

Library of Congress Cataloging in Publication Data
White, Stuart, 1966-
The civic minimum : an essay on the rights and obligations of economic citizenship / Stuart White
p. cm. – (Oxford political theory)
Includes bibliographical references and index.
1. Distributive justice. 2. Public welfare. 3. Democracy. 4. Economic policy. I. Title. II. Series.
HB523 .W48 2002   330–dc21   2002067175
ISBN 0-19-829505-7

1 3 5 7 9 10 8 6 4 2

Typeset by Newgen Imaging Systems (P) Ltd, Chennai, India
Printed in Great Britain
on acid-free paper by
T.J. International Ltd., Padstow, Cornwall

PREFACE AND ACKNOWLEDGEMENTS

What are the proper distributive goals of the state in the economic sphere? Do citizens have certain rights that derive from, or which constrain the pursuit of, these goals? What responsibilities do citizens have to make productive contributions to their society? To what extent may and should the state enforce these responsibilities? These are the questions I explore in this volume. I outline and defend a conception of economic justice: justice as fair reciprocity. I offer an account of the concrete rights and responsibilities that I think necessary to meet the most urgent demands of justice, so understood—an account of what I term the civic minimum. And I argue that the civic minimum represents a feasible, though demanding, prospect for reform in the circumstances of (at least some) contemporary, advanced capitalist societies. On the substance of economic justice and the civic minimum, I will say more in the chapters below. Here I would like to take the opportunity to make more explicit some of the background concerns and aims that underlie the volume, and to give thanks to the many colleagues and (other) friends who have helped me in the course of its writing.

One underlying concern of the volume, which I discuss further below, is to try to bring political philosophy closer to contemporary political debate. I do not think that all political philosophy should be done with an eye to immediate political relevance. It certainly should not be distorted by concerns of immediate political feasibility, for there is no obvious reason for thinking that what is truly just will be politically feasible (now, or perhaps ever). But it is important to explore how political philosophy can inform contemporary political debate, to consider what light it can shed on policy controversies that may be animating political life. Historically, much political philosophy, even that which does not advertise its contextual relevance, has in fact been written in this spirit. In recent years, however, there has been a tendency for political practice and political philosophy to drift apart. This tendency is a general one, but is perhaps particularly acute on the left of politics. Responding to the perceived intellectual crisis of socialism and social democracy, some political philosophers have given deep consideration in recent years to the underlying aims of egalitarian politics. Politicians, responding to the electoral defeats of the left in the 1980s, have engaged in their own reconsideration of aims and values, as well as of policy commitments. From the standpoint of the philosophers, the efforts of the politicians often seem opportunistic, lacking coherence and integrity. From the standpoint of the politicians, the efforts of the philosophers often seem utopian, or at least far removed from urgent policy questions and the imperatives of winning elections. At its worst, the latter attitude leads to a rejection of political philosophy. It is seen as a feature of an era of ideology that has now been superseded by a purely pragmatic, managerial politics. But inattention to political philosophy has only led, as one commentator has put it, to an 'acute debasement of the language of political debate'.[1]

Political philosophers have now begun to address the gap between theory and practice. Some of them (one thinks, to cite just a few examples, of Bruce Ackerman and Anne Alstott, Philippe Van Parijs, the 'Real Utopias' project organized by Erik Olin Wright, and the 'New Democracy Forum' organized by the *Boston Review*) have outlined concrete proposals for reform that present or future governments of the left might take up, while explaining how these proposals serve the values that the philosophers have worked to elucidate. This book also tries to address this gap. Taking the practice of some notionally left governments as a starting point, in particular their shift towards 'workfare' and contractualist forms of welfare provision, it tries to show how core egalitarian values might be brought to bear in the evaluation of this practice, and how practice will likely have to be modified and, in certain respects, radicalized, to respect these values.

A second underlying concern of this book, in many ways the flip side of the first, is to bring policy evaluation closer to political philosophy. If we go back to the turn of the last century in Britain, it is noticeable how much debate over the emergence of the welfare state was informed and driven by arguments within political philosophy. While the technical side of policy analysis was relatively undeveloped, it was widely acknowledged that one could not discuss welfare policy, or tax policy, without outlining one's underlying philosophy of citizenship and, therefore, one's understanding of what makes for a just state. The debate was, as Jane Lewis puts it, 'imbued with moral purpose' (a purpose frequently linked with the cultivation of an ideal type of character).[2] Even at the time of the Beveridge report in the 1940s, policy discussion and advocacy still went hand in hand with the effort to outline a supporting philosophy of citizenship. Beveridge clearly believed that he had to make sense of what he was proposing in terms of such a philosophy, and that his civic philosophy would properly set limits on the kind of policies he could propose. In the post-war period, however, policy analysis became increasingly free of explicit attention to, or detailed analysis of, normative issues. Arguments 'became more technical, economistic, and administrative'.[3] Of course, all policy evaluation has to rest on some normative assumptions, and in this respect is always at least implicitly committed to a philosophy of citizenship and a theory of justice. But, in Britain, there appears to have been for many years an underlying consensus on normative issues, at least among the main body of professional students of social policy, and this allowed policy evaluation to proceed without a return to the explicit discussion of citizenship, of rights and duties, that characterized the respective eras of T. H. Green, Leonard Hobhouse, and even William Beveridge. As I explain in Chapter 1, the rise and partial success of the New Right in the past two decades, combined with important social and economic changes, has made it impossible to sustain this indifference to underlying philosophies of citizenship and theories of justice. Hayek, Nozick, Friedman, and their circles of supporters have put basic normative questions about the role of the state in the economy back on the table. Contemporary economic and social pressures—post-industrialism, demographic change, the maturation of historic welfare commitments, the liberalization of labour markets, increased inequality (the list could go on)—increase their urgency and salience. There is, in consequence, a need for students of social policy to re-engage with political philosophy, and for those sympathetic to a broadly social democratic model of society to rediscover the tradition of philosophically grounded policy argumentation that we find in writers such as Leonard Hobhouse.

This brings me to a third, and perhaps more implicit, underlying concern of the volume. This is to bring closer together two eras and bodies of work in egalitarian political theory. One era, largely pre-war, is represented by Hobhouse and his associate J. A. Hobson, and by later democratic socialist thinkers such as R. H. Tawney. The second era starts in 1971 with the publication of John Rawls's *A Theory of Justice* and continues to this day. Rawls's work has stimulated a huge and deeply reflective literature on the subject of economic justice, in particular on the level and kind of equality that justice requires. The two eras and bodies of work are not wholly unconnected. Rawls explicitly refers, albeit briefly, to Tawney's work in *Theory*. And, as I explain briefly in Chapter 1, the functionalist theory of justice developed by Hobson and Hobhouse roughly anticipates Rawls's famous 'difference principle'. But thinkers like Hobson, Hobhouse, and Tawney are not often directly alluded to in contemporary political theory. One aim of this book is to try to connect the two eras of sustained reflection on justice and equality, to explore how we might learn from, and integrate, the best from both bodies of work into our own substantive thinking about economic justice and citizenship. There is, to be sure, much that is unsatisfactory about the thinking of the earlier era. But it may help us get a handle on some issues that are raised, but not much addressed, by the contemporary literature. Rawls, for example, is explicit that those who enjoy a share of income and wealth at or above the minimum available under the difference principle should make a minimum productive contribution to the community in return. But he only begins to sketch out a conception of what would constitute an appropriate, reciprocal productive contribution. Thinkers such as Hobson and Hobhouse published a lot more on this issue, and so may have something to add to a contemporary effort to address this topic.

In writing this book I have accumulated a very large number of debts of gratitude. My first thanks go to Amy Gutmann and Alan Ryan who supervised my dissertation at Princeton University. This book is not that dissertation, but this book would not exist without it, and I am very grateful to Amy and Alan for sagely guiding those first efforts to pull my thoughts together. I should have listened to more of their advice. I must thank Amy a second time, along with Brian Barry, David Miller, and Andrew Williams, for reading an earlier draft of the entire book and for providing me with excellent comments. I am not sure I have risen to the challenge of all of their comments, but the book would certainly be a lot poorer without the stimulus they provided. A number of people have supplied written comments on material I have used for particular sections of the book and/or have engaged me over the past few years in a sustained, ongoing conversation about its themes, and I would also like to thank them. They include Selina Chen, G. A. Cohen, Joshua Cohen, Jurgen De Wispelaere, Cécile Fabre, Susan Giaimo, George Kateb, Christopher Lake, William Leblanc, Meira Levinson, Lawrence Mead, Marc Stears, Steven Teles, Peter Vallentyne, Philippe Van Parijs, Frank Vandenbroucke, Robert van der Veen, Gijs van Donselaar, and Albert Weale. Diana Gardner helped me clarify ideas through many discussions of the book, and gave me a lot of encouragement to stick at it, for which I am very grateful. Additional thanks to Josh Cohen who, as head of the Political Science Department at Massachusetts Institute of Technology, enabled me to take a reduced teaching load for one term when I needed to focus on writing, and who, along with many other members of that Department, helped to make my time at M. I. T. a supportive and stimulating one. Much initial work for the book was done while I held a Prize Research Fellowship a Nuffield College, and I would like to thank Nuffield collectively for its support, and David Miller in particular for his interest in the project. Thanks also to Bruce Ackerman, Daniel Attas, Clancy Bailey, Lawrie Balfour, Sammy Basu, Linda Bazarian, Dario Castiglione, Matthew Clayton, Judy Failer, Michael Freeden, Jeremy Goldman, Bob Goodin, Lock Groot, David Halpern, Kyle Hudson, Matthew Humphrey, Bill Jordan, Desmond King, Elizabeth Kiss, Jeroen Knijff, Daniel Kryder, Eugenia Low, Pratap Mehta, Donald Moon, Carey Oppenheim, Alan Patten, Thomas Pogge, Andy Sabl, Debra Satz, Jason Scorza, Ian Shapiro, Amrit Singh, Adam Swift, Eugene Torisky Jr., Ramon Vela, Steven Warner, Ralph Wedgewood, Martin Wilkinson, Jonathan Wolff, Stewart Wood, Erik Olin Wright, Loretta Yin, Amos Zehavi, Ross Zucker, Perri 6, and an anonymous reader for Oxford University Press – all of whom (of those I recall) contributed to the evolution of the book at some point, in some way, through helpful comments and well-targeted questions. Dominic Byatt has been a wonderfully patient and supportive editor, and I would like to thank him, Amanda Watkins, and Gwendolen Booth at Oxford University Press for their efforts. Thanks to Diane, Gordon and Samantha, my parents and sister, for their love and support throughout. Final and joyful personal thanks are to Katherine Wedell: for asking me the right questions, stilling the tempest, and infusing me with her revivifying love.

I would also like to thank Cambridge University Press for permission to use material from the following articles in writing this book:

White, S., 'Social Rights and the Social Contract: Political Theory and the New Welfare Politics', *British Journal of Political Science* 30 (3): 507–32, 2000.

White, S., The Egalitarian Earnings Subsidy Scheme', *British Journal of Political Science* 29 (4): 601–22, 1999.

Stuart White
Oxford
August 2002

CONTENTS

CHAPTER 1

Introduction: The Politics of Economic Citizenship

Paine's Questions

> The present state of civilization is as odious as it is unjust.... The contrast of affluence and wretchedness continually meeting and offending the eye, is like dead and living bodies chained together.
>
> Take New York City.... some zip codes have average incomes higher than any other place in the United States, perhaps the world. Yet New York also has the greatest number of welfare recipients per capita in the country. Some of the world's richest and poorest people live within a few short city blocks of each other.

The first of these two quotations is from Tom Paine.[1] Paine penned these words in the winter of 1795–6, at the beginning of the democratic era. He wrote in response to a fierce debate in post-revolutionary France about the nature of economic citizenship. The revolution propounded the values of liberty, equality, and fraternity. But the revolutionaries continued to disagree about what these values implied for their society's economic arrangements. What, in the name of liberty, equality, and fraternity, do the 'rights of man' (and woman) add up to in the context of the economy? The second of these two quotations, which strikingly echoes the one from Paine, is from a recent study of wealth distribution in the United States.[2] Although material inequalities have narrowed since Paine's day, this study confirms that the 'contrast of affluence and wretchedness' of which Paine spoke is still very much a feature of contemporary capitalism. And so too are the questions which this contrast prompts. Does an economic system which generates such contrasts really live up to values like liberty, equality, or fraternity, values that are widely thought to be central to the modern democratic project? Ought we to restructure the terms of economic cooperation better to realize one or more of these values? Can we better realize one of the values without sacrificing the others? If so, how? These questions prompt us to consider, as Paine did, just what are the fundamental rights and obligations of economic citizenship.

The nature of these rights and obligations is the subject of this volume. In Part I (Chapters 2–5) I consider in more detail the values that properly inform debate over the nature of these rights and obligations. I might be said to offer an elaboration of liberty, equality, and fraternity, and of how these values fit together into a theory of justice. In Part II (Chapters 6–8) I explore the institutional and policy implications of the theory of justice presented in Part I. I use the theory to evaluate the merits of alternative proposals that feature in contemporary social policy discussions, including 'workfare', unconditional basic income, and proposals for 'asset-based welfare'. Through a critical evaluation of these proposals, based on the theory of justice developed in Part I, I try to develop an account of what I call the civic minimum: the concrete rights and obligations of economic citizenship, embodied in specific institutions and policies, necessary to make a market economy acceptably (though not absolutely) just. In Chapter 9 I summarize the policy agenda suggested by the discussion in Part II, and briefly consider how this agenda might yet find purchase in the contemporary politics of economic citizenship; how political theory might yet constructively connect with political practice.

For this book has been shaped, in no small part, as an engaged response to a contemporary, ongoing political struggle over the terms of economic citizenship. My aim, in this first chapter, is to clarify the aim and motivation of the book by explaining the nature and situation of this struggle. Section 1.1 briefly sets out the political and socioeconomic background to the emergence of this struggle. As I explain there, it is very much a struggle between competing ideas; at its centre there lies an intense and urgent debate between competing philosophies of economic citizenship. In Section 1.2 I therefore outline the philosophies of economic citizenship that presently confront each other in this debate, and I identify the key issues over which their advocates disagree. This sets the stage for Section 1.3, in which I explain, albeit in a very preliminary and schematic way, how the philosophy of economic citizenship to be developed in this volume differs in its approach to these issues from other, perhaps more familiar philosophies.

1.1   *The Emergence of the Debate: The Crisis of Welfare Capitalism*

In Britain, and in many other advanced capitalist countries, the Second World War was followed by a fundamental restructuring of the relationship between state and society. The state accepted a commitment to maintain full employment and to provide reasonably generous and universal protection against contingencies such as unemployment, ill health, and old age. In an important lecture in 1949 the sociologist T. H. Marshall argued that the British people had acquired, or were in the process of acquiring, a new set of 'social rights': rights in relation to health care, education, housing, and decent levels of income.[3] Marshall argued that these rights of 'social citizenship' would mitigate and balance the class inequalities reproduced in the marketplace. According to Marshall, their emergence represented a distinct stage in the development of modern citizenship, preceded by the universalization of civil and political rights. Social rights would complement these more traditional rights, increasing their effectiveness. In due course welfare capitalism became the norm across the advanced capitalist countries, though with much, and important, institutional variation.[4] Writing in the 1970s, Ralf Dahrendorf felt able to speak of a 'revolution in life chances' that the welfare state, harnessed to a steadily growing, full-employment economy, had achieved for millions of people in the advanced capitalist countries during the post-war years.[5] Though social analysts of the 1960s located alarming pockets of residual poverty in these countries,[6] one could be forgiven for thinking that, within these fortunate countries at least, the 'contrast between affluence and wretchedness' of which Paine spoke was on its way to becoming a thing of the past.

Dahrendorf was writing, however, at a time when economic growth in these countries had slowed, distributional conflict had intensified, and the post-war welfare capitalist settlement was consequently under severe strain.[7] In some of the nations of so-called Anglo-Saxon capitalism, such as Britain and the United States, politicians came to office at the end of this decade who explicitly repudiated the post-war philosophy of welfare capitalism. In government they sought, often with great controversy, to restore social order and economic growth by ending the commitment to full employment in favour of price stability, and by making concerted efforts to reduce public spending in general and welfare spending in particular.[8] By the early 1990s some commentators began to speak in terms which suggested that Dahrendorf's 'revolution in life chances' had stalled and, for many millions of citizens across the advanced capitalist world, gone into reverse.

Four developments in particular caught the eye of the critics. First, they pointed to statistics that seemed to indicate a substantial increase in inequality of earnings, income, and wealth. In Britain the Gini coefficient for incomes, which economists standardly use as a measure of inequality, rose by almost 10 percentage points between 1979 and 1993, from 0.25 to 0.34, an unprecedented rate of change. While the share of income (before housing costs) of the lowest-income decile fell from 4.1 per cent to 2.9 per cent in the decade up to the early 1990s, the share of the richest decile, which had been stable at around 21 per cent since the early 1960s, rose sharply to 26.2 per cent.[9] Inequality in expenditure did not increase by as much as inequality in income; but it too increased, suggesting that the observed rise in income inequality in part reflected increased inequality of lifetime incomes, and not just increased volatility in people's incomes over time.[10] The United States also experienced a rise in income inequality over this period, the Gini coefficient creeping steadily up by an average of more than 0.2 percentage points a year between 1974 and 1992.[11] A major contributor to widening income inequality in both countries during the 1980s was widening earnings inequality, as shifts in relative labour demand attributable to technological changes and trade competition pulled up the wages of the skilled and pulled down those of the unskilled.[12] In Britain the real wage rates of those in the bottom decile of male earnings were actually lower in 1992 than in 1975.[13] In the United States, even more dramatically, the real hourly earnings of less educated workers fell by 20 per cent between 1979 and 1989.[14] Widening income inequality was also accompanied by widening inequality of wealth. The Gini coefficient for inequality of financial wealth stood at 0.92 in 1992 as compared with 0.88 in 1962. In 1983 the richest 1 per cent of US households collectively owned 33.8 per cent of total net worth, while the bottom 40 per cent owned 0.9 per cent; in 1993 the corresponding figures were 37.2 per cent and 0.2 per cent.[15] In Britain the distribution of wealth was more stable during the 1980s, though there was a problem of indebtedness among low-income households.[16]

Against the background of increasing inequality, the critics pointed, secondly, to an increase in poverty rates. There is disagreement among poverty specialists as to how to specify the poverty threshold, but many in Britain take the proportion of households with incomes (equivalized for household composition) below half the national average as one relevant measure of the poverty rate. Between 1979 and 1993/4, as the background level of income inequality rose, the proportion of the British population living below this threshold increased from 8 per cent to 19 per cent. The number of people living at or below the minimum level of income which is supposed to be provided by the social security system also increased.[17] In the United States, the official poverty rate rose from 11.7 per cent in 1979 to almost 15 per cent in 1992.[18] Other indicators, such as statistics on homelessness, pointed to growing problems of absolute deprivation. Roughly eight people in a thousand were homeless in Britain in the early 1990s, with the number of homeless growing at an estimated rate of 16 per cent per year between 1989 and 1994.[19]

Thirdly, critics pointed to increases in, and persistently high levels of, unemployment and non-employment.[20] Growth in income inequality and poverty over this period was less pronounced in continental European countries than in Britain (and, in most cases, than in the USA).[21] But many of these countries experienced high levels of un/non-employment and a severe problem of long-term unemployment. Across the European Union (EU) as a whole, the unemployment rate rose from an average level of around 3 per cent in the early 1970s to an average of over 10 per cent in the early 1990s. Nearly one-half of those unemployed in the EU at this time, moreover, had been unemployed for over one year.[22] Not that problems of unemployment were confined to continental welfare capitalisms. In Britain the male unemployment rate rose from 5.1 per cent in 1979 to 9.4 per cent in 1991, averaging about 8.5 per cent in the 1980s.[23] Moreover, the official unemployment figures increasingly understated a problem of non-employment among certain social groups, such as men in late middle age and single parents. The United States had a lower unemployment rate than the EU average in the early 1990s, but, again, this statistic obscured the true level of inactivity among the working-age population.

The fourth concern of the critics concerned the overall effect of these developments on the prospects and quality of life of certain sub-communities. A word from a supposedly bygone age, the 'underclass', acquired a new vogue as commentators struggled to come to terms with the consequences of geographically concentrated economic disadvantage coalescing in many cities.[24] The sociologist William Julius Wilson, while critiquing conventional theories that the urban poor have a distinctive 'culture of poverty', argued that the concentration of joblessness in these areas, and the related, growing isolation of these communities, facilitated the spread within these communities of antisocial or self-destructive behaviours.[25] In Britain the term 'social exclusion' was increasingly fastened on to refer to the problem posed by this mix of economic disadvantage, social isolation, and dysfunctional behaviour.[26]

These developments challenged Marshall's vision of the good society as a society of inclusive social citizenship, in which generous social rights work to substantially mitigate market inequality. This was all the more striking given that Marshall's original, hugely influential essay on social citizenship contained a strong dose of what one might call social democratic teleology: social citizenship was understood, at least by many of Marshall's later interpreters, as a destination towards which democratic industrial societies would naturally tend to evolve. But if as these developments imply, history is not necessarily on the side of social citizenship, then this has profound implications for the kind of analysis and advocacy that supporters of social citizenship engage in. They will have to explain why history *ought* to go in their preferred direction. To this end, technical policy analysis, important as it is, will not suffice. Social democrats are confronted with the need to make a case, in ethical terms, for a system of generous social rights. Meanwhile, the libertarian or near-libertarian critics of social democracy, whose voices sounded so anachronistic in the 1950s and 1960s, can take heart from the fact that history is apparently not necessarily set against them. Their ethical and efficiency-based critiques of social democracy have connected, in a rough-and-ready way, with electorates at points in the recent past. Why not again? As the teleological assumptions underpinning Marshall's analysis have lost credibility, normative philosophical debate over the justice and content of social rights has become correspondingly more important.

Of course, in the past the problems of welfare capitalism might have increased the credibility of those arguing for a complete revolutionary break with capitalism. But Marxist teleology is no less discredited today than that of the social democratic kind. And the traditional model of socialism, based on public ownership of the bulk of the means of production and central planning, has little to recommend it.[27] For socialists, the relevant question now is how to make a market economy work in a way that is consistent with the historic egalitarian aims of socialism. In order to get a handle on this question, socialist theoreticians have had to consider more closely the character of these ambitions, i.e. have had to think more systematically about the values that animate their vision of the good society. In addition, they have had to pay much closer attention than in the past to questions of institutional design. The orthodox Marxist vision of socialism as a wholly distinct economic system to capitalism, destined to emerge because of its superior efficiency, has given way to a conception of socialism that has more in common with Eduard Bernstein's revisionism: socialism as a process of ongoing, institutional modification to capitalism, aimed at a progressive reduction in class inequalities, and explicitly grounded in a theory of social justice.[28] Marxists, and post-Marxists, are therefore also increasingly drawn into normative debate over the rights and obligations of economic citizenship.[29]

This debate is not likely to wane any time soon. There are too many pressures at work on the economies and welfare states of the advanced capitalist countries to allow it to do so. One frequently cited supposed source of pressures is that associated with the increased internationalization of economic activity, or 'globalization'. Recent years have indeed seen a steady expansion in international trade,[30] and a prodigious growth in international capital flows.[31] However, the significance of these developments for taxation, public spending, and systems of social rights is frequently misunderstood (a point to which I shall return in Chapter 9). Probably more important for the future of social rights are pressures that are largely internal to national welfare states, and somewhat independent of globalization.[32] These include: deindustrialization, the continuing shift from a manufacturing- to a service-based, 'post-industrial' economy;[33] demographic change, in particular the process of population ageing;[34] and the costly maturation of many existing welfare programmes, introduced in the 1950s and 1960s to meet problems which were salient then but which are sometimes poorly calibrated to contemporary needs.[35]

Moreover, the problems of inequality, poverty, un/non-employment, and social exclusion referred to above have by no means disappeared in the last few years. In some countries, such as Germany, high levels of economic inactivity remain an urgent problem, particularly in view of population ageing. In Britain income inequality continues to hover around the level to which it rose during the 1980s.[36] By the usual measure (proportion of the population with incomes, before housing costs, below half the national average), the poverty rate actually seems to have increased during the 1990s, rising to no less than 25 per cent of the population in 1998/9.[37] In the United States, the official poverty rate fell during the 1990s.[38] But child poverty rates remain high in absolute terms.[39] Employment growth was steady over the decade, but the pattern of growth reinforced polarization in the labour market: growth in both high- and low-quality jobs contributed substantially to the overall employment expansion, but there was relatively little expansion in jobs of intermediate quality.[40] There continued to be a significant pay divide between workers with and without higher education.[41] And wealth inequality continued to increase. By 1995 almost 50 per cent of financial wealth (net worth minus owner-occupied housing) in the United States was owned by the richest 1 per cent of the population; the poorest 80 per cent collectively owned less than 10 per cent of this wealth.[42] Critics of so-called 'Euro-sclerosis' point to the inactivity levels and strains on welfare spending in countries like Germany to justify the adoption of more market-oriented, US-style institutions. But this raises the question of whether it is possible to get the benefits of these institutions without the costs in terms of inequality.

1.2   *Three Philosophies of Economic Citizenship*

The contemporary debate over economic citizenship is heavily value-laden, animated not only by conflicting interests, but by competing philosophies of economic citizenship. What are these philosophies? What do they identify as the key issues in thinking about economic citizenship? And how do they differ in their response to these issues? It is possible, I think, to identify three broad philosophies that presently shape the debate. I shall refer to these philosophies here as libertarianism, communitarianism, and real libertarianism. In identifying these philosophies as shapers of the debate, my eye is most immediately on the British case. But I think similar philosophical perspectives frame the debate in the United States and, to some extent, in continental Europe. Needless to say, my characterization of these philosophies here is somewhat impressionistic, and one that certainly does not capture much of the detail and nuance of particular thinkers whose work I see as representative of these philosophies. So this characterization should be regarded only as a preliminary one, intended to bring out the basic positions in the debate and the most important points on which they disagree. I will go into greater depth with respect to specific key authors at later points in this volume.

1.2.1   *Libertarianism and the New Right*

According to the first of these three philosophies, Marshallian social citizenship is intrinsically undesirable. This is the view we find expressed by theorists of the 'New Right', whose ideas guided and inspired governments in Britain, the United States, and elsewhere, in the 1980s. As an intellectual movement, the New Right contains a number of currents, but all of these currents share a conception of the good society as based on the institutions of private property, the free-market economy, and a limited but strong state: limited in that its functions are narrowly confined to the definition and protection of private property rights; strong in that it must have the capacity to carry out these limited functions effectively. What the state may not do is step beyond these functions in order to pursue goals of economic equality, e.g. through the redistribution of income and wealth. Such action is variously condemned in the literature of the New Right as destructive of individual liberty; as violating the claims of distributive justice; and as undermining economic efficiency and/or diminishing overall social utility.[43] The job of good government, therefore, is to liberate citizens from the iniquitous and disabling burden of bogus social rights by cutting welfare commitments, lowering taxes, and reining in various other forms of government intervention in the economy. In this way, it is claimed, we can move closer to a truly free, just, and economically dynamic society.

This ambition finds its clearest, least compromising expression in the work of libertarian thinkers, and the libertarian position is perhaps most impressively developed in Robert Nozick's influential book *Anarchy, State, and Utopia*.[44] Nozick's libertarianism is grounded in his 'entitlement theory' of justice. Nozick argues that, morally speaking, each of us is, in the first instance, the morally rightful, exclusive owner of our own body and abilities (the principle of self-ownership). In a world where external resources have not yet been allocated between different owners, Nozick holds that individuals may freely use their self-owned powers to privatize unowned parts of the external world. A given act of privatization is justified, Nozick claims, provided it does not leave any person worse off than she would be in a world where all external resources remain unowned (the principle of justice in acquisition).[45] Members of later generations may find no unowned external resources left to appropriate. But this is not objectionable, in Nozick's view, if their welfare prospects in the society into which they are born are no worse than they would be had all external resources remained unowned. Individuals are then entitled to whatever they produce with their initial resource entitlements and/or acquire through the free exchange of such products and initial entitlements. And every subsequent distribution of 'holdings' is just provided it emerges from a prior just distribution in a manner that is itself just, i.e. involving no force or fraud (the principle of justice in transfer). In principle, then, a free-market capitalist economy, in which the state is confined to the nightwatchman function of securing public order, results in a perfectly just distribution of income and wealth.[46] Efforts to maintain equality or a pattern of distribution according to some criterion of merit or equality will, Nozick argues, ride roughshod over the free choices that individuals make as to how to deploy their resources. Nor may one try to reconcile freedom with equality via redistributive taxation. Such taxation violates the property rights of some people in order to advance the welfare of others. But treating people in this instrumental way, as if, as Nozick puts it, they are 'mere means' instead of 'ends', is to fail to respect the inviolability they have in virtue of their dignity as human beings.[47]

Other libertarians, such as Charles Murray, present efficiency-based and utilitarian arguments against the redistributive state.[48] Redistribution damages the incentive to work hard, or to be entrepreneurial, and this, in turn, reduces aggregate social utility. Indeed, by cushioning those with low earnings, redistribution will tend to undermine their motivation to do what they can to improve their lot, thus moulding their character in the direction of a degrading 'dependency' on the rest of society. As a result, the supposed beneficiaries of redistributive policies may well end up worse off than they would be in the absence of such policies.[49] With aggregate social utility depressed, and the supposed beneficiaries of redistribution damaged in this way, redistribution threatens to make everybody worse off than they would be under a libertarian dispensation.

The libertarian position is admittedly very radical, and other currents within the New Right, drawing on the work of Friedrich Hayek and Milton Friedman, more readily accept a role for the state as provider of a 'safety net'.[50] But provision of this safety net is not seen as a demand of social justice. In Friedman's view, for example, state provision of this safety net is justified as a way of overcoming coordination and assurance problems among philanthropists.[51] It is emphatically not a way of acknowledging supposed 'social rights'. Friedman tells us that 'if the objective is to alleviate poverty, we should have a program directed at helping the poor', i.e. employ means-testing. He adds that 'so far as possible the program should . . . not distort the market or impede its functioning'.[52] This implies low benefits and/or punitive eligibility conditions.[53] The model of the safety net which emerges is much more akin to that of the Victorian Poor Law than to the expansive welfare state of the post-war, Marshallian kind.

Libertarian and near-libertarian theory has been subject to considerable, and quite powerful, criticism in recent years, and I shall take note of some of this criticism in the course of this book.[54] Nevertheless, the centre of intellectual gravity on the political right in Britain and the United States is probably even closer to these New Right perspectives at the beginning of this century than it was when conservative politicians such as Margaret Thatcher and Ronald Reagan began to articulate their disagreement with post-war welfare capitalism in the 1970s. And these ideas may also be finding new support in countries like Germany, where some now advocate the dismantling of the German model of 'Rhineland capitalism' in favour of a more Anglo-American, free-market form of capitalism.

1.2.2   *Communitarianism and the New Centre-Left*

However, while libertarian and near-libertarian perspectives on economic citizenship remain influential, they do not go uncontested, and they certainly do not command clear majority support even in relatively 'liberal' (i.e. free-market) capitalist societies like Britain and the United States. In no small part this is because many citizens in these countries continue to find substantial economic inequality and 'social exclusion' morally unacceptable, and because the ideas of the New Right are also widely seen as being partly responsible for these phenomena (or at least as offering no adequate response to them).[55] We have witnessed a growing concern about 'social cohesion' and a renewed sense of the need for an activist, interventionist government to secure this cohesion in the face of market forces. In the course of the 1990s electorates across the advanced capitalist world frequently rejected parties oriented to the New Right in favour of governments drawn from political parties on the traditional left and centre. Many of these governments, including Britain's so-called 'New Labour' government, came to power pledged to halt and reverse the problem of social exclusion allegedly produced by the policies inspired by the New Right in the 1980s.

Associated with the revival of these parties of the left and centre (or 'centre-left' as they are now often called) is the emergence of a second philosophy of economic citizenship, a philosophy that I shall here call, for want of a better term, communitarianism.[56] I call this philosophy communitarian because if there is a central organizing idea or value in the rather inchoate body of thought I have in mind, it is perhaps that of 'community', often associated with cognate ideas of 'social cohesion' and 'social inclusion'. Economic citizenship cannot, on this communitarian view, be collapsed into the market; the very point of economic citizenship is to embed the market, to constrain its processes and outcomes, so that society remains cohesive and inclusive—remains a community.

What do the goals of cohesion and inclusivity demand at the policy level? In contrast to the libertarians, communitarian thinkers associated with the new centre-left argue that the state has a responsibility to ensure that all citizens have genuine access to a wide range of basic goods such as education, training, health care, and a decent minimum of income. This is essential to put a floor under rising economic inequality and, relatedly, to prevent the evil of social exclusion (as defined above). The state need not necessarily provide all of these goods itself, but it should certainly act to ensure that each citizen has ready access to them. However, having accepted that the state has this set of responsibilities, questions can now arise as to the appropriate terms on which individual citizens ought to enjoy access to these basic goods. A key claim advanced by communitarian thinkers is that the individual citizen who stands in potential receipt of these goods also has a set of responsibilities parallel to those of the state. Moreover, across a wide range of cases, the state may, and should, condition eligibility for the goods on the individual's performance of (or demonstrated willingness to perform) these responsibilities. The dominant metaphor for capturing this idea is that of the *welfare contract*: social rights are one side of a contract between citizen and state on the other side of which stand certain responsibilities; these are centrally related to work, and the citizen must perform them as a condition of enjoying the benefits secured by these rights. In the 1980s such ideas were largely the property of a section of the self-styled 'civic conservative' wing of the political right.[57] But in the 1990s, beginning perhaps with Bill Clinton's presidential election campaign in 1992, politicians of the new centre-left have increasingly sounded contractualist themes in their efforts to build firmer electoral coalitions in support of the welfare state. Thus, in the British case, the rhetoric of 'balancing rights and responsibilities' became central to the 1994 report of the Commission on Social Justice (established under the auspices of the then opposition Labour Party). And, in due course, this rhetoric has become central to the policy documents and literature of the Labour Party. As the Labour Party leader, Tony Blair, put it, writing before the election of 1997, 'the rights we enjoy [must] reflect the duties we owe'.[58] Nor did this way of conceptualizing and describing welfare disappear following the 1997 election. In the words of the British government's 1998 Green Paper *New Ambitions for our Country: A New Contract for Welfare*: 'At the heart of the modern welfare state will be a new contract between the citizen and the government, based on responsibilities and rights.'[59]

In the United States, this emphasis on balancing rights and responsibilities in social policy has found support at the theoretical level in the writings of 'New Paternalists' like Lawrence Mead[60] and associates of the Communitarian Network such as Amitai Etzioni and William Galston.[61] These writers have also had some influence in Britain, and similar themes have been explored in writings by the Labour MP (and ex-Minister for Welfare Reform) Frank Field and by the sociologist Anthony Giddens.[62] In France the theme is developed in the work of the influential social theorist Pierre Rosanvallon.[63] While there are differences between these writers, they mostly subscribe to the contractualist view that the state should provide the benefits of the welfare state as a quasi-contractual return for responsible behaviour. Making eligibility for unemployment benefits more tightly conditional on work-related activity, such as active job search, is perhaps the most familiar expression of the contractualist view. But contractualism can express itself in other ways, e.g. in proposals to make parents' welfare benefits conditional on preventing truancy by their children; or to make welfare recipients seek treatment for drug addiction; or to make young single mothers move into supervised housing as a condition of assistance.[64]

So community, the building of a cohesive and inclusive society, is taken to require universal access to a range of basic goods and, at the same time, the enforcement of various civic responsibilities, particularly in the case of those receiving some form of special assistance from the state. Is communitarianism, then, an egalitarian philosophy? In his classic work *Equality* the British social democratic thinker R. H. Tawney argued that inequality in income and wealth is justified only to the extent that it is necessary to bring forth productive functions for the common good.[65] In holding that inequality must be of benefit to all, Tawney anticipates John Rawls, who argues in his hugely influential *A Theory of Justice* that economic inequality is justifiable only to the extent that it benefits the group that is worst off under this inequality: the so-called difference principle.[66] In defending this principle, Rawls argues that the differential market earnings derived from the application of unequal endowments of natural ability are not intrinsically deserved (and, therefore, are not intrinsically just). Nobody deserves their position in the distribution of natural ability, Rawls asserts, and to allow natural ability endowments a privileged place in determining citizens' access to 'primary goods' like income and wealth would be to make citizens' life chances differ on the basis of something which is fundamentally 'arbitrary from a moral perspective'.[67] In Britain Rawls's theory was initially received enthusiastically by some influential social democratic politicians and thinkers as improving upon the articulation of egalitarianism contained in the canonical writings of thinkers like Tawney.[68]

Contemporary communitarian thinking on economic citizenship, however, is not egalitarian in Tawney's or Rawls's sense. In the British case, an early intimation of a shift away from this type of egalitarianism was provided by one of the interim reports of the aforementioned Commission on Social Justice, *The Justice Gap*.[69] This report, which attempted to set out the conception of economic justice that would underpin the Commission's policy deliberations, explicitly rejected Rawls's theory in favour of an eclectic view of economic justice. The Commission held, for example, that the more naturally gifted are inherently 'deserving' of, or 'entitled' to, at least some of the differential reward that they are able to obtain through application of their distinctive talents in the marketplace.[70] More recently the political theorist John Gray has argued that the new centre-left should accommodate itself to what he sees as an emerging 'liberal consensus' in British society, a consensus that eschews the 'old social democratic view' of equality in favour of a commitment to bring all citizens within reach of a minimally decent level of lifetime opportunity and needs satisfaction. Gray associates this perspective 'not [with] the egalitarian liberalism of Rawls, but the New Liberalism advocated in Britain by L. T. Hobhouse, T. H. Green, and John Maynard Keynes in the early decades of this century'.[71] Subject to this floor constraint, which, according to Gray, 'need not [involve] more than very moderately progressive' taxation, meritocracy should reign. The communitarian view, now so prevalent on the centre-left, finds no better expression, I think, than in the following passage from the writings of the young Winston Churchill: 'We want to draw a line below which we will not allow persons to live and labour, yet above which they may compete with all the strength of their manhood. We want to have free competition upwards; we decline to allow free competition to run downwards.'[72]

To be clear, the communitarian view, echoed in much literature of the new centre-left, is that there are not only limits of feasibility or efficiency in regard to how far market-based inequalities should be reduced, but also as a matter of fundamental moral principle.[73] It is immoral, on this view, to require the advantaged to solidarize with the less fortunate beyond provision of a basic, universal floor of welfare and opportunity for all.[74] Of course, if the floor is set high enough, then in practice there may not be that much difference with an egalitarian like Rawls or Tawney. But how is the level of the floor to be determined? Many critics worry that contemporary communitarian thinking is too influenced, at the level of principle, by what is thought to be politically feasible in the relatively short run:[75] that the tendency is to take the level of acceptable taxation of the advantaged as the given—and, moreover, as being relatively close to the level of taxation inherited from past, non/anti-egalitarian governments—and then to work back from this given to a view about what kind of floor of welfare and opportunity the state ought to provide. The worry is that politics is driving the formulation of communitarian theory, rather than theory being developed on its own terms and then used to guide political action.

1.2.3 *Real Libertarianism and the Radical Left*

Welfare contractualism, championed by communitarian theorists, is highly controversial. It is rejected by many on the left who see in the steady shift to welfare contractualism a fundamental reorientation of the welfare state away from the broadly emancipatory purposes supported, as they see it, by the philosophy of social citizenship articulated by T. H. Marshall, towards an older and less admirable conception of welfare: welfare as an instrument for the maintenance of social order in the context of highly unequal society.[76] What welfare contractualism represents, on this view, is merely the revival of the spirit of the Victorian Poor Law: welfare that polices the poor, in the interests of an exploiting class, instead of liberating them. The similarities between the communitarians and social-policy thinkers of the near-libertarian New Right are said to be more obvious than the differences.[77] Egalitarian critics might ask whether certain background conditions, e.g. concerning the distribution of wealth and opportunity, have to be satisfied before it is legitimate, as a matter of social justice, to demand certain kinds of behaviour (in particular, a certain level of work effort) from all citizens in return for the welfare benefits they receive. Critics also worry about the way in which notions of civic responsibility and social contribution get operationalized in contractualist policy thinking. Is there, in particular, an unwarranted emphasis in contemporary contractualist policy proposals on paid work to the neglect of other forms of social contribution, such as forms of care work that typically go unpaid in societies like our own?[78]

The most radical critics call into question the inherent desirability of structuring social rights so that access to welfare benefits is tightly conditional on allegedly responsible behaviour. The point of social rights, argue these critics, is to expand individual freedom: specifically, to facilitate freer, more experimental ways of being than would be possible under a laissez-faire capitalist system in which most people are subject to what Marx termed the 'dull compulsion of economic forces'. Social rights fail as instruments of freedom, however, if access to the relevant benefits is made conditional on conforming to conventional standards of responsible behaviour. Work-related eligibility conditions in the welfare system are undesirable, for example, because they demand conformity to a conventional, employment-centred way of life. This reproduces the servitude of wage labour instead of emancipating citizens from it.

At this point the reaction against welfare contractualism links up with growing interest in and support for a radically different policy approach. Appalled by the problems of rising inequality, poverty, unemployment, and social exclusion reviewed above, many policy thinkers in the 1980s and 1990s have been drawn to the idea of unconditional basic income (UBI): an income grant paid to each citizen as of right without any test of means or willingness to work or to make any other form of productive contribution to the community.[79] Many proponents of UBI argue that the long-term goal should be to replace most existing conditional welfare benefits with a simple grant of this kind set at or close to a level sufficient to meet citizens' basic needs. The unconditionality of the proposal is directly linked by many of its supporters to the objective of personal freedom. In the words of the political philosopher Philippe Van Parijs, UBI serves the objective of securing 'real freedom for all'. Real freedom, Van Parijs argues, requires more than the formal liberty of action to which the conventional libertarian is committed. It also requires that individuals have assured command over scarce resources, and it is argued that an UBI, set at the highest sustainable level, is the fairest way of assuring such command.[80] Within the movement for UBI we can thus discern another philosophy of economic citizenship. Following Van Parijs, we may refer to this as the philosophy as real libertarianism.

Real libertarians clearly differ with communitarians on the conditionality of social transfers. In addition, they are typically more egalitarian in their ambitions than communitarian theorists. The connection is most explicit in the aforementioned work of the philosopher Philippe Van Parijs, who has sought to provide a philosophical justification for the UBI proposal grounded in a theory of egalitarian justice which, as Van Parijs emphasizes, owes much to the work of John Rawls (as well as other egalitarian philosophers such as Ronald Dworkin).[81] More intuitively, the introduction of an UBI, set at a generous level, can be expected to have a profoundly equalizing effect on power relations between workers and employers in the labour market, as well as, perhaps, between men and women within the home. It is not altogether unfair to say that, as socialism has gradually faded from the left's political agenda, the UBI proposal has taken its place as the main means by which post-socialists envisage they can advance their egalitarian objectives.

1.3   *A Fourth Philosophy?*

We are now in a position to list some of the key questions concerning the rights and obligations of economic citizenship. Firstly, should citizens enjoy 'social rights' that temper market-based inequality? If so, what exactly should these be rights to? Secondly, what civic responsibilities do citizens have in return for these rights? To what extent, if at all, is it legitimate to condition the enjoyment of the goods covered by such rights on the performance of these responsibilities? (Another, related question: Is such conditionality compatible with the very notion of social rights?) Finally, relevant to both former sets of questions: What are the ultimate distributive goals that should inform the determination of these rights and responsibilities? In particular, is substantial economic equality the appropriate goal, or something more modest?

The libertarians answer the first question in the negative and so, for them, the other questions do not really arise. The communitarians and real libertarians both answer the first question affirmatively. But real libertarians tend to be suspicious of efforts by the state to regulate citizens' behaviour in the name of civic responsibility. On the other hand, the communitarians advocate such regulation. Real libertarians often (though not, perhaps, always) have quite radical egalitarian ambitions; communitarians tend to aim at a moderation of market-based inequality that is more modest. The philosophy of economic citizenship that I shall outline and defend in this book can be understood in contrast to these latter two philosophies. It shares with the communitarians an emphasis on the responsibilities that accompany citizens' social rights. But it is closer to some real libertarian thinkers in its commitment to a radical form of economic egalitarianism. In short, it holds that: (i) citizens are properly possessed of various social rights; (ii) these rights are instrumental to an ultimate distributive goal that is radically egalitarian; and (iii) where these rights work to secure citizens a sufficiently generous share of the social product, and sufficiently good opportunities for productive contribution, citizens have definite, potentially enforceable obligations to make a productive contribution to the community in return. This volume outlines the conception of justice that underpins this alternative philosophy of economic citizenship— *justice as fair reciprocity*—and considers the policies and institutions necessary to satisfy the most urgent demands of justice, so conceived.

In Part I, I outline and defend the conception of justice as fair reciprocity.[82] Chapter 2 introduces and defends some of the main elements of this conception of justice: a commitment to respect and protect what I call the integrity interests of the citizen, implying a set of basic civil liberties; a commitment to protect citizens from specific types of disadvantage that otherwise compromise genuine equality of opportunity; and a related commitment to protect citizens against market vulnerability (situations of economic dependency that put the citizen at risk of exploitation and abuse). These commitments mark justice as fair reciprocity out as a liberal and egalitarian conception of justice. In this respect, fair reciprocity has much in common with many other conceptions of justice that political theorists have articulated in recent years (and my indebtedness to these theorists is clear). In Chapter 3, however, I introduce another key element of this conception of justice, one which is more distinctive than the commitments introduced in Chapter 2, or which at least receives greater emphasis and closer attention in this book than in much recent work on social justice. This is the reciprocity principle. Stated in its most general, abstract form, this principle holds that each citizen who willingly shares in the social product has an obligation to make a relevantly proportional productive contribution to the community in return. This simple idea can, however, be elaborated in radically different ways. Chapter 3 identifies and defends a particular conception of reciprocity that, so I contend, features implicitly in many past egalitarian accounts of the good or just society: the fair-dues conception of reciprocity. This version of the reciprocity principle can be stated as follows: where the institutions governing economic life satisfy other demands of justice (such as those reviewed in Chapter 2) to a sufficient extent, citizens who actually claim the high minimum share of the social product necessarily available to them under these institutions have an obligation to make a decent productive contribution, proportional to ability, to the community in return. In rough, intuitive terms: in a context of otherwise sufficiently fair economic arrangements, everyone should do their bit.

Chapter 4 brings together the ideas outlined in Chapters 2 and 3 into a provisional overall statement of justice as fair reciprocity. A society satisfies justice as fair reciprocity, in its ideal form, when the demands of reciprocity are made in the context of policies and institutions that, among other things, prevent or fully correct for unequal access to the means of production and unequal endowments of marketable talent. This ideal form of fair reciprocity is, however, unfeasible for the foreseeable future. It is necessary to explore non-ideal forms of fair reciprocity, in which society satisfies a threshold of absolute and relative economic opportunity somewhat lower than that associated with fair reciprocity in its ideal form. Specification of this threshold is a controversial matter, but I outline and defend an account of this threshold, linking it to: (i) non-immiseration (centrally, no citizen suffers poverty of income due to forces beyond her control); (ii) market security (citizens have adequate protection against market vulnerability and associated risks of exploitation and abuse); (iii) self-realization (citizens have real opportunity, over the course of their working lives, to relate to their work as a site of intrinsically valuable challenge); and (iv) minimization of class inequality (reduction of inequalities in initial endowments of wealth and educational opportunity to a reasonable minimum). Where the ground rules of economic cooperation satisfy these (and a few other) criteria, all citizens will have access to a high minimum share of the social product, and good opportunity for productive contribution; and, against this background, those citizens who do claim this share of the social product have an obligation to make a decent productive contribution to the community in return. This is what justice as fair reciprocity demands, in its non-ideal form.

But what does a decent productive contribution consist in? Even where political thinkers emphasize the importance of citizens' reciprocity-based, contributive obligations, they seldom look closely at the question of exactly what they must do to meet these obligations. In Chapter 5 I do my best to answer this question. The citizen's contributive obligation should be primarily understood, I argue, as an obligation to satisfy a basic work expectation: a socially defined lifetime minimum of paid employment. But such expectations should be adjusted, I argue, for specific kinds of care work, typically unpaid in societies like our own, which should also be regarded as labour of a kind that counts in satisfaction of the citizen's contributive obligation. I also consider, albeit very briefly and tentatively, how far the provision of capital might count as a form of productive contribution in satisfaction of the citizen's reciprocity-based contributive obligation. This completes my outline and defence of the basic theory of justice as fair reciprocity.

In Part II, I turn to the policy and institutional implications of this theory of justice. I attempt to give an account of what I call the *civic minimum*: the kind of policies and institutions that would be necessary to satisfy the demands of fair reciprocity in its non-ideal form. To focus discussion I take as a starting point one of the major policy developments of the recent past, the shift in countries like Britain and the United States towards welfare contractualism. In Chapter 6 I discuss what support might be found for welfare contractualism in the conception of justice as fair reciprocity, and I explain how an approach to welfare contractualism grounded in this conception of justice differs from the communitarian approach (paying particular attention to the 'New Paternalist' approach developed by Lawrence Mead). Chapter 7 then examines the alternative to welfare contractualism put forward by real libertarians: UBI. In the first half of this chapter I evaluate real libertarian arguments to the effect that there is a fundamental right to UBI, focusing in particular on the argument recently presented by Philippe Van Parijs.[83] Having found these arguments largely unpersuasive, I consider in the chapter's second half some variants on the UBI proposal which can be defended from the standpoint of justice as fair reciprocity—not necessarily as full-blown alternatives to welfare contractualism, but certainly as possible supplements to it.

Chapter 8 develops this line of thought further. Having first presented a critique of the conventional institution of inheritance, I then make the case for an alternative form of social inheritance: a universal capital grant as a basic right of economic citizenship. This grant might appropriately be tied, in part, to specific activities that are closely linked with productive participation in the economy. But I argue that it is also desirable on balance, that some portion of this grant be available as a form of time-limited UBI that citizens can use periodically at their discretion to supplement income from other sources. In short, Chapter 6 offers some reasons, grounded in the conception of justice as fair reciprocity, to be cautious of the practice of welfare contractualism; Chapter 7 rejects arguments which, in effect, seek to defend UBI as an alternative to welfare contractualism; and Chapters 7 and 8 then consider a range of variants on the original UBI proposal which, I argue, might complement welfare contractualism—indeed, some of which may well have to complement it if welfare contractualism is to be consistent with the demands of fair reciprocity (in its non-ideal form).

Having laid out the theory of justice as fair reciprocity in Part I, and having discussed the institutional and policy implications of fair reciprocity in Part II, I conclude in Chapter 9 with a brief discussion of the politics of fair reciprocity. In light of the policy discussion in Part II, I outline, in broad terms, some of the main elements of a reform programme that would enable societies like Britain and the United States to approximate the demands of fair reciprocity in its non-ideal form. Implementing such a programme would involve radical policy innovation in these countries, and this naturally raises questions as to the political feasibility of such a programme, and thus, also, as to the practical utility of its animating philosophy. I argue that the political obstacles to such a reform programme are real but not obviously insurmountable. I argue that the reform programme associated with the civic minimum addresses the real and urgent needs of many citizens in these countries, and that the underlying philosophy of fair reciprocity resonates with popular values in a way that could serve to consolidate and extend support for such a reform programme.

PART I

Fair Reciprocity

CHAPTER 2

───

Integrity, Opportunity, and Vulnerability

A conception of citizenship is defined by the rights and obligations we think people ought to have as members of a given polity. Our account of these rights and obligations will depend on what we take to be the shared basic interests of citizens, and on our understanding of the principles that properly articulate how we should uphold these interests. In short, any conception of citizenship must rest, philosophically, on a conception of justice (for a conception of justice simply is, at the end of the day, an account of the shared basic interests of citizens and of the principles that should govern the protection and promotion of these interests). My aim in Part I of this volume, beginning in this chapter, is to outline and defend the conception of justice that will inform my discussion of economic citizenship, a conception I call justice as fair reciprocity. I should stress at the outset that, for those who are already knowledgeable about contemporary political theory, the terrain covered in this particular chapter will be, on the whole, rather familiar. Many of the ideas discussed here play a central role in contemporary liberal egalitarian thinking about social justice. This chapter represents my own effort, drawing on a wide range of existing literature, to articulate some of these ideas, which I see as essential to any credible conception of justice. With this preliminary groundwork done, I will then turn, in Chapters 3–5, to a discussion of other ideas that are, I think, more distinctive and specific to the conception of justice as fair reciprocity (or which have at least been less thoroughly explored in recent literature).

As Section 2.1 explains, the conception of justice as fair reciprocity is founded on the thesis that the good society is, fundamentally, a community of mutual concern and respect. More precisely, the good society is viewed as a society that exhibits democratic mutual regard: in such a society individuals seek to justify their preferred political and economic institutions to others by appealing to shared basic interests, and to related principles that express a willingness to cooperate with their fellow citizens as equals. What shared basic interests, and related principles, must the members of a political community acknowledge, then, if they are to determine their major, life-shaping institutions in a way that satisfies the ethos of democratic mutual regard? The rest of Part I is a response (and an incomplete one, at that) to this question.

The response begins in Section 2.2. Here I argue that citizens' basic interests centrally include what I term their integrity interests: interests in bodily integrity, in expressive freedom, and in having the capacity and opportunity for informed deliberation about the ideals that animate their personal lives. Mutual respect and concern for these interests, embodied in a generous scheme of civil freedoms, is one fundamental expression of democratic mutual regard.

Citizens also have important opportunity interests: interests in access to the resources necessary for pursuing the ideals that animate their personal lives and, more basically, for what I term their core well-being. Mutual concern for these interests will also be a feature of a community guided by the ethos of democratic mutual regard. But what sort of distributional principle, or principles, best capture this concern? I argue in Section 2.3 for a strong egalitarian understanding of this concern. The institutions governing economic life should protect citizens against certain morally objectionable forms of discrimination and, ideally, should also prevent, correct, or appropriately compensate for, certain types of 'brute luck' disadvantage: for example, disadvantage in access to income and wealth due to differences in class background. Egalitarianism of this type is certainly not endorsed at present by the majority of citizens in countries like Britain and the United States. (Indeed, as I noted in Chapter 1, even many parties of the left have recently repudiated this type of egalitarianism.) Therefore, in Section 2.4 I review some of the more familiar arguments against this type of egalitarianism. I argue that these arguments are not convincing, though they do help refine our understanding of what egalitarianism of this type involves. I conclude that popular indifference to this type of egalitarianism is not philosophically well grounded.

In Section 2.5 I introduce another consideration that should inform design of the institutions that govern economic life. In economic relationships individuals can sometimes find themselves in positions of vulnerability and dependency which carry risks of exploitation and abuse. Such vulnerability threatens both integrity and opportunity interests, and a commitment to protect citizens against it is therefore another necessary expression of democratic mutual regard. Section 2.6 concludes.

2.1 *Democratic Mutual Regard*

The conception of justice I shall outline and defend in this book, justice as fair reciprocity, takes as its starting point the thesis that the good society is a community of mutual concern and respect. More exactly, the good society is one in which individuals exhibit *democratic mutual regard*. As citizens, coming together to determine their shared laws and other common institutions that will regulate their life together in a fundamental way,[1] individuals do not seek merely to impose their preferred institutions on others. For the purpose of designing these institutions, they regard one another as equals, and as possessing certain shared basic interests that these institutions must respect and protect. As citizens, they form their preferences across institutions, and seek to justify their institutional preferences to other citizens by offering reasons that appeal to their status as equals and, relatedly, to their shared basic interests. Institutions are subject to a test of reasoned justification by reference to a norm of citizen equality and a public conception of shared basic interests.

The idea of democratic mutual regard is more specific, we should note, than that of mutual regard *simpliciter*. It is perfectly possible, after all, for individuals to have mutual concern and respect even though they also perceive themselves to be unequal in their fundamental civic standing. The 'master' and the 'servant' can reciprocate a non-democratic form of mutual regard in which each respects a dignity that is specific to her respective position and role.[2] What one might call modernist political morality—the political morality which perhaps first found imperfect expression in the Leveller movement of the English Civil War, and, later, again imperfectly, in the philosophies of the American and French Revolutions—repudiates this hierarchical understanding of mutual regard. Democratic mutual regard, the ethos that I think is foundational to modernist political morality, expresses the now familiar idea that citizens share a more fundamental dignity than that connected with their immediate social positions, an intrinsic dignity rooted in their common humanity.[3] It represents one elaboration and application of the concept of human dignity that has played such a major role in the thinking (or at least the rhetoric) of modern movements for political and social emancipation.[4]

This modernist rejection of traditional, hierarchical conceptions of mutual regard—at least as regards specifying the common institutions that will regulate citizens' lives together in a fundamental way—presupposes, of course, that individuals do not have a *need* for hierarchical differentiation. Some political philosophers, such as Thomas Hobbes, seem to have believed that a desire for eminence is intrinsic to human nature.[5] According to this view, human beings have by nature a desire for esteem, for the recognition of their worth by others, which can be satisfied only by their being acknowledged as superior to others. If this view of human nature is correct, then the ideal of democratic mutual regard may well appear utopian: it demands something of people that is contrary to their deepest instincts. The gambit underpinning advocacy of this ideal, then, is that, while people do have a basic need to have their worth affirmed by others in the design of their common institutions, this need can be satisfied if others recognize and affirm one's status as an equal; that self-respect does not depend, necessarily, on the subordination and humiliation of others (or, more exactly, does not depend on such subordination and humiliation being built into the common institutions that regulate citizens' lives together in a fundamental way).[6]

I have spoken here of certain institutions being determined in accordance with an ethos of democratic mutual regard. 'Institutions' is an ambiguous term. But to make just one point of clarification here, I do not intend the term to refer here solely to the formal, legal arrangements that govern citizens' lives together. As G. A. Cohen has recently emphasized, important social outcomes, e.g. the final distribution of income and wealth, can be affected not only by the formal legal rules that govern economic life, but also by the social norms that influence how people choose to act within the formal legal set-up.[7] In view of this, I shall assume here that the ethos of democratic mutual regard not only should apply to the design of formal, legal arrangements, but should also be expressed directly in the authoritative social norms that more informally govern economic life. These norms can also be understood as institutions that regulate citizens' lives together in a fundamental way, and which thus call for justification of the appropriate, mutually regardful kind. At the same time, however, it is not claimed that all social institutions should conform to the ethos of democratic mutual regard. It is not my claim, for example, that the ethos must be respected, in all its aspects, in the internal life of all voluntary associations within society, though adherence to this ethos might well demand some limitations on the internal arrangements of such associations (e.g. limitations necessary to ensure that individuals retain an effective right to leave associations). Thus, while the ideal of democratic mutual regard has substantive moral content, which will impact in various ways on citizens' personal lives, it is not what John Rawls would call a 'comprehensive' moral or ethical doctrine,[8] intended to serve as a complete account of personal morality or ethics.

It is not difficult to connect this idea of democratic mutual regard to the revolutionary trinity cited at the beginning of Chapter 1: liberty, equality, fraternity. What distinguishes democratic mutual regard from more hierarchical forms of mutual regard is, as said, that it is founded on a sense of the fundamental equality of the parties to the civil relationship: an equality of status that must, in turn, be manifest in various substantive ways in the common institutions that govern their life together in a fundamental way. Fraternity is implicit in the attempt to consider how institutional proposals are likely to affect the basic interests of others, conceived as equals, and in an attendant willingness to eschew institutions that, while advantageous for oneself, risk injury to the basic interests of others. Liberty, finally, enters into the picture when we stop to think about the content of the interests that citizens will be attending to when they evaluate institutional proposals in accordance with the ethos of democratic mutual regard (a point I shall develop shortly, in Section 2.2).

These comments represent only a beginning, however, in elaborating what democratic mutual regard demands. My aim in Part I of this book is to offer a more detailed account of the principles that I think best express the concern and respect citizens should have for each other and, relatedly, of the shared interests that are the proper focus of this concern and respect. I shall discuss how these can be integrated into a conception of justice that can then, in turn, inform contemporary debate about the rights and obligations of economic citizenship. In this way, I hope to bring real-world decision-making, specifically about the rights and obligations of economic citizenship, closer to the ideal of democratic mutual regard. The aim is not to displace 'democracy' with 'philosophy',[9] but to use philosophy to consolidate democracy, on a specific conception of what democratic decision-making involves: not the brute assertion of majority will, but collective decision-making informed by the ethos of democratic mutual regard.[10] So understood, political philosophy can be seen as a kind of democratic underlabouring, as an effort to bring democratic society to a better self-understanding. Democratic underlabouring is, nevertheless, critical work. Popular views of justice can reflect ideological distortion connected with the protection of special interests. The political theorist, as democratic underlabourer, must be ready to challenge popular views where these seem inconsistent with the ethos of democratic mutual regard, and to explain the deficiencies in the arguments that are put forward in defence of special interests.[11]

2.2   *Liberty and Integrity Interests*

As I noted above, democratic mutual regard does not amount to a comprehensive morality: that is, to a full account of how one's personal life is best lived. There are many ethical questions, and related theological and philosophical questions, which sincere and intelligent citizens may disagree about, even if they share the ethos of democratic mutual regard. Thus, a society based on an ethos of democratic mutual regard may nevertheless be characterized by what John Rawls calls reasonable pluralism, by a diversity of reasoned religious and related views about how life is best lived, held by citizens who are nevertheless committed to living together on terms that express mutual respect for each other as (religiously and philosophically diverse) equals.[12] Even in this pluralistic context, however, citizens share certain basic interests, which will form the focus of their mutual concern and respect. Specifying these interests is, of course, a controversial matter (indeed, my claim that citizens have such interests at all is itself controversial). I shall contend here that these interests should be understood to consist centrally in certain basic integrity and opportunity interests. I will discuss integrity interests briefly in this section, before considering opportunity interests in Section 2.3.

Let us refer to a citizen who has a conception of how life is best lived, perhaps grounded in some religion or analogous belief system, and who endeavours to live in accordance with this conception, as an ethical agent. Citizens who differ on the nature of the good life are nevertheless all ethical agents in this sense. And, as agents of this kind, citizens can plausibly be said to have a common, and quite fundamental, interest in ethical integrity: in being able to live, without fear, in authentic accordance with their respective views of how life is best lived, views that they are able, moreover, to test and shape through informed reflection.[13] This is a substantial claim, and I shall now proceed to explain and, in part, defend it, by distinguishing three more specific interests that are connected with this general interest in ethical integrity.

Firstly, each citizen has a physical-integrity interest: an interest in having the effective power to draw some elementary boundaries between her physical self and other people, and to regulate the movement of others across these boundaries. To lack such power is to be deprived of crucial physical and psychological conditions for ethical agency. Note that, as I have defined it here, the physical-integrity interest is violated not only by actual non-consensual acts of aggression or interference by others, but also by relationships in which individuals are vulnerable to such aggression or interference at the discretion of another. Even if the master does not beat the slave, the master–slave relationship renders the slave vulnerable to beatings at the whim of the master, and this suffices to violate the slave's interest in physical integrity.[14]

Secondly, each citizen has an interest in what I shall call expressive integrity. Expressive integrity is a matter of being able to live in authentic accordance with one's view of how life is best lived. Expressive integrity is violated when the individual is pressured to adopt a way of life, or to profess commitment to a set of beliefs about the nature of the good life, that she does not genuinely endorse; or when she is simply prohibited from acting in accordance with what she perceives to be the requirements of her sincerely held ethical beliefs, including communicating these beliefs to others, without necessarily being forced into outward conformity with another determinate way of life.[15] The resulting state of inauthenticity entails a sharp dissonance between what the individual perceives as true or valuable on the one hand, and her behaviour on the other. Because of this, no ethical agent can seriously deny the fundamental importance of expressive integrity in her own case. And if, as we here assume, she follows the ethos of democratic mutual regard, she must put herself in the position of other citizens, who may have different conceptions of how life is best lived, and perceive thereby how the interest matters no less to them. (This does not mean, of course, that citizens can do whatever they like in the name of expressive integrity: the claims of expressive integrity are bounded by the duty to respect the expressive integrity and other basic interests of one's fellow citizens.)

Thirdly, each citizen has a basic interest in having adequate opportunity to reflect and deliberate critically about matters that pertain in a strategic or more fundamental way to her ethical agency. We may refer to this as her deliberative interest.[16] This encompasses her interest in being able to reflect critically on how her beliefs about the good life are most effectively put into practice. More controversially, it also encompasses her interest in being able to consider and evaluate alternative views about what the good life is.[17] Some critics will argue that, in saying this, I am biasing my account of citizens' basic interests towards a sectarian, autonomy-loving 'liberal view of life'. But I do not think the considerations which underpin my argument at this point are narrowly sectarian ones. It is surely not sectarian to say, firstly, that as ethical agents, our deepest interest lies in leading a life that is genuinely good. Nor is it sectarian to point out, secondly, that the beliefs on this matter that we inherit or currently have may not point us in the right direction, that error is possible. Moreover, thirdly, no individual can claim comprehensive knowledge of the good life on grounds that all reasonable people will find compelling; in this area of human inquiry, no one can show themselves, beyond all reasonable doubt, to be beyond error.[18] If this is so, surely no citizen can reasonably demand the authority to substitute his own judgement on such matters for the judgement of another. Each individual must be able to venture an independent judgement on such matters, even if the judgement she makes is to surrender her judgement to someone whom *she regards* as having superior insight. This interest in having the capacity and opportunity for independent judgement on questions about the content of the good life is central to the citizen's deliberative interest. As an ethical agent, any citizen should perceive the fundamental importance of this interest in her own case and, following the empathetic demands of democratic mutual regard, should also recognize its importance for others.[19]

These integrity interests represent, then, one major focus of the concern and respect that citizens owe to each other in a society governed by the ethos of democratic mutual regard. The commitment this implies can be expressed as follows: All citizens have basic integrity interests (physical, expressive, and deliberative) and the common institutions that govern their life together in a fundamental way must respect these interests and protect individual citizens against their violation. In accordance with this principle, each citizen needs to consider how alternative institutional proposals are likely to affect the integrity interests of herself and others. A proposal that threatens to frustrate these interests on the part of some group in the community will be suspect for that reason. For, according to the ideal of democratic mutual regard, no self-respecting citizen should ordinarily consent to a violation of her own basic interests; and, acknowledging other citizens' appropriate self-regard, no citizen should ordinarily expect a fellow citizen to consent to a proposal which has this likely effect. Each must respect the basic interests of all.

This principle obviously demands more elaboration than I can give it here. But some implications of the principle seem fairly clear. Adequate protection of integrity interests will require certain basic liberties and securities, in particular rights to security of the person, and expansive freedoms of conscience, expression, and association.[20] These basic liberties and securities thus form an assumed part of the institutional context in this book. A commitment to uphold these basic liberties and securities is a primary commitment of justice as fair reciprocity, and this commitment will enter as a factor into my discussion below of what fair reciprocity demands and/or permits in other areas that are more directly connected with economic citizenship.

2.3   *Equality and Opportunity Interests*

I have said that in a society built around the ethos of democratic mutual regard, citizens must accept and affirm one another as equals in the design of the common institutions that are to govern their life together in a fundamental way. Accordingly, the institutions that regulate economic life, including social norms that exert a major influence on economic activity, must acknowledge and make manifest the equal worth of each citizen. Each citizen must be able to see in the operation of these institutions a recognition of her equal worth. This is easily said, but what, more concretely, does it imply?

In contemporary politics, talk of equality *simpliciter* is increasingly rare, but there is still widespread nominal adherence to the goal of 'equality of opportunity' (though even this idea is increasingly displaced by the potentially less demanding 'opportunity for all'). Does this provide us with any handle on the question? I think the notion of equality of opportunity does provide some helpful initial orientation, but not much more than that. For of course, underlying the nominal consensus on the importance of equality of opportunity, there lurks considerable disagreement both about what this goal consists in as a matter of principle, and about what it requires by way of institutional design. One might say, rather abstractly, that equality of opportunity obtains when no citizen suffers morally arbitrary disadvantage in her access to certain morally significant goods. But which kinds of disadvantage are morally arbitrary? Which goods are relevant to assessing whether, or how far, equality of opportunity obtains?

The question we really need to start with, I think, is this: What should citizens have equal opportunity *for*? What interests are (or ought to be) fundamentally at stake when we speak of equality of opportunity? There is a tendency to think of equality of opportunity in terms of the relative access citizens enjoy to specific goods such as education and employment. This is not exactly wrong, but it does not fully capture the interests that are fundamentally at stake. Education and employment matter because of the contribution they make to the satisfaction of other, more basic interests. What we need to identify are these deeper interests.

It is tempting, firstly, to identify these interests with the aforementioned capacity for ethical agency. What matters fundamentally, it might be said, is the individual's prospects for agency of this kind. Equality of opportunity should be understood centrally to consist, perhaps, in equality of access to income, wealth, and other goods that fundamentally determine our prospects for such agency. However, I am not sure that the interests fundamentally at stake here are entirely reducible to the citizen's basic interest in ethical agency. Consider someone, a small child, say, who is suffering from hunger. Certainly one reason why this hunger matters, morally speaking, is that it may impair the child's development of capacities that are important for ethical agency: hungry in the classroom, the child cannot focus on her schoolwork, and so fails to learn to read. And this, in turn, severely limits her ability to engage critically with alternative conceptions of how life is best lived. But this impairment of her capacity for ethical agency, while obviously important, surely does not exhaust the moral significance of the hunger the child suffers. The child's suffering is a bad, and establishes an urgent moral claim upon us, *in itself*, quite independent of any effect it may have on her immediate or future capacity for ethical agency. The example shows, in other words, that we have some morally significant, justice-relevant interests that, while typically connected with our interest in ethical agency (such that damage to the former implies damage to the latter), are also intrinsically important. As Amartya Sen puts it: 'there is an essential and irreducible "duality" in the conception of a person in ethical calculation. We can see the person, in terms of *agency*, recognizing and respecting his or her ability to form goals, commitments, values, etc., and we can also see the person in terms of *well-being*, which too calls for attention.'[21] A plausible account of citizens' basic interests must, I think, attend to both the agency and the well-being dimensions of human life, and not try to reduce the significance of either entirely to the other.[22]

Now of course, what exactly constitutes 'well-being' is one of the things that individual citizens, pursuing their respective philosophies of life, will disagree about. But, notwithstanding these disagreements, citizens surely can and should share a conception of what we might call *core well-being*. Roughly speaking, core well-being obtains for a given individual when she is in good health and, more generally, has physical and mental capacities that place her within the range of normal human functioning. In Sen's terminology, it derives from a range of basic 'functionings' and 'capabilities', including being adequately nourished, adequately rested, having good mobility, and so on (this is obviously a very incomplete list).[23] A little schematically, we may thus speak of citizens having two major opportunity interests, additional to the integrity interests discussed in Section 2.2: an interest in the goods that fundamentally affect prospects for ethical agency; and an interest in core well-being. The significance of core well-being is derived partly from its vital contribution to the individual's prospects for ethical agency, but also, quite independently, from its importance to another fundamental human interest, an interest in the avoidance of involuntary suffering. The concept of equality of opportunity should, I think, be elaborated by reference to these two major opportunity interests.

This is still very abstract. To make the idea more concrete, it will help to consider some of the ways in which people may be put at an objectionable disadvantage with respect to satisfying these opportunity interests. A first possible source of objectionable disadvantage is the practice of discrimination: that is, conditioning access to goods, such as education or employment, on characteristics, such as race, gender, or religion, that are, in the case at hand, irrelevant as qualifications for making effective use of the good. To achieve equality of opportunity, therefore, the state must itself ordinarily refrain from discrimination. In addition, the state must also protect citizens from discrimination at the hands of non-state agencies who happen to wield control over access to resources that are strategically important for core well-being and/or ethical agency. This latter claim is more controversial because it involves placing a limitation on property rights and associational liberties. As I have argued elsewhere, respect for citizens' integrity interests may require that the state give priority to associational liberty over preventing discrimination in some cases, but respect for these interests does not preclude the enforcement of anti-discrimination norms over a wide range of cases.[24]

Even in a discrimination-free environment, however, individuals can still end up with unequal access to core well-being and/or the goods which determine prospects for ethical agency because of what we may call, following Ronald Dworkin and G. A. Cohen, brute luck inequalities.[25] A brute luck inequality in, say, income, is an inequality in income that would emerge in a non-discriminatory (and, in the sense to be defined in Section 2.5, a non-exploitative) environment but which nevertheless derives from forces over which the disadvantaged individual can exercise no control, e.g. differences in social class. Brute luck inequality along a given dimension is to be contrasted, therefore, with inequality along this dimension that is attributable to different lifestyle and economic choices between individuals facing similar opportunities. Such choice-based inequalities include inequalities attributable to differential option luck where individuals genuinely volunteer to take some risk and the risk turns out differently for different people.

Three types of brute luck inequality seem particularly important in affecting core well-being and prospects for ethical agency and will therefore feature prominently in this book. Firstly, there is inequality in endowments of external wealth due to unequal inheritances. A second significant type of brute luck inequality is that between individuals in their endowments of marketable talent: inequalities in individuals' respective abilities to earn income, under competitive market conditions, from the productive deployment of their talents, where these inequalities are attributable to differences in their family backgrounds and educational opportunities and/or to different genetic endowments. Even in a world of equal inheritances and marketable talent, however, individuals might still suffer unequal access to core well-being and unequal prospects for ethical agency due to handicaps. A handicap is here understood as a deviation from the normal range of physical or mental capacity that impairs core well-being, and prospects for ethical agency across a very broad spectrum of beliefs about the nature of the good life. Individuals with handicaps will typically need more resources than others to achieve core well-being and to actualize particular projects.

I thus propose the following as a provisional, working definition of what equality of opportunity demands: (i) a prohibition on practices of discrimination in relation to employment and education, to be respected by the state and enforced by the state against (most) private sector agencies; and (ii) the prevention, correction, or appropriate compensation of significant forms of brute luck disadvantage, understood to consist centrally (though not exclusively) of disadvantageous endowments of external wealth, marketable talent, and handicaps.[26]

2.4   *Some Objections: Intention, Self-Ownership, Desert, and the Bottomless Pit*

This working definition of equal opportunity is by no means uncontroversial. Concerning part (i), there is, as noted, some controversy as to how far the state may prevent private actors from practising discrimination. But it is part (ii) of this working definition that is most controversial. The idea that we should design the institutions that govern economic life, so as to prevent or correct for brute luck inequality in marketable talent is not one that commands widespread support in contemporary capitalist societies.[27] Moreover, many political theorists also dispute the justice of preventing or fully correcting for this and other kinds of brute luck disadvantage. In this section I shall review some of the chief objections that critics have raised against this conception of equal opportunity. If, as I shall argue, these objections can be met, then the tendency to reject this conception of equal opportunity may be less well founded than is often thought. Considering these objections will also help to clarify certain aspects of this conception of equal opportunity; in particular, I hope to clarify why, and in what sense, brute luck disadvantage sometimes warrants what I have referred to as 'appropriate compensation' rather than prevention or full correction.

A first challenge questions the link I have asserted between equal opportunity, understood along the lines just set out, and the deeper, underlying ethos of democratic mutual regard. Of course, the critic says, the state should not make laws that, for example, ban women from certain occupations, or which set a ceiling on how much blacks can earn relative to whites. Such rules obviously do not reflect the mutual regard that should obtain between citizens who think of themselves as equals. But the rules of something like laissez-faire capitalism are perfectly consistent with the absence of formal state discrimination of this kind. To be sure, under such rules some citizens may do quite poorly because of the meagre endowments they bring to the market. But so what? If a given citizen has a low income because of her poor endowment of marketable talent, rather than because the state has legally restricted how much she may earn, then surely her disadvantage does not reflect a deliberate intention to do her down; and, therefore, it does not reflect a failure of the mutual regard that ought to obtain between citizens. She may be the victim of bad luck; but not, according to this view, of a lack of the respect that is due to her as an equal. The ethos of democratic mutual regard does not, so this argument claims, necessarily point us beyond the rather formal conception of equal opportunity espoused by libertarians and near-libertarian advocates of limited government.

But this argument will not do. If some of us push for institutions that, while advantageous for us, will predictably result in significant brute luck disadvantage for some of our fellow citizens, then we *are* intentionally and deliberately doing these fellow citizens down. We are consciously choosing institutions that enhance our prospects, our opportunity interests, at the expense of others. And so we would not be showing all of our fellow citizens the regard they are due as equals; and these potentially disadvantaged citizens would show insufficient self-regard were they to acquiesce in our efforts to put them at a disadvantage. It might be argued in reply that a move away from laissez-faire institutions towards more egalitarian institutions also involves some citizens improving their prospects 'at the expense of others' whose prospects are correspondingly diminished. This is true, but begs the critical question: Why should we take laissez-faire institutions as the relevant baseline for evaluation? Any set of institutions will produce its own distribution of opportunity, making some better or worse off relative to other possible sets of institutions. As citizens, we have to select one set of institutions from the full spectrum of possibilities. If our deliberations on this are guided, as they should be, by the ethos of democratic mutual regard, then the relevant presumption should be the moral presumption that each citizen has equal standing and, as such, a presumptively equal right to see her opportunity interests satisfied. And given this moral presumption, the appropriate institutional presumption would appear to favour a conception of equal opportunity like that outlined above.[28] It is movement away from this baseline that carries the burden of special justification, not movement towards it.

But perhaps this burden of special justification is one that the critic can bear. A libertarian critic might argue that we should eschew egalitarian institutions because of their likely cost to individual liberty. A forceful elaboration of this objection is provided by Robert Nozick, whose ideas I briefly reviewed in Section 1.3.1. As noted there, Nozick takes as one of his premises that each person is the morally rightful and exclusive (initial) owner of her body and abilities: the legal rights a slave-owner has over a slave are rights that, morally speaking, each person initially has over herself.[29] Self-ownership, in this sense, seems highly desirable, and something we should indeed respect, in view of its apparent link with the integrity interests and associated freedoms discussed above (see Section 2.2). To be owned by another, after all, is to be highly vulnerable to interference and direction by another, violating one's physical integrity, and threatening one's expressive and deliberative interests. So we might be tempted to think that the best way to provide protection for these basic interests is by giving each citizen full rights of private ownership in her own body and abilities. But it appears we cannot both affirm the principle of self-ownership and demand equality of opportunity in the sense outlined above. Implementing equality of opportunity in this sense will typically require the government to tax those with favourable endowments of marketable talent and then to redistribute towards those with less favourable endowments of marketable talent.[30] The libertarian points out that such redistribution gives the less talented a property right in the marketable skills of the more talented, thereby making them part-owners of the talented. The talented are in this respect akin to slaves; as Nozick famously asserts, 'taxation of labor incomes is on a par with forced labor'.[31]

Egalitarian thinkers have spent considerable energy evaluating this objection in recent years. One response, which I shall not explore here, is provisionally to concede the illegitimacy of taxing labour incomes and to advocate the redistribution of non-labour assets as a way of achieving egalitarian ends.[32] But some egalitarians, seeking to justify taxation of labour incomes, have questioned the principle of self-ownership itself.[33] They have pointed out that 'ownership' is not a relationship reducible to a single, simple right, but involves a complex cluster of rights (and duties).[34] Building on this insight, they have questioned whether all of the rights constitutive of full self-ownership are necessary for the individual to retain the kind of real, meaningful freedom in relation to work that the slave obviously lacks. Concretely, if the talented individual is subject to a redistributive tax when she chooses to go to work, then the return she can expect on her work is certainly reduced. But this does not mean that she has given up her right to determine whether to work at all, how long to work for, and to take a particular kind of job that she finds most pleasing. Even with the tax in place, her status as a free labourer is substantially intact. The property right that the untalented effectively have in her skills is not, like that of a slave-owner, a right to command whether and how she works, but, more modestly, a right to receive a share of the earnings she generates should *she* make the decision to work. All the key decisions about working remain in her hands. The claim that egalitarian redistribution of labour incomes converts the talented (or whoever carries the burden of redistribution) into slaves thus seems, at least, wildly exaggerated. It seems plausible only if we fail to distinguish different kinds of ownership rights.[35]

This is not to deny that there may indeed be some genuine conflicts between important liberties, linked to citizens' integrity interests, on the one hand, and the conception of equal opportunity outlined above. Nor is it to say that, in the face of such conflicts, the liberties should be sacrificed to the demands of equal opportunity. In the course of this volume I will identify some cases where such a conflict arises, and where I think the claims of liberty have priority.[36] But we should be wary of assuming a general conflict of this kind, and we should certainly reject the claim that redistributive taxation of labour incomes is illegitimate because it conflicts with the principle of self-ownership. It does indeed conflict with this principle. But, as we have seen, this does not necessarily indicate a deeper, genuinely worrying conflict between egalitarian redistribution and individual liberty.

A third objection to the conception of equality of opportunity outlined above also questions the legitimacy of redistributing labour incomes. This objection appeals not to the idea of self-ownership, but to the idea of desert. Because the talented make more valuable product-ive contributions to the community when they deploy their talents, they are often said to deserve proportionately higher rewards, making it unfair to tax their higher earnings away (at least completely). It is this desert-based objection which seems to underpin popular scepticism concerning the justice of egalitarian redistribution.[37] As I remarked in Chapter 1, a more or less explicit acceptance of this type of desert-based defence of inequality is also a feature of much contemporary 'centre-left' communitarian thinking about economic citizenship. It is especially important, then, to see why this widespread desert-based defence of inequality is unconvincing.

The key claim, recall, is that because the talented make more valuable productive contributions to the community when they deploy their talents, they deserve proportionately higher incomes than others as reward.[38] Egalitarians are typically unimpressed with this claim. They reply that the talented—that is to say, the naturally gifted—do not deserve higher income for their superior productivity because they are not responsible for having the talent that explains their superior productivity. The force of their point can be illustrated by means of a simple example. Imagine two people, Kelly and Ingrid, who work as widget-makers. When they arrive at work in the morning, each is assigned a machine. It so happens that Kelly's machine is newer and more efficient than Ingrid's, and so, though both work at equal inten-sity, Kelly produces twice as many widgets as Ingrid in the course of the working day. It seems odd to say that Kelly deserves a higher reward than Ingrid, given that her higher productivity is entirely explicable by the fact that Ingrid was restricted to working a less efficient machine. But now let us vary the example slightly. Kelly and Ingrid are endowed with identical machines, but Kelly has been blessed by nature with more dexterous hands than Ingrid, which enable her to produce twice as many widgets as Ingrid for the same effort. This is precisely the kind of case in which, according to the desert-based defence of inequality we are here considering, Kelly is deserving of, and so should receive, a proportionately higher income than Ingrid as reward for her higher productivity. But what is the morally significant difference between this case and the previous case? In both cases, Kelly is advantaged in her productive potential, relative to Ingrid, by a kind of mechanical good fortune. If she is not deserving of higher reward in the first case, how can she be deserving of such reward in the second? Why is it significant that in the one case the mechanical good fortune inheres in Kelly's own body, while in the other, it inheres in an external object? Is the difference not a completely arbitrary one?

We cannot leave the matter at that, however. For it is just too counter-intuitive to claim, as a general matter, that someone cannot be deserving of special reward unless they are themselves fully responsible for that which explains their superior performance. Does a brilliant pianist not deserve greater applause than a less accomplished pianist even if her brilliance reflects innate genius rather than harder work?[39] It is hardly plausible to say that she does not. But are we not then accepting the basic principle of talent-based desert, that people can be genuinely deserving of special reward in virtue of superior performance even when the superiority of their performance is due to greater talent for which they are not themselves responsible? And haven't we then effectively conceded the argument to the desert-based defender of inequality in earnings and incomes?

In fact, we have not. While conceding that the better pianist does indeed deserve her warmer, longer applause, we can still question why superior pianists and the like deserve not only greater applause but *also* the higher level of income that they may be able to command. We can accept that over our society as a whole there will be, perhaps ought to be, some spheres or practices in which people deserve differential rewards due to superior performances where the specialness of their performance is at least partly attributable to personal qualities for which they are not themselves responsible. We may organize athletic competitions, for example, and allow superior athletes to take home gold medals even if their victories reflect, in part, the capricious gifts of nature. However, this still leaves entirely open the question of whether, or to what extent, we should regard the distribution of income and wealth as properly regulated by talent-based desert claims. From the fact that the ablest sprinter deserves the gold medal, it does not necessarily follow that we should regard economic life as a race for a prize. Why would citizens committed to living together in accordance with the ethos of democratic mutual regard wish to do so? Why treat the economy as a race for a prize, when you know that some of your fellow citizens will, through no fault of their own, have no chance of winning? How would that be to show them the regard they are due as equals, with opportunity interests no less weighty than your own?[40]

A fourth objection to the conception of equality of opportunity outlined above focuses on the proposed obligation to compensate for handicaps. If this is understood as an obligation to correct fully for the disadvantage caused by handicaps, it may well bankrupt society for very little positive result: to meet the obligation, society will have to pour huge amounts of resources into raising the prospects of the most handicapped, even if the results are only very marginal improvements in their living standards. We begin to discern here the nightmare vision so often painted by critics of egalitarianism: egalitarian society as a society of universal levelling-down to a state of uniform misery or mediocrity. To meet this objection, the egalitarian must refine the account of what counts as appropriate compensation for handicaps.[41] One possible approach to the problem is that suggested by Ronald Dworkin, and, with slight variation, it is this approach that I shall adopt for the purposes of this book.[42]

Imagine a world in which each person has equal marketable talent and equal access to means of production like land and capital.[43] Each person thus has the same potential income: anyone can obtain the same level of income as anyone else for a given level of productive effort. Each person in this world also knows the population-wide probability of acquiring specific handicaps, but does not know her own likelihood of developing any specific handicap. Imagine that in this world various insurance companies offer insurance packages against the eventuality of developing specific handicaps. People may choose between very low-cost packages that offer very limited compensation if handicaps eventuate and higher-cost packages that offer higher compensation should handicaps eventuate. All insurance premiums are debited against the individual's potential income. Thus, people can choose to reserve the bulk of their potential income for other purposes, rather than buy a decent insurance policy, though they may live to regret this if they turn out to have a serious handicap. At the other extreme, they can buy very expensive insurance policies which provide generous compensation for handicaps. But they will then have to work flat out just to earn the income to pay their insurance premiums. For what level of compensation, and against what handicaps, would people choose to insure themselves in this imaginary world?

Of course, people's chosen levels of insurance in such a situation would doubtless differ. However, Dworkin contends that in the case of 'general handicaps . . . that affect a wide spectrum of different sorts of lives', most people would take out roughly similar insurance policies, and that we can thus make some tolerable assessment of what insurance package 'the average member of the community [would] purchase'.[44] He suggests that this average level of insurance for compensation can then serve as our guideline in setting levels of tax-financed disability benefits and in deciding upon a tax-financed package of universal health-care entitlements. (Note that while the insurance premiums are flat-rate in the imaginary world, there may be strong equity reasons for making the real-world taxes to finance these benefits proportionate or progressive in relation to income, rather than flat-rate lump sums, to the extent that our society has not in fact achieved the equality of wealth and talent assumed in the imaginary world.[45]) When I speak of providing appropriate compensation for brute luck inequality in handicaps, then, this may be understood to refer to a level and pattern of compensation determined by asking what sort of insurance package the average person would be likely to buy in a hypothetical insurance market of this kind. Compensation at this level will not carry the same risk of creating a bottomless pit in which to pour society's resources. But the limits it places on the level of compensation seem consistent with the underlying ethos of democratic mutual regard, in particular with the duty to acknowledge and affirm all citizens as equals. For the limits on appropriate compensation approximate the insurance choices that individuals would make when placed in a hypothetical situation of equality, both in terms of initial resources and exposure to risk.

Of course, as Dworkin acknowledges, the judgement we come to about the level of insurance chosen by the 'average member of the community' will be speculative. But the model of the hypothetical insurance market at least provides a framework within which citizens can steer a course between the bottomless pit and the unacceptable policy of providing zero compensation. Note also that compensation ought not to be thought of solely in terms of cash benefits, or in terms of in-kind therapies and treatments that alleviate handicaps. It can and should be understood to include policies of social integration that facilitate participation by handicapped citizens in mainstream social life. By asking what proportion of our potential income we would be willing to spend in the hypothetical insurance market to promote integration we can perhaps get some idea of how much as a society we ought collectively to spend.

I should not be understood as saying that there are no problems with the conception of equal opportunity outlined above. A key issue, not considered at all here, concerns incentives: Would the attempt to implement this conception of equal opportunity dampen the incentives of the more talented to employ their talents, perhaps making everybody worse off? Another issue not considered here, more closely related to the incentives issue than might appear, is whether this conception of equal opportunity does not make excessive informational demands of the state: Could the state possibly know enough about citizens' respective talents to design a fair scheme of redistribution between them? I shall not ignore these issues in this volume; I shall return to them at some length in Section 4.1. But I hope in this section to have cast doubt over some of the familiar objections to this conception of equal opportunity. I hope to have shown that in the design of the institutions that govern our economic life there ought at least to be a presumption in favour of this form of equal opportunity; and that at least some of the usual reasons that are cited as grounds for rejecting or relaxing the presumption are unpersuasive.

2.5 Vulnerability and Dependent Exchange

Concerns over discrimination and brute luck disadvantage lie at the centre of egalitarian thinking about economic citizenship. There is, however, a further concern that, while related to these first two concerns, is not wholly reducible to them. This is the concern over market vulnerability and the consequences of exchanges entered into in circumstances of vulnerability. In this section I will seek to clarify the nature of this problem, and why it ought to be a vital concern for citizens animated by the ethos of democratic mutual regard.

Let us begin by clarifying the concept of market vulnerability. To this end, imagine two parties in the marketplace, Peter and Paul, whose relationship has the following three features. Firstly, Peter urgently needs some good over which Paul has control; we may call this the urgency condition. Secondly, Paul is the sole feasible supplier of the good which Peter needs; we may call this the monopoly condition. Thirdly, Paul does not similarly need a good of which Peter is the effective monopoly supplier; this is what we may call the asymmetry condition. When these three conditions obtain (urgency, monopoly, asymmetry), then we may say, roughly following Robert E. Goodin,[46] that someone in Peter's position suffers from market vulnerability with respect to the person in Paul's position. Note that market vulnerability is not necessarily an either/or thing. We may speak of degrees of vulnerability depending on the extent to which the three conditions are simultaneously satisfied.

The reverse side of market vulnerability is power. In an economic environment characterized by perfectly competitive and fully clearing markets, there may be profound inequalities in access to income and wealth due to unequal endowments of talent and capital, but, as transactors, all individuals are equally power*less* price-takers. However, while this model of a perfectly competitive market-clearing economy has many heuristic uses in economic and political theory, real-world market economies are characterized by various departures from the competitive norm. Moreover, decentralized exchange occurs in time and in space and, where it is consequently impossible or very costly to bring all buyers and sellers together instantaneously, little islands of vulnerability and power can and do arise.[47] Individuals on the strong side of vulnerability relationships can then use their resulting power for personal advantage in ways that are morally objectionable. Specifically, they can use their power to exploit and/or to abuse weaker parties. Trades that are entered into from a position of vulnerability, and which thus carry risks of exploitation and/or abuse, I shall refer to as dependent exchanges, in view of the obvious and acute dependency that the weaker party has on the goodwill of the stronger party. In addition to any exploitation and abuse that may actually occur, this state of dependency is arguably itself a bad, a form of unfreedom that compromises the integrity interests of the dependent party.

Let us first consider the problem of exploitation. Where one party is vulnerable, in the sense defined above, the party on the strong side of the vulnerability relationship can use his resulting power to exchange goods and services with the weaker party at prices that deviate from the prices that would obtain in a competitive equilibrium, to the advantage of the stronger party and to the disadvantage of the weaker. The weaker party then suffers from an exploitative exchange. The stronger party is able, and makes a deliberate choice, to extract a rent of vulnerability from the weaker party owing to the latter's difficult circumstances. The exploiter is then better off than he would be under competitive market-clearing conditions, given the background distribution of assets and preferences, and the exploitee is worse off than she would be under such conditions.

An example may help to illustrate the idea. Imagine a group of black immigrants to a predominantly white and racist society. When the immigrants apply for jobs, try to rent rooms, or apply for loans, they routinely find themselves turned away on racist grounds. Now imagine a member of the white majority called George, who is not racist, but who is dedicated to maximizing his own income and wealth. Perceiving the predicament of the immigrants, George approaches a group of them and offers to provide them with the loans they need to purchase a house. Being ruthlessly self-interested, however, he holds out for the highest rate of interest he can get on the loans. Having been turned away by a long succession of racist white bank managers, the immigrants see George as probably their only source of finance, and so they are reluctantly forced to agree to the relatively high rate of interest he demands—a rate considerably higher than that which prevails for whites in the regular credit market. George thus exploits the immigrants, extracting a rent of vulnerability equal to the difference between the interest they pay for the loan he provides and the prevailing rate on the wider loan market. This example is not at all far-fetched. It roughly describes how the housing market functioned for West Indian immigrants to Britain in the 1950s.[48]

The overall moral judgement we make of any given case of exploitative exchange must surely take into account the distributional consequences of the exploitation. Thus, an exploitative exchange seems especially unjust if the effect of the exploitation is to intensify the absolute disadvantage suffered by an individual or group who would be unjustly disadvantaged even in the absence of this exploitation (i.e. individuals who have poor initial endowments of talent, capital, etc.); and it seems even more objectionable if the effect of the exploitation is to push the exploited party below, or even further below, a basic threshold of material decency, i.e. if exploitation of this kind is immiserating.[49]

Let us now turn to the notion of abusive exchange. Thomas Pogge offers one striking imaginary example of what I mean by an abusive exchange. A person is extremely ill and seeks treatment from the nearest doctor. Both parties are aware that the sick individual will die (or at least both think he will die) if he is not treated immediately. In this desperate situation, and assuming a libertarian property rights regime, the doctor could conceivably offer the patient a contract which exchanges treatment for slavery.[50] If the sick individual agrees to this exchange, but would reject this exchange were an acceptable alternative available, then the slavery contract constitutes what I am calling an abusive exchange. Less extreme cases of abusive exchange might involve the sale of body parts; the sale of sexual or reproductive services; or agreement to work under conditions that are physically hazardous to the worker. What makes an exchange abusive is the violation of integrity interests it involves. In some cases, it may be the physical integrity of the citizen that is violated, as when someone agrees to work under physically hazardous conditions rather than starve. But expressive and/or deliberative interests might also be violated. Think, for example, of a case where the employer, on the strong side of the exchange, insists that the vulnerable party attend prayer meetings at work as a condition of receiving desperately needed employment, meetings that conflict with the worker's own religious beliefs. Sometimes, as in the slavery case, all integrity interests might be violated.

We are only entitled to say that such interests have been violated, however, and thus that abuse has occurred, if the exchange in question is not genuinely consented to by its putative victim. In a formal sense, of course, all exchanges are consented to. But we routinely distinguish between genuine consent and the kind of consent that is given under duress, and that (or a very similar) distinction is also relevant here. The first condition which must be met for us to say that an exchange has not been genuinely consented to is that the exchange is made in a situation where the putative victim of abuse lacks an acceptable alternative to the exchange. Following G. A. Cohen, we may say that an alternative is unacceptable if it is 'thoroughly bad' in an absolute sense;[51] if, say, it would push the individual below the threshold of core well-being or deprive her of minimally decent opportunity for ethical agency.[52] The second condition is that the putative victim would not enter into the exchange if he did have an acceptable alternative available. To see the relevance of this second condition, imagine that someone offers you a job ironing shirts. In return for just five hours of labour a week, she will pay you a sum that is three times the societally average level of weekly pay. Your only alternative to the job is, let us say, starvation. This is not an acceptable alternative. However, what would you do if you were offered an acceptable alternative, an alternative that is not thoroughly bad in an absolute sense, such as working at a checkout for thirty hours a week for a societally average level of weekly pay? If, faced with this acceptable alternative, you would still take the job ironing shirts, then surely you do genuinely consent to take this job even though, as a matter of fact, you have no acceptable alternative but to take it.[53]

Even if no actual abuse occurs, the vulnerable party in an exchange relationship remains acutely dependent on the goodwill of the stronger party and, as suggested above, it can be argued that this situation of dependency is itself a threat to the integrity interests of the vulnerable party. For to be dependent in this way is to live in a situation of uncertainty that may inhibit one's pursuit of the good life as one conceives it, and which may incline one to strategic deference towards others in an effort to win and hold their goodwill. ('I had better not go to those gay clubs any more because if my boss finds out he might sack me, and I will then be destitute. Instead, I had better go to the Young Conservatives' Association to impress him.') One ceases freely to follow one's own intimations of the good, and starts to live to please others. In this way, the situation of dependency results in a kind of unfreedom.[54]

2.6   Conclusion: Three Basic Commitments

My aim in this and the next three chapters is to outline and defend the conception of justice in terms of which I believe we should discuss the rights and obligations of economic citizenship. I call this conception justice as fair reciprocity, and it has been my aim in this chapter to outline some of the main presuppositions and commitments of this conception of justice. Before moving on to consider other, and perhaps more distinctive, aspects of fair reciprocity, it may help to summarize three of these commitments.

Firstly, as explained in Section 2.2, there is the commitment to respect and protect citizens' integrity interests (physical, expressive, and deliberative) and to maintain a scheme of basic civil liberties and securities that is adequate to this task. I have not said very much here about the exact content of this scheme of civil liberties. I shall return to the issue as seems necessary in the course of the discussion below. But otherwise I shall work with a very general, familiar formulation of these basic civil liberties as including freedoms of conscience, expression, and association, the rights associated with a fair trial, and securities against arbitrary arrest and imprisonment; in short, as Rawls puts it, the 'specific rights and liberties ... found ... in various bills of rights and declarations of the rights of man'.[55] Secondly, as explained in Sections 2.3 and 2.4, there is the commitment to prevent discrimination and to prevent, correct, or appropriately compensate for significant forms of brute luck disadvantage. Significant forms of brute luck disadvantage centrally include disadvantage in initial access to external wealth, in marketable talent, and in handicaps. This commitment will feature prominently in the book, and I will say more about it in Chapter 4, as well as at various points in Part II. Thirdly, there is the commitment to protect citizens from market vulnerability, and from the dependency, and risks of exploitation and abuse, to which such vulnerability gives rise. This commitment will also feature prominently in the discussion below.

Thus, against a background of an adequate scheme of basic civil liberties, fair reciprocity requires that the institutions governing economic life prevent discrimination, significant brute luck disadvantage, and market vulnerability. There is, however, at least one further, crucially important commitment of fair reciprocity which remains to be discussed. This is the subject of the next chapter.

CHAPTER 3

—

The Reciprocity Principle

I have not yet introduced the commitment that helps give the conception of justice as fair reciprocity its name: the commitment to substantive economic reciprocity. In short, and roughly stated, if one willingly enjoys the fruits of one's fellow citizens' labours, then, as a matter of justice, one ought to provide some appropriate good or service in return. An injustice occurs when citizens share in the social product in violation of this reciprocity principle. The aim of this chapter is to outline and defend a particular version of this principle and to explain why we should regard satisfaction of the principle as a requirement of justice.

I begin in Section 3.1 by reviewing two broad conceptions of reciprocity that have featured prominently in past thinking about social justice. The first conception is embodied in the view that justice demands nothing less than a strict equivalence or proportionality, in value terms, between entitlements to the social product and contributions to it: one may take out in value only what one puts in, or, relative to others, only in strict proportion to the value of what one puts in. But many political theorists have rejected this account of justice and the conception of reciprocity it embodies. And some of these have advanced an alternative view of the kind of substantive economic reciprocity that the just society should embody. I refer to this as the fair-dues conception of reciprocity. The basic idea is that where the institutions that govern economic life are sufficiently fair in terms of the opportunities they afford for productive contribution, and the awards they apportion to it, those citizens who claim the high share of the social product available to them under these institutions have an obligation to make a decent productive contribution, proportionate to their abilities, to the community in return. The relevant ethos is not that of putting in just what you take out, but of doing one's bit in a context that is sufficiently fair in other crucial respects; not that of precise tit-for-tat, but of mutual service in a context of sufficient social and economic equality.

In Section 3.2 I turn more directly to the question of why we should regard substantive economic reciprocity, of the fair-dues kind, as a requirement of justice. I argue that the mutuality of productive service associated with this kind of reciprocity is one fundamental expression of the ethos of democratic mutual regard that I have taken as my starting point for this book. A degree of substantive reciprocity, along the lines of the fair-dues conception, is something that mutually regardful equals properly expect of each other in the economic context. The historical salience of the fair-dues conception of reciprocity in egalitarian political thought naturally prompts further questions, however, about the precise relationship between reciprocity and other, more familiar egalitarian concerns. Addressing some of these questions in Section 3.3, I argue that the motivation for substantive economic reciprocity is (to some extent) independent of that underpinning these other concerns: it stands as a demand of justice in its own right. In Section 3.4 I complete my defence of the reciprocity principle, understood in its fair-dues form, by outlining some of the instrumental considerations which support public enactment of the principle. If we take it as a given that citizens do have expectations of substantive reciprocity, then it can be argued that major social institutions ought manifestly to respect these expectations so as to facilitate other social objectives, including large-scale egalitarian redistribution.

3.1 *Two Conceptions of Reciprocity*

It is often claimed that economic justice consists in, or at least centres on, a principle of substantive economic reciprocity. Stated roughly, and in its most general form, this reciprocity principle holds that people who willingly share in the social product (the flow of goods and services intentionally generated by the combined industry of the members of a society) ought to make a return for this in the form of a relevantly proportional productive contribution of their own. However, as with the apparent consensus over the importance of equal opportunity, widespread endorsement of this principle is misleading. For the principle can be, and is, elaborated in radically different ways by different political theorists and ideologies. There is a multiplicity of different conceptions of substantive economic reciprocity, each of which elaborates the core idea in a different way. I cannot attempt anything like a comprehensive review of these various conceptions here. But it will help to distinguish two broad conceptions of reciprocity, and of how reciprocity links with justice, that have featured prominently in political thought. For ease of reference, I shall refer to these as the strict-proportionality, and the fair-dues, conceptions of reciprocity.

Let us look first at the strict-proportionality conception. According to some political theorists, justice requires a strict proportionality, if not strict equivalence, between the value of an individual's productive contribution to the community and the value of the goods and services that she is entitled to claim from the community in return. If Alf contributes to the value of x and Betty to the value of y, then they are entitled to benefits of exactly x and y respectively (strict equivalence) or at least to benefits in the ratio $x : y$ (strict value proportionality).[1] Justice consists in 'taking out' in exact proportion or equivalence to the value of what you 'put in'. If you wish to take out up to a certain value, then it follows from this conception of justice that you must be prepared to put in value of a strictly proportionate or equivalent amount. You must contribute to the value of x to be entitled to benefits of value x (strict equivalence), or, if Alf has to contribute z value to be entitled to benefits of value x, then Betty too must contribute up to z value to be entitled to benefits of x value (strict value proportionality). In short, justice simply *is* the reciprocity principle, understood in the following, very specific sense: those who share in the economic benefits of social cooperation have a corresponding obligation to make a productive contribution to the community that is strictly proportional (or strictly equivalent) in value to the benefits that they enjoy.

Of course, disagreement can arise over what is the relevant metric of value here, and different views on this question can lead in turn to different views about what sort of things count as entitlement-building productive contributions. There is, for example, a tradition of socialist thought that identifies justice with strict value proportionality in distribution, but which takes some measure of embodied labour as the relevant metric of value, and which, relatedly, regards labour as the only form of productive contribution that establishes legitimate claims on the social product. According to this tradition of socialist thought, distributive justice consists in ensuring that each individual receives benefits from production that are perfectly proportional (or strictly equivalent) in labour-value to the individual's labour-value contribution to production. 'Labour-value' here might be measured by the time standardly necessary for the production of goods with hours of different types of labour typically weighted to reflect skill (so that one hour of skilled labour contributes more value than one of unskilled labour). For some early socialists, such as the British so-called Ricardian socialists,[2] this conception of justice was to be realized by radical reform of the market economy. All goods would be priced in terms of the respective labour-times necessary to produce them, and all producers would receive vouchers representing the labour-time embodied in the goods they had produced. In such an economy each producer would consequently consume no more than precisely what he had contributed to the community through his labour. Capitalism stood condemned in the eyes of these early socialists precisely because it appears to be a system of 'unequal exchange' in which non-working capitalists, by paying workers less than the value of what they produce, are able to consume goods in spite of having made no personal labour contribution to production. Other socialists, while agreeing that capitalism was exploitative in this way, believed that the way to realize this conception of justice was through public ownership and planned control of the means of production, making all workers employees of the state to be remunerated in proportion to the respective values of their labour contributions. This is how Karl Marx envisaged the 'lower stage' of communist society.[3] But whereas Marx regarded this only as an interim stage on the road to a higher stage of social development, other socialists believed that this form of strictly proportional reward for labour contribution should be the ultimate socialist objective.

Marx, for his part, famously critiqued this particular socialist vision for remaining, as he alleged, fundamentally within the framework of 'bourgeois right'.[4] This was perceptive on Marx's part, for there certainly is a core structural similarity between the socialist conception of justice described above and other conceptions of justice that have been invoked in defence of the capitalist economy. Some classical liberal or libertarian defenders of capitalism argue along the following lines: under competitive conditions, each factor of production in a capitalist economy receives a return equal to the value of its marginal product; the value of the marginal product of a given factor of production is a measure of its contribution to production; thus, each individual factor-supplier in such an economy receives an income strictly equivalent to the value of the productive contribution that he makes (where 'his' contribution includes the contribution of the non-labour factors of production that he happens to own); therefore, competitive capitalism produces a perfectly just distribution of income. The argument has a long pedigree stretching back at least as far as the turn-of-the-century economist John Bates Clark.[5] More recently it has been employed by Milton Friedman, who suggests that a competitive capitalist economy will tend automatically towards distributive justice because it will tend to generate a pattern of reward that satisfies the maxim 'To each according to what he and the instruments he owns produces'.[6] Clearly, the metric of value here is competitive prices rather than some measure of embodied labour-time; and the notion of what counts as a productive contribution by an individual has been unreservedly extended from personal labour to include contributions from all the 'factors of production' that individuals happen to own (land, capital, and so on). These mark fundamental differences with the socialist conception of justice described above. However, what remains the same is the idea that justice consists in achieving a strict proportionality (or even equivalence) between the value of an individual's productive contribution and the value of the social product that he enjoys. What also remains the same, therefore, is the implication that someone who enjoys a specific share of the social product has a corresponding obligation to make a productive contribution to the community that is strictly proportional (if not equivalent) in value to the share he enjoys.

What Marx arguably was getting at when he criticized the aforementioned socialists for remaining within the confines of 'bourgeois right' was the inegalitarian thrust which this conception of justice has, whether in its socialist or classical liberal form. In both forms, unequal capacities to make a productive contribution will translate directly into unequal shares of social product. In the classical liberal version, unequal endowments of land and capital may be largely responsible for this; in the socialist version, unequal endowments of skill will come to the fore. As Marx put it, the socialist version of strict proportionality 'tacitly recognises unequal individual endowment and thus productive capacity of the worker as natural privileges'.[7] Egalitarian theorists tend, therefore, to reject the strict-proportionality conception of justice on the grounds that its implementation would unfairly disadvantage individuals who, through no fault of their own, happen to have poor capacity to contribute value through productive activity. In the terms introduced in Chapter 2, an insistence on strict proportionality would result in a brute luck, and therefore unjust, inequality of income and wealth between citizens.

Nevertheless, egalitarian theories of the good or just society frequently emphasize the moral desirability of productive contribution in return for a share of the social product. Indeed, it is often presented in the writings of egalitarian thinkers as a necessary condition of income entitlement for most (all adult, able-bodied) citizens. I would like now to illustrate this point by reference to some major egalitarian thinkers, and then consider what alternative conception of reciprocity their writings suggest.

Robust economic egalitarianism combined with an insistence on universal productive contribution (for short, a contribution ethic) is, firstly, a notable feature of utopian communist thinking in the early modern period. A key difference between the economically egalitarian society depicted in Thomas More's *Utopia* and More's own society is the obligation to labour which characterizes life in Utopia. Whereas in More's England 'many noblemen live in idleness like drones on the labor of others', in Utopia goods are distributed equally, while special executive officers, the syphogrants, 'take care that no one is idle'.[8] A similar perspective informs the work of the 'Digger' or 'True Leveller' theorist and agitator of the English Civil War, Gerrard Winstanley. In Winstanley's ideal commonwealth, as described in the mature statement of his political theory, *The Law of Freedom*, all land is owned and worked in common, and the resulting products transferred to common storehouses, from which all citizens are free to draw to meet their needs (which Winstanley clearly assumes are quite basic and static).[9] What, however, if somebody takes from the storehouse and then refuses to do any work? Winstanley is in no doubt about the injustice of this and of what ought to be done to prevent it. He writes that if a particular individual 'refuse[s] to work' and so seeks to 'feed and clothe himself with other men's labours', then 'he shall be reproved'; 'if he still continue idle . . . whipped'; and, if he should still continue to consume without working, he is to be 'delivered to the task-master's hand, who shall set him to work for twelve months, or till he submit to right order'.[10] Thus, for Winstanley, a just society is not simply one with common ownership of the means of production and an equal division of the social product. It is, in addition, a society in which each able-bodied member participates in the endeavour to create this product, gives something of themselves, in the form of labour, to it. Indeed, each member carries an enforceable obligation to make such a productive contribution, as well as the right to take what he needs from the common storehouse.

There are, of course, many important differences between the agrarian communist utopias of More and Winstanley and the socialist philosophies which emerged in response to the industrial revolution. But a point of commonality lies precisely in the picture of a just society as one which combines an egalitarian division of the social product with a strong contribution ethic. I have argued elsewhere that Marx's writings contain a broadly consistent conception of distributive justice which includes the idea that rightful claims on the social product carry, for the able-bodied, a corresponding obligation to make a productive contribution back to the community through work.[11] As Marx writes in *The Civil War in France*, 'with labour emancipated, every man becomes a working man, and productive labour ceases to be a class attribute'.[12] A fundamental human need according to Marx is free time (time free from the drudgery of necessary labour). Access to free time can only be equalized, he argues, if individuals shoulder the burdens of production equally, and thus if all those sharing in the social product make some appropriate labour contribution to it.[13] This emphasis on the obligation to work in return for one's share of the social product, and related moral criticism of unearned income, was to become a central feature of Marxist critique and advocacy in the twentieth century. A good example of this is contained in the following words of Rosa Luxemburg, written in 1918 on what she hoped was the eve of a socialist revolution in Germany, with a view to clarifying the task of social reconstruction that prospectively lay ahead

in order that everyone in society can enjoy prosperity, everybody must work. Only somebody who performs some useful work for the public at large, whether by hand or by brain, can be entitled to receive from society the means for satisfying his needs. A life of leisure like most of the rich exploiters currently lead must come to an end. A general requirement to work for all who are able to do so, from which small children, the aged and sick are exempted, is a matter of course in a socialist economy.[14]

In their attachment to this contribution ethic, Marxist thinkers and activists reflected the wider socialist culture in which they worked and helped construct. We can gain a good deal of insight into the assumptions and prejudices of this culture by looking at Robert Tressell's classic socialist novel *The Ragged Trousered Philanthropists*.[15] Particularly interesting for present purposes is the chapter of this novel entitled 'The Oblong', in which Tressell pictures the hero of the novel giving a lecture on the causes of poverty to his fellow workers. In the course of the lecture the hero draws a rectangle on the wall and divides the rectangle into productive and non-productive social classes, the poverty of the working-class being explained by the hero as a consequence of the maldistribution of the social product between these two social classes. When listing who is included in the unproductive classes, the hero chalks up, in addition to landlords and capitalists, 'tramps' and 'beggars'. When challenged with the remark that landlords and capitalists are typically very rich, while tramps and beggars are typically very poor, the hero responds that categorizing them with capitalists and aristocrats is

the proper place for them. They belong to a loafer class. They are no better
mentally or morally than any of the other loafers in that division; neither
are they of any more use. Of course when we consider them in relation to
the amount they consume of the thing produced by others, they are not so
harmful as the other loafers, because they consume comparatively little. But
all the same they are in the right place in that division. The section represents
not individuals—but the Loafer class.[16]

That is what socialism is about for activists like Tressell: not just
the elimination of poverty or inequality, but the elimination of a
'Loafer class'. A socialist society is one of reciprocal productive
service, reciprocal work, in a context of social and economic equality.

Not only revolutionary socialists, but also reformist social democrats of this period, saw the good society in these terms, and they therefore voiced similar criticisms of unearned incomes (while also being
more discriminating about what constitutes a genuinely unearned
income). John Stuart Mill, in some ways a father of British social democracy, looked forward in his *Autobiography* to a future state in which
'society will no longer be divided into the idle and the industrious;
when the rule that they who do not work shall not eat, will be applied
not to paupers only, but impartially to all'.[17] The more radical New
Liberal thinkers, such as J. A. Hobson and Leonard Hobhouse, argued
that private-property rights are not absolute, unconditional claims to
resources but instruments for the performance and reward of socially
useful productive functions.[18] R. H. Tawney's work *The Acquisitive
Society* vividly restates their critique of 'functionless property': that is,
rights of ownership and reward that are detached from the performance of some socially useful productive function.[19] Following the leads
of John Stuart Mill and Henry George, these British social democrats
saw the income rights accruing from the mere ownership of land as the
paradigm case of functionless, and therefore illegitimate, property.[20]
But they quickly expanded the category to include the income rights
accruing from inherited wealth, from various forms of 'speculative'
capital gains, and the 'rent of ability' that skilled workers are able
to extract by virtue of the scarcity of their talents (payments over
and above those strictly necessary to 'call forth' the requisite kinds
of skilled labour to meet social needs). A social democracy would
eliminate these various forms of functionless property through a combination of taxes on unearned increments to land values and ground
rents, inheritances and bequests, capital gains, and progressive taxes
on earnings, and would then distribute the proceeds back to citizens

in the form of various social benefits. In distributing these benefits, however, the state would have to take care not to create just another form of functionless property. As Harold Laski, also writing in this functionalist tradition, put it:

[An individual] can claim ... such a share of the national dividend as permits him at least to satisfy those primary material wants ... which, when unsatisfied, prevent the realization of his personality. ... But the right is relative to a duty. If I receive it must be in order that I return. Society cannot maintain me for the privilege of my existence. I must pay my way by what I do. ... No man ... has a right to property except as a return for functions performed.[21]

This functionalist conception of distributive justice continued to influence the political theory of British social democracy into the second half of the twentieth century. For example, in the revisionist classic *The Future of Socialism* we find Anthony Crosland defining distributive justice in terms that still echo Hobhouse: 'An equitable distribution ... requires first that wealth should be a reward for the performance of a definite service or function, and secondly that all should have an equal chance of performing the function, and so of earning the reward.'[22]

Critiques of functionless property have featured less prominently in recent theories of egalitarian justice. However, if one looks carefully one can sometimes see an echo of the contribution ethic we find in earlier egalitarian writings. Particularly notable in this respect, I think, is John Rawls's theory of justice as fairness.[23] As noted in Chapter 1, Rawls argues that the distribution of the economic benefits of social cooperation ought to be regulated by the difference principle. This requires that inequalities in primary goods, such as income and wealth, be arranged so as to maximize the 'index of primary goods' enjoyed by the class of citizens who are to have the lowest index of such goods.[24] Inequality in primary goods that goes beyond this 'maximin' point is unjust. Some early critics of Rawls's theory claimed that some of those in the 'worst-off group'—roughly, the group with the lowest index of income and wealth—might be 'surfers' who are poor because they have chosen a life of ocean-skimming leisure over work. Are these surfers really entitled, the critics asked, to the minimum income share apparently guaranteed to them under the difference principle?[25] Rawls has responded to this objection by modifying his original account of primary goods, i.e. his account of what it is that the difference principle aims to maximin. In Rawls's own words, we are to 'include in the index of primary goods a certain amount of leisure-time, say sixteen hours per day if the standard working day is eight hours. Those who do no work have eight extra hours of leisure and we count those extra hours as equivalent to the index of the least advantaged who do work a standard day.'[26] Thus, if an individual chooses not to work, then she may not still claim the minimum income share guaranteed under the difference principle. For in terms of her overall index of primary goods she is, by stipulation, already as well off as those individuals who give up a day's leisure to acquire this income share. The implication is clear: if a citizen wishes to claim the minimum income share guaranteed under the difference principle, then she must be willing to perform a certain minimum of work in return. Thus, Rawls concludes, 'Surfers must somehow support themselves.'[27]

Elsewhere, Rawls writes in a similar vein that 'Those who were unwilling to work under conditions where there is much work that needs to be done (I assume that positions and jobs are not scarce or rationed) would have extra leisure stipulated as equal to the index of the least advantaged. So those who surf all day off Malibu must find a way to support themselves and not be entitled to public funds.'[28] A problem with this formulation, however, is that there could be 'much work that needs to be done' even if jobs are 'scarce or rationed'. (There is, after all, much work that 'needs to be done' in a classic Keynesian slump in which jobs are scarce.) I take it that, on Rawls's view, someone who is unemployed but who would not be willing to work even if a job that 'needed to be done' were offered to him is in the same position, morally speaking, as the 'Malibu surfer', and is therefore also not 'entitled to public funds'. As it stands, Rawls's specific proposal for including leisure time in the index of primary goods is not without its problems,[29] but I am less interested here in the merits of the specific proposal than in noting the underlying concern Rawls has to develop his theory so that it more clearly 'expresses the idea that all citizens [sharing in the social product] are to do their part in society's cooperative work'.[30]

I have spent some time illustrating the strong contribution ethic that features in the writings of many egalitarian thinkers. As egalitarians, these thinkers do not accept that justice consists simply in reciprocity, understood as a strict equivalence or proportionality between the value of income shares and productive contributions. But they nevertheless hold that a form of substantive economic reciprocity is important. How are we to characterize the form of reciprocity they endorse? Of course, on further analysis we will doubtless find important points of difference between these various thinkers, and any definition of reciprocity I offer here cannot claim to capture exactly what each of them thought. But it is possible, I think, to identify a way of thinking about substantive economic reciprocity that captures the basic idea at work in at least some of these writings, and which reflects the broad ethos that they more generally express.

The conception of reciprocity I have in mind may be stated roughly as follows: where the institutions governing economic life are otherwise sufficiently just, e.g. in terms of the availability of opportunities for productive participation and the rewards attached to these opportunities, those who claim the generous share of the social product available to them under these institutions have an obligation to make a decent productive contribution, suitably proportioned and fitting to ability and circumstances, to the community in return. I term this the fair-dues conception of reciprocity.

When we reject the view that justice consists simply in strict proportionality or equivalence between benefits and contributions, we accept that there are other demands of justice in addition to reciprocity so understood, such as the demand that citizens be protected from certain forms of brute luck disadvantage. This raises the question of how we are to integrate the claims of reciprocity with these other demands of justice. The fair-dues conception of reciprocity offers one plausible way of doing this. It says that in the context of economic arrangements that meet these other demands of justice to a sufficient extent and which, in view of this, provide citizens with sufficiently good opportunities for productive participation and sufficiently generous access to the social product, citizens who claim the generous share of the social product available to them under these institutions should indeed 'do their bit', productively, in return. It is this conception of reciprocity, closely akin, I think, to that we find in Rawls's theory of economic justice, that will inform my discussion of the rights and obligations of economic citizenship in this book.

3.2 *Reciprocity as an Expression of Democratic Mutual Regard*

Why does reciprocity—substantive, economic reciprocity—matter? Why ought people to make some personal productive contribution to their society in return for the share of the social product they enjoy?

One possibility is that non-reciprocation is a bad, and to be discouraged, because it is in some way harmful to the non-reciprocator. A life of non-reciprocating idleness may be bad for bodily health, or for the development of valuable personal faculties, and should be discouraged, perhaps even penalized, for this reason. This idea has certainly played its part in egalitarian critiques of unearned income. Thus, we find the early twentieth-century social democrat J. A. Hobson commenting that it is

the normal and necessary effect of living upon another's property ... [that o]ne by one the higher faculties are debilitated, and cease to work; the attempt to consume without producing, to enjoy without effort, at once lessens the quantity and lowers the quality of life.... Nature imposes the obligation of work as a condition of enjoyment, and it belongs to a well-ordered society to enforce this obligation.[31]

A related line of argument focuses on the link between reciprocation and self-esteem.[32] Self-esteem is, as Rawls puts it, a primary good, underpinning each individual's capability for forming and pursuing conceptions of the good (in the language of Chapter 2, it under-pins one's capability for ethical agency).[33] If self-esteem depends on proper reciprocation for benefits received, then it is in the indi-vidual's own interests to reciprocate. If myopia and/or weakness of will threaten to undermine her efforts to reciprocate, then perhaps the community ought even to enforce reciprocation. Similar arguments inform contemporary advocacy of 'workfare' (programmes which make work-related activity a condition of receiving state welfare pay-ments). According to Lawrence Mead, whose ideas I shall consider in Chapter 6, it is in the best interests, material and psychological, of the welfare poor that they work; and it is, in part, this strictly paternalistic consideration that supposedly justifies forcing them to work.[34]

Paternalist arguments for productive participation should not be dis-missed, and I will try to integrate them into my analysis in Part II (see especially Section 6.6). However, paternalist considerations do not get to the bottom of why the kind of reciprocity we are interested in mat-ters. Indeed, some of the above arguments are not really arguments for reciprocity at all, but simply arguments for work. Hobson's wor-ries about the debilitating effects of idleness on personal health and the development of personal faculties would presumably apply just as much to an isolated Robinson Crusoe character, tempted to live idly off the fat of the land, as to people living in a community, receiving goods and services from others. And the argument from self-esteem begs the critical question. If non-reciprocation jeopardizes self-esteem, that is probably because it is dishonourable, or at least is perceived to be so either by the non-reciprocator or by someone whose opinion she cares about. But why is failure to reciprocate dishonourable? One can reply that it is dishonourable because it is unjust. But why, we can then ask, is reciprocity something that justice demands?

In approaching this question, let us begin with a relatively straightforward case. Imagine a society consisting, say, of a thousand people. These people earn their living by fishing in the sea off their island. There is a problem of fishing boats regularly breaking against rocks on the shore in foggy conditions, so one day the fisherfolk's government sends each of them a request for funds to build a lighthouse. Nine hundred of the fishers send funds in, and the resulting sum is sufficient to build the lighthouse. All of the 1,000 island inhabitants subsequently benefit from the lighthouse, including the 100 fishers who also wanted the lighthouse built, and who, we shall assume, were no less able to contribute to its cost, but who refrained from sending in any funds. The non-contributing fishers thus enjoy a so-called free ride. It is widely thought that such free-riding, under conditions of the stipulated kind, is morally objectionable. By refusing to make a contribution to the cost of the benefits that he willingly enjoys, the free-rider chooses to offload a definite share of these costs onto others. This seems to express a lack of respect for these others. Certainly, citizens who have democratic mutual regard for each other would, as an expression of their regard for other citizens as their equals, want to share these costs and not offload them onto others.

Now this is, of course, an example which concerns collective effort to provide what economists call a public good, a good that has the characteristic of non-excludability in that it is impossible or prohibitively costly to exclude those who don't contribute to its cost from enjoying it.[35] Most goods and services do not have this characteristic of non-excludability. However, in egalitarian pictures of the good society, the tendency is to view the whole social product as having a quality of normative non-excludability that is analogous to the excludability characteristic of public goods. The social product is, if not a public good, what we might call a shared good: a good that everyone is presumptively entitled to share in to a more or less equal (or more or less equally needs-satisfying) extent. Every output is assumed to be in the collective pot (or, to follow Winstanley, warehouse) for all to share equally in. When the social product is viewed in this light, however, worries analogous to those about public-goods free-riders arise. The thought arises that, as with public goods, if the benefits of collective effort are going to be shared, so too should be this effort. To eschew participation in this collective effort is a form of disrespect to those who do engage in it. An intuition of this sort may be what underlies the contribution ethic that we have seen at work in so much egalitarian thinking about the just society. With this preliminary thought in place, let me now try to delve further into what I think motivates (or ought to motivate) the concern for reciprocity.

Non-reciprocation, by which I mean failure to satisfy a contributive obligation of the kind associated with the fair-dues conception of reciprocity, seems to violate what I shall contend is a basic norm of mutually respectful, mutually dignified, social cooperation: a norm of *reasonable mutual advantage*. According to the norm of reasonable mutual advantage, any member of the community who is a willing beneficiary of cooperative industry (that is, a willing claimant on the social product intentionally generated through the combined industry of members of this community) must make a reasonable effort, given his or her endowment of productive capacities, to ensure that other members of the community also benefit from and (the flip side of this) are not burdened by his or her membership of this scheme. As a matter of their dignity, other citizens have the *right* to expect you to make this effort. Failure to do so treats them in an offensively instrumental way; or, as we more usually say, it *exploits* them. There is, note, no claim here that one must necessarily match the benefit one creates to the benefit that others provide for you. You must, according to this norm, make a reasonable effort to make good the contribution of other citizens to your material well-being and/or opportunity through their creation of a social product in which you share (and, as the flip side of this, make a reasonable effort to avoid imposing a material burden upon them). What a reasonable effort is for you will depend partly on the degree of benefit one takes from others (the size of the share of the social product that you claim) and partly on one's relative capacity to produce reciprocal benefits.[36] At the limit, your capacity in this respect may be non-existent, in which case the obligation to make such an effort entirely lapses. For it cannot be considered a failure of respect for another to fail to provide a reciprocal good or service for them when one is simply incapable of doing so.

Now, how does one make a reasonable effort to ensure that others are not burdened by, indeed benefit from, one's membership of the same economic community? Ordinarily, one will do so by making a suitably weighted productive contribution in return for the share of the social product that others provide (or by refraining from claiming a share of the social product if one is unwilling to make such a contribution), a suitably weighted contribution being one that takes account of one's respective capacity and opportunity to produce valuable goods and services.[37] I suggest, then, that the reciprocity principle, in its fair-dues form, is best understood as a more concrete expression of the norm of reasonable mutual advantage, a norm which, I contend, expresses the ethos of mutual respect between equals that I have taken as a starting point for this book.

The injustice involved in non-reciprocation is sometimes expressed using the language of parasitism. Such language is often used rather loosely, but David Gauthier and Gijs van Donselaar offer a more precise definition of a parasitic distributional arrangement: an arrangement is parasitic if it allows one party to the arrangement, Smith, to make himself better off than he would be in the absence of a second party, Jones, while Jones, by virtue of this arrangement, is at the same time made worse off than he would be in the absence of Smith.[38] This notion of parasitism is certainly one that we have to handle with care. Some might argue, for example, that we should minimize redistribution from the able-bodied to the handicapped because such redistribution is likely to be parasitic in the foregoing sense: the handicapped will likely be better off than they would be in the absence of the able-bodied, while the able-bodied are worse off than they would be in the absence of the handicapped. I do not think that redistribution of this sort is in fact necessarily morally objectionable; indeed, I think such redistribution is justified by the commitment to protect citizens from significant brute luck disadvantage (see Section 2.3). However, if the putative parasite imposes a net cost on the consumption possibilities of his fellow citizens, making them worse off than they would be if he were absent from the scene, and this net cost is one that the putative parasite could avoid imposing by making a reasonable productive effort (in the sense described above), then an injustice arguably has occurred. This person is not being sufficiently attentive to how other citizens are affected by his membership of the community, and this expresses a lack of proper respect for them. Once again, what counts as a reasonably avoidable burden will depend on individuals' respective capacities and opportunities to avoid claims on the social product and/or to produce offsetting benefits, and thus on their respective endowments of handicaps, talents, and so on.

In the contemporary philosophical literature the most extended discussion of reciprocity is probably that provided by Lawrence Becker.[39] Becker starts from a consideration of what people need to develop and flourish as rational agents. One thing they need is the help and assistance of others. To sustain relationships of the requisite kind, however, individuals will need to practise reciprocity. We must, Becker says, 'return good for the good we get from agents who are trying to produce benefits for us' so as to 'sustain the sort of equilibrium necessary for productive [i.e. need-fulfilling] social intercourse'.[40] More specifically, we ought to be disposed as a general matter, in all social contexts, to make *fitting* and *proportionate* returns for the goods we receive from others.[41] Reciprocity, in this sense, is not merely desirable; we ought to be disposed to make such reciprocation a moral obligation. As Becker puts it, 'The capacity for balanced exchanges must be preserved, against the effects of opposing tendencies, by insisting that overall actual balances be preserved. ... insisting on actual balances means making them required.'[42] Finally, Becker argues, our social structures should be designed to be consistent with the obligations of reciprocity and, relatedly, so as to cultivate the disposition to reciprocate, fittingly and proportionately.[43] What Becker has in mind is illustrated in a subsequent article, where he argues in favour of work obligations in the welfare system: welfare recipients ought to return the good they receive in the form of their welfare benefits, and a fitting and proportionate return, Becker claims, is for them to produce valuable goods and services.[44]

Let us take a closer look at the notions of proportionality and fittingness at work in Becker's theory of reciprocity. A first question: Is a return proportionate if it produces equal benefit for one's benefactor as her original effort provided for you? Or is proportionality a matter of making a return that imposes an equal sacrifice to that incurred by one's benefactor? The question arises, of course, because for one person to produce a benefit of equal value to that received from another may require much greater sacrifice than that made by the person who provided the original benefit. According to Becker, since the aim of reciprocity is to create 'balanced' social exchanges, with a view to sustaining exchange over time, proportionality should be understood as aiming primarily at an exchange of equal benefits (which points towards what I referred to above as the strict-proportionality conception of reciprocity).[45] However, if the effort to reciprocate on these terms would impose considerable inequality of sacrifice between the parties, Becker accepts that 'the level of sacrifice should be controlling', even though this is 'a second-best option' that, he claims, may chill interaction between people with unequal capacities to produce benefits for others.[46] A fitting return, for its part, must be in some way commensurable with the benefit we receive (or else we will be unable to assess whether or not it is a proportionate return).[47] Where we have benefited from another's efforts in the context of an ongoing social practice or institution, a fitting return may well be one that contributes to the maintenance of this practice or institution and need not necessarily be made directly to the original benefactor herself.[48] For example, if I have benefited from an anonymous donor to a national blood bank, then an appropriate return for this good received may well be for me to give blood to the bank, so helping to maintain the supply of blood from which I have benefited. Where, by contrast, it is appropriate to make the return directly to the benefactor, the benefactor's perception of what has value will also be relevant to the issue of what constitutes a fitting return: 'since the point of being disposed to reciprocate is to create and sustain balanced social relationships, the good returned will have to be good *for the recipient*, and (eventually) perceived by the recipient both *as a good* and *as a return*'.[49]

Becker's analysis is in some ways complementary to that I have offered, and I shall refer back to Becker's ideas about fittingness in my discussion of what citizens need to do to satisfy the fair-dues conception of reciprocity (see Section 5.1). But three points of difference between Becker's analysis and my own may be worth noting. A first difference is one of focus. Becker is fundamentally concerned with reciprocity understood as an encompassing personal virtue, an action-guiding disposition that, in his view, ought to manifest itself in all areas and types of social interaction. I am much more narrowly concerned with a specific obligation to work, or otherwise contribute productively, in return for a share of the social product, something Becker would regard as just one expression (albeit an important one) of the encompassing virtue of reciprocity. The second difference is more substantive. For Becker, it is simply the case that social cooperation withers when benefits are not reciprocated. He does not arbitrarily assert, or speculatively assume, this; he cites solid evidence in support of the claim.[50] But some philosophers might argue that merely pointing to this fact begs the important question. For perhaps people act wrongly when they cease producing benefits for non-reciprocators. Perhaps it is the task of moral philosophy to explain this, and to make the case for more generous, unconditionally altruistic behaviour. In short, we need to say *why* it is acceptable, perhaps even desirable, for people to stop providing benefits for others when their efforts go unreciprocated. A plausible response to this challenge will, I think, have to appeal to some notion of dignity and appropriate self-regard. As intimated above, non-reciprocation can be understood as producing a kind of dignitary harm, as a failure to show appropriate respect to benefactors. Scaling down one's efforts on the non-reciprocator's behalf can then be understood as an assertion of one's own dignity ('I am not a doormat'). Moreover, in doing this, one also indirectly affirms the dignity of all actual or potential benefactors ('People, in general, ought not to be treated as doormats'). Looked at in this light, the withdrawal of social cooperation in the face of non-reciprocation is not a mere brute fact to which moral and political theory must accommodate, but a legitimate consequence of individuals' efforts to cooperate on terms that express, and uphold, principles of universal dignity and mutual regard. Thirdly, I do not think we should give as much emphasis as Becker does to strict equality of exchange (equal benefit for benefit) in considering what would constitute a proportionate return for good received. What shows disrespect for a benefactor, I suggest, is a failure to make an equal effort to benefit her *relative to* one's respective capacity for producing benefits. A proportionate return should thus be understood, at least as a first approximation, as one that realizes one's respective capacity to create benefits to the same proportional extent as one's benefactor realized her capacity in benefiting you. Depending on what our respective benefit-producing capacities happen to be, a proportionate return might consequently be of smaller or larger value than that we received. The fair-dues conception of reciprocity embodies this alternative understanding of proportionality. In this respect it may in fact be somewhat revisionary with regard to what people in societies like our own currently tend to expect in reciprocation for their efforts.

A final point, which Becker also notes,[51] concerns the distinction between substantive and formal reciprocity. Institutions and proposed conceptions of justice exhibit formal reciprocity when they require people to acknowledge that the claims they are entitled to make of others can also be made by others of them. But formal reciprocity need not entail substantive reciprocity between people: actual, ongoing, predictable promotion of each other's good. Consider, for example, a society that is governed in accordance with a utilitarian theory of justice, a theory which says that institutions must be designed to maximize average social utility. A liberal critic of utilitarianism, such as Rawls, will point out that average social utility could conceivably be maximized by institutions under which the basic interests of some are routinely sacrificed for the benefit of others without any return, e.g. by enslaving a small proportion of the population. Yet this failure of substantive reciprocity is quite compatible with formal reciprocity. For every citizen has to accept, under this utilitarian dispensation, that she may have to sacrifice her good for that of others in the same way that others may be required—and some currently are required—to sacrifice theirs for her. It is crucial to my argument that citizens motivated by an ethos of democratic mutual regard will not be satisfied with institutions that satisfy a merely formal reciprocity. They will expect, as a matter of dignity, to see actual returns for the benefits they provide for their fellow citizens, and, putting themselves empathetically into the shoes of others, will likewise expect to see others receiving actual returns for the benefits they provide. Only then will all be able to assent to these institutions without undignified self-abnegation.[52]

3.3   *Reciprocity and Egalitarianism*

Imagine a citizen who addresses her fellows, saying, 'I exist to create benefits for others, but others need make no effort to create benefits for me.' As intimated above, this smacks of servility, of seeing oneself as intrinsically less worthy than others. On the other hand, she might say, 'I exist to enjoy benefits created by others, but I need make no effort to create benefits for them.' This, for its part, smacks of aristocracy, of seeing oneself as somehow intrinsically more worthy than others. Neither standpoint, that of servility nor that of aristocracy, is compatible with the ethos of democratic mutual regard, an ethos which insists that, in the design of their society's ground rules and basic institutions, individuals regard one another as equals. In this respect, the concern for reciprocity is, as I have emphasized, an egalitarian concern, one that derives from a picture of the good society as a community of mutual respect between equals.

However, is the concern for reciprocity (or, more exactly, the concern for a form of reciprocity such as that expressed in the fair-dues conception of reciprocity) perhaps egalitarian in another sense? Could it not be argued that the concern for reciprocity is, in fact, simply derived from the concern for some form of equality of opportunity? The thought here is this. Across a wide range of cases, an insistence on substantive economic reciprocity will equalize opportunity for or access to various kinds of advantage. Think, for example, of Marx's argument that all should work so that all can have equal access to free time. Perhaps it is simply this equalization of access to advantage that ultimately matters, not reciprocity for its own sake. Reciprocity, on this view, is not itself an axiom of justice, but is more like a theorem derived from some kind of equal-opportunity axiom. I think the link between substantive economic reciprocity and various forms of equality of opportunity is undeniable. And I speculate that this also goes a long way towards explaining why so many egalitarian thinkers have endorsed a commitment to substantive economic reciprocity (and, indeed, why we ought to). But I am not convinced that the moral significance of reciprocity is exhausted by this connection. A case can be made that it ultimately stands as an independent demand of justice, as a primary virtue of shared productive endeavour in its own right.

To begin with, we should note how widespread concerns over economic free-riding and parasitism do not depend, as is sometimes suggested, on there being unequal opportunities to free-ride or to act parasitically.[53] In the simple islander example presented above, each islander had exactly the same opportunity to free-ride. The situation on the imagined island would certainly be *more* objectionable if some citizens had no choice but to contribute while others had the opportunity to avoid contributing. But the situation described, in which all could choose to free-ride, but only some take advantage of the opportunity, is objectionable as it stands even though there is equal opportunity to free-ride. What matters is that the free-rider offloads the costs of provision onto other citizens when it is reasonably within his power to share them.[54] Similarly, I suggest that parasitism, in the sense defined above, does not become morally acceptable just because two citizens have the same opportunity to act parasitically. Parasitism and free-riding are akin to a wrong like pollution in this respect: it is wrong to engage in such practices even if everyone has the same opportunity to do so.[55]

Does the concern for reciprocity perhaps stem from, and reduce to, a concern for inequality in the ownership of assets, such as land and capital? This is one way one might interpret the import of John Roemer's early work on the concept of exploitation. Roemer sought in this work to reorient the Marxian understanding of exploitation away from a concern with the unequal exchange of labour for goods towards a concern for inequality in asset endowments.[56] Failures of reciprocity, it might be argued, are just a symptom of what is of real significance: unequal endowments of external assets.[57] However, it is striking that in his (to date) last word on this subject, Roemer retreats somewhat from the view presented in his earlier work.[58] He does so, moreover, for a reason which I think suggests that a concern for reciprocity has an important, independent role in our understanding of exploitation.

Roemer asks us to imagine two simple hypothetical economies in which there is a single kind of productive asset which, combined with labour, produces a single kind of output ('corn'). We are to assume that in both economies all citizens have the same capacity and opportunity to work. In one economy each citizen has an equal, privately owned share of productive assets. Some citizens do no work and live off the return to their share of productive assets. In the second economy, productive assets are collectively owned and each citizen receives a share of the social product in proportion to the labour he supplies. While both economies satisfy the asset-equality criterion for the absence of exploitation, Roemer acknowledges some uncertainty as to whether the first economy can really be described as non-exploitative. For property rights in this economy clearly do allow some citizens to live off the labour of other citizens when, by assumption, all citizens have equal capacity and opportunity to labour. Roemer is unsure as to what possible principle of distributive justice might underpin the judgement that living off the labour of others in this way is unfair. But perhaps the notion of substantive economic reciprocity that I am exploring here offers an answer. Some citizens in the first economy we imagined deploy their control over productive assets to extract a share of the social product without making a personal productive contribution in return. Their fellow working citizens would be unambiguously better off (in narrow economic terms) if these non-working citizens did not exist for they could then work the same assets at the same rate and get a higher income because they would no longer have to carry the burden of the latter's unreciprocated consumption. If Roemer is right to have 'second thoughts' about his original theory of exploitation, perhaps that is because there is a legitimate concern to see reciprocity of productive contribution between citizens that is (to some extent) independent of the concern to prevent brute luck inequality in endowments of land, capital, and so on.[59]

It might alternatively be argued that the concern for reciprocity is simply tracking, and is ultimately reducible to, a concern for equality of welfare, or for equality of opportunity for welfare.[60] In many instances, an insistence on reciprocation, or restriction on parasitism, can be expected to equalize welfare, or opportunity for welfare. If, for example, we understand welfare in roughly Benthamite terms as a state of subjective good feeling, based on the balance of pleasures and pains, insistence on reciprocity could in some circumstances equalize welfare levels. Think again of the sort of expectations Marx probably had of the day when 'every man becomes a working man and labour ceases to be a class attribute'. The pains of the many would be eased as former bourgeois 'idlers' take up some of the strain of production; and the pleasure-filled life of these idlers would come to an end. The overall distribution of welfare would thus be more equal.[61]

My views on this issue remain tentative, but I do not think the concern for reciprocity is, in fact, ultimately reducible to a concern for equality of opportunity for (or access to) welfare. One reason for thinking this (and the one I feel most tentative about) is that an insistence on reciprocity can sometimes have a disequalizing effect on welfare levels, and yet it is not obvious that the claims of reciprocity lose their force in all such cases. Consider the case of two castaways, Jim and Joanne. Joanne is blessed by nature with high productivity and, moreover, with a disposition that enables her to derive much enjoyment from her work. She rises at five each morning and throws herself into a twelve-hour day of work. She produces not only for herself, but for Jim too, so that at the end of each day, as a result of her labours, each enjoys a welfare level of thirty utils, well above the baseline of ten utils, a minimally acceptable level of utility that each would enjoy in the absence of any productive activity. (Imagine that she builds shelters for the two which for some reason have to be rebuilt every day.) Jim has much less productive capacity than Joanne. There is, however, one thing he is good at, and which Joanne values. He can cook excellent meals. Were he to cook a meal for Joanne at the end of each working day, her util level would rise to thirty-five, while his own, in view of the intrinsic burdensomeness to him of the cooking, would fall back to twenty-seven. Now, should Jim cook the meal for Joanne? Is Jim *obliged*, as a matter of reciprocity, of reasonable mutual advantage, to cook the meal?

I think that he is. While the effect of reciprocation is, on the assumptions we have made, to disequalize welfare levels between Jim and Joanne, I do not think, in this case, that this constitutes a decisive objection to insisting on reciprocation. Joanne could, after all, work solely for herself, in which case she would enjoy a welfare level of, say, forty-five utils, and Jim, let us imagine, would be left to achieve a mere fifteen utils through his own efforts. My intuition is that, in these circumstances, it would be unacceptably self-indulgent (unacceptably aristocratic) for Jim to refuse to reciprocate Joanne by cooking her the meal. Joanne has done *so much* for him, at great cost to her welfare (for she could enjoy forty-five utils if she chose to work wholly for herself). How can he reasonably refuse to do something for her in return, even if it does involve some modest cost to himself?[62] This is not to imply, of course, that the claims of reciprocity always trump those of welfare equality. There is some point at which the cost to someone like Jim of reciprocation may be so large that, under any plausible understanding of the norm of reasonable mutual advantage, this person no longer has an obligation to reciprocate. But to identify this lapse point, as one might call it, with *any* departure from strict welfare equality strikes me as implausibly extreme. I readily confess, of course, that mere statement of my intuitions about this hypothetical case does not constitute a decisive argument showing the inadequacy of welfare (or opportunity for welfare) egalitarianism. But I would press ardent welfare (or opportunity for welfare) egalitarians to search their intuitions in such a case. Even if you think that strict welfare (or opportunity for welfare) equality is a highly desirable goal, how would you feel if you were in the shoes of someone like Jim? Would you feel happy not reciprocating the person in Joanne's shoes?[63] Would you really feel that the relationship between the two of you is appropriately balanced, that the person in Joanne's shoes is getting a fair deal, that you are treating her with the respect that she is due as a benefactor?

Certainly in our ordinary social lives I think many of us do regard the concern with returning good for good, or substantive reciprocity, as having some degree of independence from the concern to act so as to generate or preserve equality of welfare (or, more precisely, to prevent brute luck inequality of welfare). If a friend gives me some good at no cost to himself, and the effect of my receiving the gift is to equalize welfare levels between us, so that no act of reciprocation is required to establish welfare equality, would I—would you—feel under no obligation to reciprocate, in view of the fact that welfare equality now prevails? What if you can reciprocate, thereby raising the benefactor's welfare, at no welfare cost to yourself? Would you really think yourself not obliged to reciprocate in this case, in which reciprocation is quite painless, but nonetheless welfare-disequalizing? But if in this case, why not also in the case where reciprocation also carries a welfare cost to you, but not one that seriously reduces your welfare (like the case of Jim above)? The fact that reciprocation is welfare-disequalizing in this second, Jim-like case cannot be, in itself, a decisive objection if welfare-disequalizing reciprocation is perfectly in order in the first type of case.[64]

I have claimed that a concern for reciprocity may incline us to sanction some inequalities of welfare that a strict principle of equal opportunity for welfare would incline us to condemn. But the opposite might also be true: the principle of equal opportunity for welfare may sanction some inequalities of wealth and welfare that the concern for reciprocity would lead us to condemn. Consider, firstly, the case of those who forgo paid work in order to care for children or the infirm. Do such carers have a claim, as a matter of justice, to assistance or compensation for the income they forgo? Someone who thinks of justice as consisting solely in equal opportunity for welfare might regard assistance or compensation as unjust, on the grounds that any income and welfare loss which results from becoming a carer reflects a lifestyle choice rather than bad brute luck.[65] In contrast, a reciprocity-based perspective might incline us to condemn this income and welfare loss, and to support measures of compensation or assistance to carers. The argument would be that care work counts as a form of productive contribution to the community, and that those who perform it thereby satisfy their obligation to reciprocate in return for a decent share of the social product, and, as such, have equal right to such a share of the social product as those who meet their reciprocity-based obligations through paid employment. Of course, such a conclusion depends not only on the view that substantive economic reciprocity is a fundamental demand of justice, but also on the claim that some kinds of care work count in satisfaction of reciprocity-based obligations, a claim I have not yet defended.[66]

Consider, secondly, what one might call pure gambles, e.g. a state lottery.[67] From the standpoint of equal opportunity for welfare, the inequalities in wealth and welfare that result from games of chance are not unjust because they result from individuals' choices to expose themselves to risk, rather than from brute luck over which they have no control. Lottery millionaires are, on this view, a perfectly legitimate feature of an egalitarian society. From the standpoint of reciprocity, however, lottery millionaires might be thought to be objectionable.[68] A lottery millionaire has not earned his wealth through a productive contribution but, having acquired it, he is thereby enabled to share in the social product without making a personal productive contribution in return.[69] It might be said that this outcome is just since the lottery winner's millions are paid for out of the gamblers' combined stakes, and, in advancing their stakes, the gamblers in effect consent to the possibility that someone will end up living off their monies. But we do not necessarily have to regard this outcome as just merely because the gamblers consent to it as a possible outcome of their gamble. It is plausible to argue that we have some moral obligations to each other that cannot be lifted even in the context of a fully consensual, fair gamble. Should we regard the outcomes of fair slavery gambles ('Heads, you become my slave; tails, I become your slave') as just?[70] I might plausibly be said to have an obligation to refrain from exercising absolute, arbitrary power over others, an obligation that is not cancelled, with respect to particular people, by my entering into a slavery gamble with them, but which makes it improper for me to enter into such a gamble in the first place.[71] Similarly, a proponent of the fair-dues conception of reciprocity might say that the obligation to make a decent productive contribution to the community in return for a sufficiently generous share of the social product is binding, and that it is morally wrong for people to seek to escape this obligation through lotteries and similar kinds of gamble. In this respect, gambling is simply not the activity of a good citizen.[72]

The lottery millionaire case brings out what is, I think, the most fundamental reason for thinking that the concern for reciprocity is not ultimately reducible to the concern for equality of opportunity for welfare. Let's say we think of welfare in terms of the satisfaction of preferences, or as some kind of hedonic buzz that comes from their satisfaction. It is easy, in these discussions, to treat preferences, and the source of our hedonic buzzes, as things that are simply given to us, exogenously: 'tastes' that simply reflect how we are wired up. But this is not, as a general matter, an accurate picture. As Ronald Dworkin points out, many of our preferences reflect judgements we have made about what activities and projects have value for us.[73] But the judgements we make should surely be guided by moral considerations, by a desire to avoid disrespectful treatment of others. What sort of moral considerations should we take account of in forming our preferences? I would claim, following the argument in Section 3.2, that one of these guiding considerations should be a concern to cooperate with others on terms of reasonable mutual advantage and, therefore, of substantive economic reciprocity: we should form our preferences in a way that is attentive to the norm of reasonable mutual advantage and to the claims of fair-dues reciprocity. What is arguably objectionable about those who become, or who even seek to become, lottery millionaires is that they have not necessarily internalized these claims as constraints on their preferences; they may well be motivated by a conception of personal welfare in which the 'dream life' to which they aspire is a life in which they are elevated above their fellow citizens and the nexus of reciprocation; they desire what I referred to above as an 'aristocratic' life, in which others serve us but we are not obliged to serve them.[74] But what is the implication of saying that, as a matter of justice, people should be guided by a norm of reciprocity in forming their preferences, their conceptions of personal welfare? Surely we can't still say that reciprocity matters only because, and to the extent that, it serves the objective of equal opportunity for welfare; for we would now be saying that the objective of equal opportunity for welfare must itself be 'laundered' to accommodate the concern for reciprocity. It would now be understood to mean equal opportunity to satisfy reciprocity-respecting conceptions of personal welfare. Perhaps if an individual, through no fault of his own, cannot form such conceptions, he should be exempted from the claims of reciprocity (though I would caution against attaching too much weight to such an exceptional case). But so long as we say that the concern for reciprocity should play some role in the preference formation of those who are capable of taking its demands on board, we seem to have accorded reciprocity an independent role in our thinking about justice.[75]

A final thought: Suppose that the main claim of this section is wrong, and that the moral significance of reciprocity is, in fact, entirely reducible to a concern for some radical form of equal opportunity, e.g. opportunity for welfare. Even if this were so, it would not follow that we should dismiss reciprocity. Even if it is only, as I put it above, a 'theorem' derived from some deeper 'axiom' of equal opportunity, it may nevertheless be an important theorem, and one that we should give greater attention to in developing our understanding of economic justice.

3.4   *Instrumental Arguments for Reciprocity*

We should distinguish fundamental and instrumental arguments for reciprocity (that is, substantive economic reciprocity). A fundamental argument for reciprocity seeks to explain why citizens *ought* to have some expectation of reciprocity on the part of their fellow citizens. Thus far I have focused on this kind of argument, arguing that reciprocity (of a kind like that embodied in the fair-dues conception) is what citizens guided by an ethos of democratic mutual regard properly expect of each other in the economic context. Instrumental arguments, by contrast, simply take the expectation of substantive economic reciprocity *as a given*, as a brute fact of life, rather than as something that stands in need of justification. Instrumental arguments have the following general form: Where people do in fact have an expectation of substantive economic reciprocity, institutions and policies that violate these expectations will tend to provoke feelings of alienation and resentment. This will in turn tend to weaken the effectiveness and stability of the relevant institutions and policies. And this, in its turn, could undermine the effective pursuit of various valuable social goals. Such goals would be better served by institutions and policies that work with the grain of these expectations. Therefore, for the sake of these goals, these institutions and policies should respect reciprocity-based expectations. I shall confine myself here to one instrumental argument, one with particular relevance to the overall concerns of this volume. The argument concerns institutions and policies that involve substantial, ongoing redistribution of income and wealth.[76]

The essential point is well made by Samuel Bowles and Herbert Gintis in a recent analysis of the prospects for egalitarian reform in contemporary capitalist societies.[77] Bowles and Gintis argue that popular resistance to the American welfare state derives not from an opposition to egalitarian redistribution per se, but to redistribution that enables citizens to evade the contributive responsibilities that derive from a widely shared norm of 'strong reciprocity'. Bowles and Gintis start with the observation, confirmed in a variety of experimental settings, that individuals tend not to conform to the standard model of 'Homo economicus', who rationally pursues his self-interest without regard to any norms of fairness. The evidence rather supports an alternative model of 'Homo reciprocans'. People tend not to be rational egotists, or unconditional altruists, but conditional cooperators, willing to do their bit in cooperative ventures to which they belong provided they are assured that others will also make a reasonable contribution. Their commitment to such norms of fairness is such that they are often willing to accept costs to themselves rather than see such norms violated with impunity. (One might interpret this, in line with my argument above, as a willingness to pay a price in order to assert one's dignity.) Widespread adherence to the norm of strong reciprocity may be explicable in evolutionary terms: communities in which Homo reciprocans predominates may find it easier to solve important problems of trust and collective action, and so survive and expand, than communities in which Homo economicus predominates.[78] If, however, commitment to the norm is so deep-rooted, then, Bowles and Gintis argue, egalitarians must frame their reform proposals in a way that explicitly acknowledges and upholds it.

A similar argument concerning the necessary conditions under which citizens will grant their 'contingent consent' to egalitarian social policy is made by Bo Rothstein in relation to European universalistic welfare states.[79] According to Rothstein, citizens will support programmes that are quite strongly redistributive, even if they are not (or not clearly) net beneficiaries, if they are assured that all other beneficiaries will also make a reasonable contribution to the costs of the programme. Where social policies are universalistic in the sense that there is an inclusive share-out of both benefits and contributions, these policies will consequently have greater perceived legitimacy and, Rothstein argues, will thus be relatively resistant to the politics of welfare state retrenchment. The apparent importance of substantive reciprocity in promoting solidaristic action is also attested to by much of the work that social psychologists have done on the determinants of helping behaviour. In a wide range of experimental settings psychologists find that the probability of one person assisting another is increased where they have previously received help from that other; and the likelihood of assistance also tends to decrease where the needy other has previously hindered the subject.[80]

In short, given widespread expectations of substantive reciprocity, the creation and maintenance of redistributive policies and institutions is made easier if the policies and institutions work in a way that makes such reciprocity manifest. Of course, it does not obviously follow from this that egalitarians ought to embrace the specific conception of reciprocity sketched in this book. But designing policies and institutions in accordance with something like the fair-dues conception of reciprocity is certainly one way to make substantive reciprocity manifest, and this gives us a further reason to include a commitment to reciprocity of this kind in the conception of justice we use to frame our discussion of economic citizenship.

CHAPTER 4

Justice as Fair Reciprocity

Q. What is the alternative to the present unequal distribution of
work and good things?
A. That all should be obliged to do their fair share of the work,
and to content themselves with a fair share of the good things.

(J. L. Joynes, *The Socialist Catechism*[1])

In this chapter I shall bring together the ideas introduced in Chapters 2
and 3 and summarize the conception of justice which animates the
philosophy of economic citizenship presented in this book: justice as
fair reciprocity. Fair reciprocity centres on a commitment to substantive economic reciprocity. But it integrates this commitment with those
of the kind presented in Chapter 2: the commitments to respect and
uphold basic civil liberties, and to protect citizens from significant
brute luck disadvantage and from market vulnerability. It holds that
where the institutions governing economic life satisfy these (and certain other) commitments to a sufficient extent, citizens who claim the
generous share of the social product available to them under these institutions have an obligation to make a decent productive contribution
to the community in return.

It is important, however, to distinguish between ideal and non-ideal
forms of justice as fair reciprocity. In its ideal form, fair reciprocity
requires that the institutions governing economic life fully prevent or
correct for brute luck inequality in access to external wealth and in
marketable talent, and compensate appropriately for brute luck handicaps. These institutions must produce what I term a comprehensively
egalitarian society. In Section 4.1 I explain the ideal form of justice
as fair reciprocity in more depth. Focusing specifically on brute luck
inequality in marketable talent, I outline a system of redistribution, the
egalitarian earnings subsidy scheme (ESS), which corrects perfectly for
brute luck inequality of this kind. However, while having considerable

attraction in theory, redistributive schemes like ESS do not appear to be very feasible in practice; and this, in turn, casts doubt on the feasibility of realizing fair reciprocity in its ideal form.

This suggests the need for something like a theory of the second-best. If justice as fair reciprocity is not to be dismissed as unhelpfully utopian, we need to outline a non-ideal form of fair reciprocity that points us in the direction of a substantially more just society without being subject to the same feasibility objections as fair reciprocity is in its ideal form. This is the task of Section 4.2. In its non-ideal form, fair reciprocity demands that the institutions governing economic life satisfy a threshold level of absolute and relative economic opportunity, a threshold set below that necessary to achieve a comprehensively egalitarian society. The key question concerns how we specify this threshold. I argue that in specifying the threshold we should attend to a long-standing aspiration of the modern egalitarian movement: the aspiration to create a society that has abolished the bads classically associated in socialist thought with the proletarian condition: brute luck poverty; market insecurity and the attendant risk of domination by others; lack of opportunity for self-realization in work; and the underlying experience of class division based on unequal access to education and inequality in initial endowments of wealth. Even in its non-ideal form, then, fair reciprocity is a demanding prospect. But it is, I suggest, a more obviously feasible one, and thus one that can more readily enter into contemporary policy debates as a guide to reform.

Having outlined the basic content of justice as fair reciprocity, in both ideal and non-ideal forms, in Section 4.3 I note a further justice-related concern that should enter into a fuller elaboration of fair reciprocity, and which will play some part in later discussion. Section 4.4 concludes.

4.1   *Ideal Fair Reciprocity: Comprehensive Egalitarianism*

Justice as fair reciprocity combines a commitment to substantive economic reciprocity with other commitments of justice, most notably those introduced in Chapter 2. Where the institutions governing economic life are sufficiently just in terms of these other commitments, citizens who claim the generous share of the social product necessarily available to them under these institutions have an obligation to make a decent productive contribution to the community in return. But to what extent, exactly, must the institutions governing economic life satisfy commitments like those described in Chapter 2? More specifically, how far must society go in preventing or correcting for significant brute luck disadvantage? Ideally, of course, the institutions governing economic life should satisfy this commitment in full. They should provide appropriate compensation for handicaps, as defined in Section 2.4, and they should prevent or correct *in full* for brute luck inequality in access to external wealth and in endowments of marketable talent. Such a society would be, as I shall put it here, *comprehensively egalitarian*. What would the economic constitution of such a society look like? How would it integrate the commitments to prevent or correct for significant brute luck disadvantage and to substantive economic reciprocity? Is comprehensive egalitarianism a feasible objective?

4.1.1 *The Egalitarian Earnings Subsidy Scheme*

I shall focus here on arrangements for coping with brute luck inequality in endowments of marketable talent. I thus set to one side for the moment the treatment of inequality in inheritances of external wealth and the treatment of handicaps (already discussed in Section 2.4). I shall also assume that we are designing arrangements for a hypothetical market economy in which all markets are 'frictionless' and perfectly competitive, thereby abstracting from problems of localized monopoly and market vulnerability of the kind I discussed in Section 2.5. I also assume that the educational system is such that everyone has full opportunity to convert whatever natural abilities they have into marketable talent. Nevertheless, owing to differences in genetic endowment, or the ineliminable consequences of differences in social background, some individuals in this society are able to command a higher market return on the deployment of their talents than others. To prevent or correct for brute luck inequality in marketable talent, the community will therefore have to tax and redistribute earned incomes in some way in order to correct for this residual inequality of talents. What form should this redistribution take?[2]

   To help fix ideas, imagine that we have two people, Alf and Betty. The maximum that Alf can reasonably be expected to earn in a full working year given his exogenously determined ability endowment is £25,000, while the maximum that Betty can reasonably be expected to earn over the same period given her endowment is £80,000. Clearly, there is a significant inequality between Alf and Betty in earnings potential, and thus, in their accessible bundles of income and leisure. This is depicted in Figure 4.1, where Alf's trade-off between income and leisure, when working at his peak-ability wage rate (the highest wage rate he can reasonably be expected to command

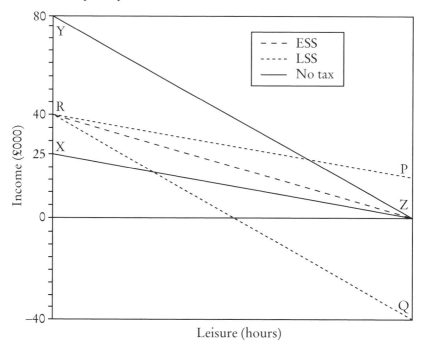

Figure 4.1. *Alf and Betty under the no tax-benefit system, LSS (lump-sum tax–subsidy proposal), and ESS (egalitarian earnings subsidy scheme)*

given his endowment of talent) is given by the line XZ, and Betty's trade-off is given by the line YZ. All the combinations of income and leisure on line YZ, and in the space between lines XZ and YZ, are in principle accessible to Betty but not to Alf. It is this inequality, deriving from the brute luck inequality in endowments of talent, that I wish to address.

Here is one way in which this inequality could in principle be addressed. Imagine that the average earnings potential across all the millions of citizens in Alf and Betty's society is, say, £40,000. For every pound that someone with Alf's earnings potential actually earns, let us give him an earnings subsidy of 60 p; and, for every pound that someone with Betty's maximum reasonable earnings potential actually earns, let us require her to pay 50 p in tax. No subsidy is paid, and no tax is due, however, until each respectively chooses actually to work and earn some income; and the final amount of the subsidy or tax that each is eligible for will depend entirely on how much income he or she chooses to earn, though the *rate* of subsidy or tax per pound earned will remain the same for each of them regardless of how long or at what wage rate they choose to work, being based on an estimate of their respective earnings potentials. We may refer to this proposal as the egalitarian earnings subsidy scheme (ESS).

The essence of ESS may be captured by a simple function:

$$y_i = (1 + s_i)w_i h_i$$

where y_i is the level of after-tax income of individual i, w_i is the individual's wage rate in whatever job he or she happens to be working in, h_i is hours worked by the individual, and s_i is the subsidy rate applied to each pound that individual i earns. The formula for s_i itself may be simply given as:

$$s_i = (t^* - t_i)/t_i$$

where t^* stands for the society's average earnings potential over, say, a full working year, and t_i stands for the individual's own earnings potential over this same period.[3] Where $t^* > t_i$, s_i will thus be positive; and where $t^* < t_i$, s_i will be negative (i.e. the individual will face an earnings tax).

In terms of Figure 4.1, the effect of ESS is to shift Betty's peak-ability income–leisure schedule down from YZ to the dashed line, RZ, and to shift Alf's peak-ability income–leisure schedule, XZ, up to this same dashed line. Alf and Betty now both have the peak-ability income–leisure schedule of someone with their society's average earnings potential. Thus, if they have unequal earned incomes, that must be because they have made different choices about how long to work and/or about how close to work to their peak-ability wage rate, i.e. different choices about how to deploy their respective talents. Thus, while there may be inequality in earned incomes, there will be no brute luck inequality in earned incomes.

It is also striking how ESS produces a distribution of reward that, under certain assumptions, corresponds directly with that demanded by an intuitively appealing conception of substantive economic reciprocity. As I noted in Chapter 3, it is clearly incompatible with egalitarian values to insist that income shares be equivalent or strictly proportional to the absolute value of the individual's productive contribution. It is not incompatible with these values—specifically, with the commitment to protect citizens from brute luck inequality of marketable talent—to insist that income shares be proportional to the extent to which the individual realizes his respective *potential* to make a valuable productive contribution. If we provisionally make two simplifying (albeit heroic) assumptions, (*a*) that an individual's productive contribution necessarily takes the form of paid labour, and (*b*) that wage rates are an accurate measure of the value to the community of different productive contributions, then we can readily see that ESS will issue in a distribution of after-tax earned income that satisfies exactly this pattern of reward. Those who work longer hours and/or in jobs closer to their peak-ability wage rates will receive proportionately more income for doing so, and will thus receive a proportionately higher reward for making a larger productive contribution *relative to their capacity to make such a contribution*. On the other hand, two people who work the same number of hours in jobs that are at, or are the same percentage below, their respective peak-ability wage rates, will receive identical earned incomes. This seems fair enough, for, given the two stated assumptions, each will have made the same productive contribution to the community relative to his capacity to make a valuable productive contribution.[4]

Moreover, although ESS imposes taxes on earnings potential, rather than earnings performance, it cannot be said to involve what is sometimes called the 'slavery of the talented'.[5] Here it is instructive to compare ESS with the more widely considered (and, following consideration, widely rejected) scheme of lump-sum taxation of earnings potential. Under this alternative scheme, denoted in Figure 4.1 as LSS, Betty would pay a lump-sum tax of £40,000, while Alf would receive a lump-sum subsidy of £20,000. Thus, in terms of Figure 4.1, Betty's income–leisure schedule, working in her highest-paying job, would shift from YZ to RQ, and Alf's would shift from XZ to RP. Although both then obtain equal earnings when working full-time in their peak-ability jobs, this scheme is demonstrably inequitable. Looking back at Figure 4.1, we can easily see that for almost any level of after-tax income that is accessible to Betty, Alf can achieve that same level of income working fewer hours than Betty. In addition, if Alf wishes to trade income for greater self-realization in work, by taking a more challenging job that pays less than his highest-paying job, this will be a lot easier for him than for Betty: Betty cannot afford to be as picky as Alf about the jobs she takes because in order to obtain almost any given level of final income she has to work closer to her peak-ability wage rate than Alf has to.[6] Under ESS, by contrast, Betty and Alf face the same trade-off between income and leisure when both work at their respective peak-ability wage rates, or, indeed, when both work at any given percentage below their respective peak-ability wage rates. And, in consequence, both face the same cost structure in deciding whether to take a relatively low-paid but more satisfying job. There is a price to be paid for trading high-paying work for lower-paid, more satisfying work, but the price is not necessarily higher for the talented than for the untalented.[7]

4.1.2   *Incentives and Information*

One of the objections to economic egalitarianism that I bracketed in Section 2.4 concerns the impact of egalitarian measures on incentives and efficiency. The usual version of this familiar objection runs somewhat as follows: 'There are people out there with high and low earnings. The egalitarian intends to tax the people with high earnings to subsidize those with low earnings. But people with above-average talents and/or energies will then have no incentive to deploy their talents and/or energies beyond some moderate point because too much of the market return from their additional efforts will be taxed away and redistributed to others. The talented and energetic will consequently withdraw their labour. Production and general well-being will stagnate.' Does this objection to egalitarianism hold good in the case of a society centred on ESS?

As far as work incentives are concerned, the effect of ESS is to give everybody the same peak-ability after-tax wage rate. Faced with this wage rate, some people will choose to work more than they would in the absence of any transfer scheme, while others will work less. The direction and extent of change for any given individual, talented or untalented, will depend on how the conventional substitution and income effects happen to balance out in that particular instance. The direction of the aggregate effect on labour supply, relative to a zero subsidy–tax baseline, is theoretically indeterminate. There is no reason to suppose that the labour supply of the talented, or the workforce as a whole, will contract in the aggregate. As far as investment in human capital is concerned, it is important to bear in mind that in estimating an individual's earnings potential for purposes of assigning her an earnings subsidy–tax rate under ESS, we take into account what she could potentially earn after undertaking the level of training that is reasonable given her underlying ability endowments. A naturally talented individual who could earn a lot after undertaking all the training of which she is capable can choose to forgo this training, but this will not affect her (relatively high) estimated earnings potential or the (relatively high) earnings tax she will have to pay under ESS. If she consequently earns well below her potential, she will end up with a relatively low level of after-tax income. While ESS suppresses differences in final incomes across the ability range, it retains differences in final incomes between differentially educated people at a given level in the ability range, and so does not deprive people at any given level in the ability range of a material incentive to invest in human capital.

However, even if an ideal scheme of egalitarian redistribution akin to ESS doesn't destroy incentives, economic arrangements closely modelled on this scheme hardly look to be a feasible proposition. A scheme like ESS obviously requires a huge amount of very detailed information about citizens' respective earnings potentials. No state is ever likely to have all the relevant information, and it may well be intolerably intrusive, violating important privacy interests, for a state to try to acquire all of this information. As Frank Vandenbroucke has recently observed, it may well be the problem of imperfect information, rather than the usual ogre of self-interest, that ultimately defeats egalitarianism of a comprehensive kind.[8] (Note, moreover, that while any two people necessarily face the same prospects for income and leisure under ESS, they might face unequal prospects for combining income with job satisfaction or self-realization in work under such a scheme.[9] Were we to try to correct for this inequality as well, the necessary scheme of redistribution would be even more complicated, requiring even more information.)

Or is self-interest in fact still the fundamental problem here? If citizens are sufficiently conscientious, can they not be relied upon to volunteer the best information they can about their respective earnings potentials? And wouldn't this make it possible for the state to introduce and operate a scheme like ESS with tolerable accuracy? To be sure, this would require a high degree of conscientiousness on the part of ordinary citizens. But many citizens in capitalist liberal democracies already accept that some egalitarian commitments can and should inform, and in certain respects constrain, how they act in their daily lives. Attitudes towards race and gender, and derivative commitments to prevent racial or gender inequality, come to mind. Why assume that citizens are incapable of firmly internalizing, and acting from, one more egalitarian commitment?

I do not think this form of egalitarian integrity, as one might call it, is beyond human nature. Moral growth, in the form of a steadily expanding recognition of the legitimate interests of one's fellow citizens, is, as John Stuart Mill emphasized, a human possibility, and there is no reason to think that the expansion of recognition need stop at the point where we confront material inequalities attributable to differential talent. Nevertheless, most citizens of contemporary capitalist societies presently do not have anything like the required level of egalitarian integrity and I think it is unrealistic to expect them to acquire it in the near future. Thus, even if the appeal to integrity shows that comprehensive egalitarianism is feasible in principle, it does little to rescue comprehensive egalitarianism from the charge of infeasibility here and now, or for the foreseeable future. Mill seems to strike the right balance between realism of the intellect and optimism of the will on this point when he writes that

Communism [which corresponds to what I have termed comprehensive egalitarianism] . . . requires a high standard of both moral and intellectual education in all members of the community. . . . I reject altogether the notion that it is impossible for education and cultivation such as is implied in these things to be made the inheritance of every person in the nation; but I am convinced that it is very difficult, and that the passage to it from our present condition can only be slow.[10]

There is, moreover, a second and perhaps more worrying problem for comprehensive egalitarianism. A scheme like ESS may be unfeasible even if citizens *do* possess the requisite kind of integrity. For regardless of how conscientious citizens are, or could be, in real-world economies they may well have a very poor sense of what their respective earnings potentials are. If the economic environment is as static as we assumed above, then over time the citizen might be able to make a fairly accurate evaluation of his or her own earnings potential. But real-world market economies are not static in this way. The pattern of demand and production is continually changing, with new goods and services appearing while other goods and services gradually disappear, and this may complicate enormously the task of estimating one's earnings potential.

Thus, even if we can parry the initial thrust of the incentives objection, our parrying move only raises further objections that cast doubt on the feasibility of achieving a comprehensively egalitarian society. Of course, any conclusion we reach here concerning the feasibility of comprehensive egalitarianism on the basis of analysing the problems associated with ESS in particular must be regarded as provisional. For there are other institutional proposals as to how we might achieve comprehensively egalitarian outcomes.[11] I suspect, however, that these proposals will encounter problems no less considerable than those that afflict ESS. Comprehensive egalitarianism is almost certainly not a feasible proposition for the foreseeable future for motivational reasons; and we may only be able to approximate it very roughly in the long run, assuming the necessary changes in motivation, for reasons of imperfect information.

4.2   *Non-Ideal Fair Reciprocity: Abolishing the Proletarian Condition*

Given the question mark which appears to hang over the feasibility of justice as fair reciprocity in its ideal form, a critic might wonder whether this conception of justice really has any contribution to make to contemporary debate about economic citizenship. In response, one can first reply that utopias are not necessarily bad things. Even if they are unrealizable, they may still describe an ideal that is worth attempting to approximate, so far as we can without undue cost. However, the critic is then entitled to ask what we take approximation of the ideal to imply. This is where the need for an account of what we may call *non-ideal fair reciprocity* comes in: an account of the most important demands of fair reciprocity which is not subject to the same feasibility objection(s), and which can therefore more credibly provide an objective for institutional design in contemporary circumstances.

Recall the essential idea behind justice as fair reciprocity: where the institutions governing economic life satisfy other demands of justice to a sufficient extent, those citizens who claim the generous share of the social product available to them under these institutions have an obligation to make a decent productive contribution to the community in return. In its non-ideal form, fair reciprocity does not require that these institutions reduce brute luck inequalities, particularly in relation to marketable talent, to the extent envisaged in the previous section. The relevant threshold of absolute and relative economic opportunity is set somewhat lower than the achievement of a comprehensively egalitarian society. But where, then, are we to set this threshold? By reference to what standard, or standards, should we attempt to specify it? It is possible to imagine different accounts of non-ideal fair reciprocity based on different answers to these questions. My aim here is to outline and defend one account of this threshold, and thus, of fair reciprocity in its non-ideal form.

I assume here that it is possible to speak of a modern egalitarian movement, a movement of ideas in politics that began to emerge in the period of the American and French revolutions, and which subsequently found its classic expression in the various currents of anti-capitalist thought that developed in the nineteenth and twentieth centuries. One way of approaching the above questions is to consider the historic ambitions of this movement. When its thinkers and activists called for a more equal society what, concretely, did they have in mind? What were they aiming to achieve, and to avoid, when they demanded greater equality? Certainly one ambition that some held was to create a society organized around the principle 'From each according to ability, to each according to need'. This ambition, which corresponds to what Marxists came to speak of as the higher phase of communist society, roughly corresponds to fair reciprocity in its ideal form.[12] But I think we can also discern a second, more limited, and perhaps more widespread, ambition underpinning the anti-capitalist commitment to equality. In no small part, the modern egalitarian movement—certainly, socialist and related currents of thought and activism—developed as a movement of protest against the condition of proletarian life in the early stages of industrial capitalism. What many in the movement sought, and intended in their advocacy of equality, was a society in which no one suffers the bads characteristic (in their eyes) of the proletarian's life under capitalism: a society which, while not necessarily free of wage labour, enables every citizen to escape the proletarian condition, understood as a condition of life characterized by these bads. This goal implies a significant reduction in the prevailing level of inequality, but not necessarily the level and form of equality that Marx and others anticipated for the higher stage of communist society. To achieve this goal, radical changes in property rights were thought to be necessary, though different thinkers and currents within the modern egalitarian movement disagreed about exactly what changes were necessary. Some, like Marx, thought that it would be necessary to abolish private ownership of the means of production. Others looked to more partial reforms, such as land nationalization, cheap public credit, and the development of an independent cooperative sector.[13] But they shared the raw intuition that the old revolutionary promise of liberty, equality, and fraternity could not be made good while some citizens languished in the proletarian condition. My proposal, then, is that we take this second ambition, the ambition to abolish the proletarian condition, as a basis for developing our account of what fair reciprocity requires in its non-ideal form. In identifying the bads that characterize this condition, I think, we thereby identify the most objectionable aspects of inequality in capitalist society, and thus the forms of disadvantage that are appropriate targets for fair reciprocity in its non-ideal form. Looking back at the writings of major thinkers in the modern egalitarian movement, one can identify at least four features of proletarian experience that were, rightly, of acute concern.

Firstly, and most obviously, is the experience of *immiseration*, the frustration of the worker's basic welfare and agency needs. One aspect of this, of course, is a low level of income making it hard to achieve core well-being and severely limiting the individual's opportunity for ethical agency. Marx argues famously that under competitive conditions investment results in growing capital-intensity of production which, in turn, works to keep the labour market in a state of excess supply, pushing wages continually down to a bare subsistence minimum.[14] But income poverty is only one aspect of immiseration. In Marx's vivid description of the proletarian experience in *Capital* we see its other aspects. In their efforts to maintain the rate of exploitation, Marx argues, capitalists try to extend the length of the working day. Consequently, the worker frequently lacks access to a decent minimum of free time. All too often her life becomes reductively a life of work, with no time for even adequate rest (let alone recreation).[15] Moreover, the working environment is often dangerous, exposing the worker to risks that also threaten her health. Marx describes cases in which long hours and unhygienic workplace environments combine to kill workers while they are at their jobs.[16] And, of course, Marx and other socialists did not hold workers themselves responsible for such deprivation: in general, they were suffering owing to forces beyond their control (in particular, owing to past efforts to detach them or their ancestors by force from their own means of production).[17] In the language of contemporary egalitarian theory, the proletarian typically suffered brute luck poverty in income and, more generally, in her capabilities for core well-being and ethical agency.

But the proletarian is not merely poor. Typically, he is also insecure, vulnerable, and dependent. Lacking independent access to the means of production, the proletarian relies on the capitalist for a living. In many contexts, the worker urgently needs the job the capitalist can provide, while the capitalist can readily substitute his labour-power for that of another worker. And so his basic structural reliance on the capitalist results in a vulnerability of the kind described in Section 2.5. Employers can take advantage of the worker's vulnerability to impose various controls on the working life of the proletarian, or, indeed, on his life outside work. To be subject to arbitrary power of this kind is bad, first, because of its likely contribution, through exploitation and abuse, to the deprivation described above. But such vulnerability is also arguably a bad because, as Philip Pettit and Quentin Skinner have recently argued,[18] it represents a kind of unfreedom. As Pettit argues, to 'suffer the reality or expectation' of subjection to the arbitrary will of another

is to suffer an extra malaise over and beyond that of having your choices intentionally curtailed. It is to have to endure a high level of uncertainty. . . . [that] makes planning much more difficult. . . . [and which] is likely to produce a high level of anxiety. . . . [it] is to have strategic deference and anticipation forced upon you at every point. You can never sail on, unconcerned, in the pursuit of your own affairs; you have to navigate an area that is mined on all sides with dangers.[19]

The demand for an end to the proletarian condition is in part the demand for an end to the *dependency* that generates such uncertainty and pressure for 'strategic deference'. Michael Sandel has pointed out how this aspect of proletarian life was of prime concern to many US critics of industrial capitalism in the nineteenth century, who saw in it a threat to the republican ideal of the self-governing citizen.[20]

A third feature of proletarian experience that provokes concern in the writings of critics of capitalism is the proletarian's typical *lack of opportunity for self-realization in work*.[21] In a sense, this is just one more aspect of the problem of immiseration. However, this concern has particular relevance in thinking about the just allocation of productive obligations, and so, given the importance of productive obligations in the theory of fair reciprocity, perhaps warrants the special attention I intend to give it here. In introducing the concept of work-related self-realization I am not making, nor am I implicitly committed to, the controversial perfectionist claim, sometimes associated with Marx's early writings, that self-realization necessarily expresses itself through work. What I in fact have in mind is better captured in Ronald Dworkin's so-called 'challenge model' of the good life. The good life, Dworkin argues, consists in formulating and responding with virtuosity to intrinsically valuable challenges: for example, acquiring a working knowledge of modern physics, playing a musical instrument, being a loving parent, and so on.[22] When I say that the proletarian lacks opportunity for self-realization in work, I mean that she is unable to treat her work, taken as a whole over the full course of a normal working life, as itself a site of meaningful, purposive challenge in Dworkin's sense.[23] Working life is, reductively, a burden to be borne, having no significance to her beyond the income it earns. By contrast, a worker with opportunity for self-realization in work is able to formulate intrinsically valuable challenges within the context of her working life, so that her work comes to have a significance to her that goes beyond the income it earns. I do not claim, as a labour-perfectionist might, that the individual ought to treat her working life in this way, still less that she should be constrained to do so. But she should have the opportunity to do so if she wants.

Underpinning these first three salient bads of the proletarian condition is the most basic fact of proletarian life: the experience of having one's life prospects, and perhaps one's self-image, fundamentally and detrimentally shaped by *class division*: that is, by social division based on unequal educational opportunity and unequal initial access to wealth. The proletarian is constrained to sell his labour-power under conditions of vulnerability that lead to poverty, strategic deference, and a lack of opportunity for self-realization in work, because he is at the sharp end of educational and/or wealth inequality. Moreover, even if these more acute symptoms of class division could be substantially reduced, educational disadvantage and poor initial access to wealth could still leave their victims substantially worse off than other citizens. Such disadvantage constrains the challenge that individuals can realistically pose for themselves in life, and in this way impoverishes the ambition and quality of their lives. Inequalities of this kind can also have an undesirable effect on how citizens view each other, diminishing their commitment to an ethos of democratic mutual regard in favour of class-specific cultures that make arbitrary distinctions and harbour resentments. These attitudes may produce patterns of discrimination that in turn work to consolidate the original inequalities.

I suggest, then, that we elaborate the non-ideal form of fair reciprocity in terms of the ambition to create a society in which citizens are able to live free of the various bads that define the proletarian condition. Fair reciprocity, in its non-ideal form, demands that the institutions that govern economic life be structured so as to satisfy at least the following core commitments:

1. *Non-immiseration.* No citizen should suffer brute luck poverty in income or, more generally, in her capability for core well-being and/or ethical agency.
2. *Market security.* Each citizen should enjoy adequate protection against market vulnerability and the exploitation and abuse to which it can lead.
3. *Work as challenge.* Every citizen who is expected to work should have adequate opportunity to make her working life a site of intrinsically valuable challenge (adequate opportunity for self-realization in work).
4. *Minimized class division.* Inequality in educational opportunity and in initial access to external wealth should be reduced to a reasonable minimum.
5. *Non-discrimination.* In addition to (4), citizens should be protected from discrimination on the basis of morally arbitrary characteristics in areas like employment and education. Such characteristics will typically include race, gender, sexual orientation, and religious belief.

Against the background of economic institutions that satisfy conditions (1)–(5):

6. *Contributive obligation (fair-dues reciprocation)*. Each citizen has an obligation to make a decent productive contribution, proportional to ability, to the community in return for claiming the high minimum share of the social product that is available to her under economic institutions that satisfy conditions (1)–(5).

The obligation described in (6) is conditional on background economic institutions satisfying conditions (1)–(5). Where they do not, those who are unjustly disadvantaged by this have a proportionately reduced obligation to contribute (they do not have to contribute as much as they would have to under institutions that meet these conditions). Other citizens, many of whom will presumably benefit from the failure of their society to meet these conditions, cannot demand, as of right, that those disadvantaged by this failure make a contribution at the same level as they would be obliged to make in a society that does meet these conditions; living at the expense of the disadvantaged as a result of this failure, they are not entitled to claim back from them the same degree of substantive economic reciprocation that they would otherwise have a right to expect. If the disadvantage is great enough, such that the effort to make a contribution is likely to expose individuals to risk of substantial harm, then these individuals have no moral obligation to make a productive contribution to the community. The class of disadvantaged individuals is, in this case, perfectly entitled to withdraw from active cooperation with the economic system (though they may still have reciprocity-based obligations to each other in the context of the struggle to replace the unjust social system, obligations which anticipate and shadow the contributive obligations they would have under a more just, reformed economic system).[24]

Undoubtedly, more needs to be said about the various commitments that define fair reciprocity in its non-ideal form. I will say more about (6), about what constitutes a decent productive contribution, in Chapter 5. Other commitments will be further clarified in the policy discussion which follows in Part II. But I should perhaps say a few words here about (4). What do I mean when I say that inequality in access to education and wealth should be reduced to a reasonable minimum?

We can answer this question by taking strict equality as the baseline and then asking what would plausibly justify movements away from this baseline. To begin with, the effort to create and sustain strict equality may be incompatible with respect for vital personal liberties (liberties that are vital to the protection of integrity interests of the kind described in Chapter 2). Maintenance of strict equality in initial access to wealth, for example, would require severe limitations on the freedom of family members to transfer resources to each other. It can be argued (and I shall argue in Section 8.2) that a limited freedom of this kind, though not necessarily anything like unrestricted freedom of transfer, is essential to the authentic expression of affection between family members, and should be respected for this reason. Of course, liberty-based arguments of this kind easily provide a cloak for special interests, and need to be treated with caution. But it would be arbitrary to presume that they never have merit.

A second consideration which might be thought to justify movement away from the baseline of strict equality is efficiency. In particular, it might be argued that the government should not seek to reduce inequality in respect to educational opportunity and initial access to wealth below the maximin level: the level at which further reductions in inequality would actually reduce the absolute level of educational opportunity or access to wealth enjoyed by those worst off in respect of these goods. However, this proposal needs to be treated with some care. I shall argue in Chapter 8 that fears over the disincentive effects of taxation of wealth transfers are probably exaggerated. Nevertheless, in the absence of a widespread, supporting social ethos, the max-imin levels of inequality in educational and inherited wealth, could be high, leaving society with clear class differences based on educational privilege and differential inheritance of wealth. On the other hand, if citizens in general accept the importance of reducing inequality in these areas, and are prepared to some extent to regulate their own beha-viour accordingly, then it is much more likely that the maximin level of inequality will in fact be quite low. A justified efficiency departure from strict equality, consistent with reducing class division to a reas-onable minimum, should be understood to refer only to an inequality prevailing when the government applies the maximin rule against the background of a strong supporting social ethos of this kind.[25] I do not think that contemporary capitalist societies like Britain and the United States currently have an ethos of this kind. But there are radical meritocratic elements in the public cultures of these societies which I think could be cultivated in this direction. (The cultivation of this, more limited kind of egalitarian ethos strikes me as much more feasible, at least in the foreseeable future, than the form of egalitarian integrity described above in Section 4.1.2.[26])

A critic might perhaps object that, in its non-ideal form, fair reciprocity does not offer a perspective on economic citizenship all that different from the communitarian philosophy I criticized in Chapter 1. Both repudiate comprehensive egalitarianism for a concern with achieving some kind of threshold level of economic opportunity. But this criticism is surely misguided. First, adherence to fair reciprocity, in its non-ideal form, involves no *principled* repudiation of comprehensive egalitarianism, as is usually the case in communitarian thinking. Quite the opposite, comprehensive egalitarianism can be (and, I have argued, should be) affirmed as an account of what justice ideally demands. The threshold level of opportunity to be achieved under the non-ideal form of fair reciprocity is to be viewed only as a second-best. Moreover, one is free to regard it, historically speaking, merely as an interim best until such time as the reigning social ethos and/or human ingenuity increase so as to make feasible the transition to a more comprehensively egalitarian society. By contrast, communitarians tend to see the threshold they espouse as exhausting the demands of justice. Secondly, the threshold level of opportunity demanded by fair reciprocity, in its non-ideal form, is ultimately more demanding and ambitious in egalitarian terms than the thresholds envisaged by most communitarian thinkers. There is not merely a concern for preventing income poverty, but a concern with the quality of working life, and, as I have just explained, a concern to achieve equality of opportunity (not just a basic level of opportunity) in areas like education and initial access to wealth.

I should also emphasize that the foregoing should be understood only as a provisional account of what non-ideal fair reciprocity requires at a minimum. In particular, while the non-ideal form of fair reciprocity does not require full correction for unequal endowments of marketable talent, it does not exclude efforts to correct for talent-based inequality. I shall certainly assume that it is perfectly legitimate to finance programmes intended to achieve goals like non-immiseration, market security, and non-discrimination at least in part from progressive taxes on earned incomes, thereby reducing the extent of talent-based inequalities in final incomes.[27] As I will further explain in the next chapter, a high degree of sensitivity to inequality of talent is built into the account of the citizen's contributive obligation under the non-ideal form of fair reciprocity: it is not expected that the less talented will make a productive contribution of the same value as that made by the talented in return for claiming the high minimum share of the social product available to them both under this form of fair reciprocity. Indeed, as I shall discuss in the next chapter, one might specify these obligations in a way that deliberately tries to compensate for residual talent-based inequalities.[28] Moreover, rough approximations of the talent taxes–subsidies described in the previous section, and rejected there as unfeasible in a pure form, may have a role to play in helping to achieve this goal.[29] But some differential reward for talent will be a feature of a society that satisfies fair reciprocity in its non-ideal form. In this respect, a society satisfying the non-ideal form of fair reciprocity more closely resembles the initial, lower stage of communist society, as Marx envisaged it, than the higher stage.[30]

4.3   *Primitive Resource Rights*

A central question of this volume is the extent to which resource claims carry corresponding obligations, in particular to make a productive contribution to the community in return for the resources claimed. Are there some resource claims that, in principle, do not carry such obligations? Here it is important to note an additional consideration of justice, not mentioned in this book so far, that should enter into a fuller elaboration of justice as fair reciprocity.

This consideration is perhaps best introduced by means of a hypothetical example. Imagine a collection of people in a state of nature on some previously uninhabited island. One group, the Lockeans, wishes to band together and form a community on the island in which members engage in production and trade. They see their productive use and development of the island as God's calling. There is a second group of people, the Hermitians, who believe that the good life consists in escaping the anguish that comes from the self-centred craving of material goods. They want to meditate on their surroundings in calm isolation, subsisting austerely on the uncultivated fruits of the soil. Now consider the following question: Do the Lockeans have an exclusive use-right, morally speaking, to the island's initial supply of natural resources?

It is surely implausible to claim that they do. The resources in question are not products of the Lockeans' combined industry, so it cannot be said that the Hermitians free-ride on or parasitically exploit the Lockeans' labours simply in virtue of the fact that they too make use of some portion of these resources. Moreover, the Hermitians do have a genuine interest in these resources. They wish to use them for purposes of contemplation and subsistence consumption. It is hard to see why, given that they have this genuine interest in using the resources, and that they cannot be considered free-riders or parasites merely in virtue of their use of them, they forfeit any rights of access and use over them simply because they wish to use them for different purposes than the Lockeans, i.e. for non-productive purposes. If we were to say that the Hermitians have no right to any share of the island's natural resources because of their non-productive inclinations, we would, in fact, be saying that they have no right to be on the island. And, as a long line of commentators from Herbert Spencer to Jeremy Waldron would be quick to point out, since the island is, we may assume, the only place they feasibly can be, we would thus be effectively denying them the right to exist.[31] Even passive meditation requires a space in which to meditate, and if the Lockeans claim all the island's space in the name of productive development, they will deprive the Hermitians of the space they need to meditate in.

What are we to conclude from this rather fanciful example? It is tempting to draw the conclusion that even those who are unwilling to participate productively in their society's scheme of economic cooperation nevertheless can have some resource rights. They can have, morally speaking, a right to what I shall call primitive resources: resources, such as undeveloped land, which exist accessibly to all prior to the community's productive endeavour. If the Lockeans and their ilk cannot provide adequate access to the resources that are covered by this right, then people like the Hermitians have a right to appropriate compensation. Respect for the primitive resource rights of all citizens should be regarded, then, as a further commitment of fair reciprocity. I shall give further consideration to the content of this commitment, and its policy implications, in Part II (see especially Section 7.3).

Each generation also inherits goods produced by predecessors and has, as a matter of intergenerational equity, a collective duty to pass on an adequate stock of such goods to future generations. I shall not consider the exact nature of this duty here, e.g. exactly what counts as an adequate stock of goods for future generations.[32] But I shall assume that there is some such duty, and that all citizens who choose to benefit from the inherited stock of produced goods share in the duty to see that their generation creates an adequate replacement product. Thus, to claim a share of the stock of these inherited goods is also, indirectly, to make a claim on the social product of one's fellow citizens (for they will have to produce an adequate replacement for the share of inherited goods that you consume). In making such a claim, one therefore acquires a reciprocity-based obligation to make a productive contribution to the community in return. (Insofar as primitive resources are destroyed in use, similar obligations will apply. However, to the extent that Hermitian-style use of these resources is essentially non-destructive, it will not generate an obligation to contribute to a replacement for future generations.)

4.4   *Conclusion: The Civic Minimum*

Let me now briefly recap the main argument of this chapter. Justice as fair reciprocity obtains when the institutions that govern economic life satisfy basic, justice-related commitments, such as those outlined in Chapter 2, to a sufficient extent, and those citizens who claim the generous share of the social product available under such institutions make a decent productive contribution to the community in return. In its ideal form, fair reciprocity requires that these institutions be comprehensively egalitarian in their operation, e.g. correcting fully for unequal endowments of marketable talent. In its more feasible, non-ideal form, fair reciprocity requires that these institutions meet a lower threshold of justice. How we specify this threshold is a matter of some controversy, but one attractive approach is to ask what these institutions would have to achieve so as to enable all citizens to avoid the bads classically associated with the proletarian condition: brute luck poverty, market insecurity and consequent domination by an employer, a lack of opportunity to treat one's working life as a site of intrinsically valuable challenge, and the more general life-shaping effects of being disadvantaged in access to education and wealth. The institutions that govern economic life must eliminate these bads. In these circumstances, the reciprocity-based obligation to make a decent productive contribution to the community applies to all those citizens who claim the high minimum share of the social product available to them.

Having now explained, at least in broad terms, the idea of fair reciprocity, we are also in a position to explain more fully the concept that gives this volume its title: the civic minimum. The civic minimum is simply that set of institutions and policies which satisfy the demands of fair reciprocity in its non-ideal form. These institutions and policies work to satisfy the high threshold of economic opportunity associated with fair reciprocity in its non-ideal form, but in a way which expects citizens to respect their contributive obligations. The content of this civic minimum will be the topic of Part II. One of the key issues I will have to address there concerns the tension between different demands of fair reciprocity, in particular between commitments to goals like market security and the commitment to see that citizens do respect their contributive obligations. Before I move on to a discussion of the civic minimum, however, I must first consider more explicitly exactly what is involved in respect for one's contributive obligation.

CHAPTER 5

The Contributive Obligation

In this chapter I shall consider one of the most crucial, yet difficult, questions that arise in developing the conception of justice as fair reciprocity: What do citizens have to do to meet the contributive obligation they have as a matter of fair reciprocity? I shall try to elaborate the citizen's contributive obligation by introducing the idea of a basic work expectation: a decent minimum of appropriate work that the community can reasonably demand of each citizen who claims the high minimum share of the social product available to him or her under economic institutions that are sufficiently just in other respects.

As I explain in Section 5.1, appropriate, reciprocity-satisfying work, or civic labour, must provide a significant good or service for the wider community. One form of civic labour, I argue, is market-generated, paid employment. However, we should not assume that only employment of this kind counts as civic labour. For one thing, some paid employment is not immediately market-generated, but the result of political decision-making and taxation, such as public-sector employment. This work counts as contributive, I argue, provided that it is geared to the production of an appropriate level of genuine public and/or merit goods. To assess whether such work is contributive, then, we need some guidance on what constitutes an appropriate level of output of these goods. I seek to identify the criteria we might use to assess whether given levels of output of these goods are excessive (or inadequate).

Section 5.2 extends the analysis, arguing that the same sort of considerations that make some tax-financed employment count as civic labour also apply to some kinds of care work that typically go unremunerated in societies like our own. Thus, these kinds of work should also be regarded, up to a point, as forms of civic labour that satisfy the contributive obligation of fair reciprocity. This sets the stage for

Section 5.3, in which I explain in more concrete terms the content of the basic work expectation. Though the exact specification of the basic work expectation is something properly left to local deliberative forums to determine, the analysis presented here does allow us to draw up some general guidelines that should be taken into account in defining the expectation for policy purposes. One important issue concerns how our specification of the basic work expectation should be adjusted to take account of the residual injustices that will characterize a society that satisfies fair reciprocity only in its non-ideal form (see Section 4.2).

For much of this discussion, the idea of productive contribution is linked to the notion of work. Not all work is contributive, in the relevant sense, but some is, and I take my brief to be that of explaining how we might distinguish work of the relevantly contributive kind. Section 5.4 considers briefly the extent to which the provision of capital, and saving, also count as relevant forms of productive contribution and, more broadly, the legitimacy of capital incomes from the standpoint of fair reciprocity.

5.1   *Civic Labour: Paid Employment*

In the previous chapter I argued that citizens have a contributive obligation: where the institutions governing economic life are sufficiently just in other respects, citizens who claim the high minimum share of the social product available to them under these institutions have an obligation to make a decent productive contribution to the community in return. How can citizens satisfy this contributive obligation? Thus far we have assumed that they can meet this obligation through work or labour (I shall use the terms interchangeably here). But, granting this assumption for the moment, what kinds of work can plausibly be seen as satisfying this obligation? For labour to count as contributive in this sense it must be what I shall call *civic labour*: roughly speaking, labour that provides a significant service for, or on behalf of, the wider community.[1] If one's labour has this quality, then it offers something back to one's fellow citizens in return for the goods and services they have provided for you. This shows appropriate respect for them, in view of the benefits they have provided for you, and diminishes or negates the net cost you impose on their consumption possibilities by appropriating these benefits. However, this response to the question with which we began obviously only raises another question: What kinds of labour count as civic labour?

The key issue in thinking about civic labour concerns the criteria we use to ascertain whether a given kind of work is sufficiently valuable to other citizens to count in reciprocation for the goods and services they have supplied. It is not enough that I regard the work I do as valuable to others. It must indeed be so, and, indeed, it must be recognizable as such by them. It may help here to recall Lawrence Becker's general point about what constitutes a fitting return for a benefit received: 'since the point of being disposed to reciprocate is to create and sustain balanced social relationships, the good returned will have to be good *for the recipient*, and (eventually) perceived by the recipient both *as a good* and *as a return*'.[2] Now one obvious test of the value, to other citizens, of the labour one performs is that provided by the market. Quite simply: Are people willing to part with their money to receive the goods and services you provide? If so, then it seems reasonable to say that the labour that went into the making of these goods and services is valued by your fellow citizens. This suggests that civic labour be understood, in the first instance, to refer to market-generated paid employment (or self-employment). Other things being equal, the longer one works in employment of this market-generated kind, the greater one's productive contribution may be said to be. Moreover, the more others are willing to pay for such work, then the more valuable it would appear to be to them (they are willing to forgo more of other things to acquire what you are offering). Thus, to the extent that increased willingness to pay is reflected in the market returns to employment, one's contribution may be said to be greater the closer one works to one's peak-ability wage rate, i.e. the more one realizes one's respective capacity to produce market value embodied in goods and services.[3]

However, I do not think we should conclude that the presence of an effective market demand for a given good or service necessarily means that the labour involved in producing it is civic labour. The production and exchange of some goods and services may be harmful to (some) citizens' basic interests. It has been argued, for example, that the sale of sexual services and the production and sale of pornography are damaging to the basic interests of women. They are said to perpetuate a perception of women as inferior, as objects for male sexual gratification, and this is said, in turn, to undermine equality of opportunity in a wide range of areas, or to threaten women's bodily integrity.[4] If the production and sale of a given good is objectively harmful to others in these ways, threatening the integrity and opportunity interests described in Chapter 2, then there is less reason to regard the labour involved in producing it as civic labour, even if there is, or would be, strong market demand for the good in question. In other cases, there may be a worry that consumption of a specific good involves an excessively high risk of self-harm, and it may be justifiable to prohibit the production and sale of the good on paternalistic grounds. Again, in this case, the reasons behind the legal ban on the relevant good service provide objective grounds for doubting the value to the community of the labour involved in its production, regardless of the level of production of the good the market would bear. If, for example, it is appropriate to prohibit a market in heroin on paternalistic grounds, then the labour of heroin-dealers does not count as civic labour even if it is highly paid. Of course, exactly which goods and services are objectionable in the first sense, or properly subject to restriction or prohibition on paternalistic grounds, is a controversial issue, and not one that I shall attempt to settle here. To the extent that there can be reasonable disagreement over whether or not the production and exchange of specific goods and services is morally or paternalistically objectionable, and properly restricted, there will also be reasonable disagreement at the margins about exactly which kinds of paid (or potentially paid) employment count as civic labour.

A second complication which arises is that much paid employment is not in fact, as we have thus far assumed, market-generated. Most advanced capitalist societies have large public sectors, and millions of people who are paid to work in the public sector. In many of these cases we cannot say that the value to other citizens of the work these workers do is validated by the fact that, as consumers, citizens freely decide to spend their income on the goods and services that these workers produce. In general, citizens are simply forced to pay taxes to fund the production of these goods and services. There are, of course, many forms of what economists call market failure (natural monopolies, missing markets, and so on) that seem to justify some degree of public intervention in the economy on efficiency grounds, and even the direct public production of some goods and services. As I shall further explain below, considerations of justice might also warrant forms of public intervention that alter the mix and level of private-sector production, or warrant direct public provision of particular goods and services. So doubtless some of this public-sector production is generating genuinely valued goods and services, and thus, the work involved in producing them can be regarded as contributive. However, we must also be attentive to problems of state failure, such as the tendency of bureaucrats and interest groups to work to expand levels of production of given goods or services in their own interest.[5] Where such state failure occurs, output of these goods and services may be driven up to levels that do not serve any genuine public interest and, in this case, some of the labour involved in their production cannot plausibly be seen as contributive. To assess how far labour in this context is contributive, therefore, we need first to assess whether or not the level of production of such goods is or is not excessive. What criteria can we use to make such an assessment? In discussing public provision of goods and services, economists usually make a distinction between merit goods and public goods, and it may help to consider provision of the two types of goods separately.[6] I shall begin with merit goods.

As David Miller points out, in a helpful analysis to which I am indebted, much of the discussion of merit goods concerns public provision that is motivated by considerations of justice: goods that people are thought to 'merit' because they have a claim to them as a matter of distributive justice.[7] Intuitively, many of the claims ventured here appeal to the concept of need. Many of us have a sense that people in certain kinds of circumstance are entitled to particular goods or services because, quite simply, they need these goods or services. Public provision of health care and personal social services, for example, seem tied up with provision for need. A typical case would be that of the physically frail elderly individual who needs a home help to clean her apartment and do odd jobs. Where public provision serves to meet clear and urgent needs there is a credible presumption that the labour involved in producing the relevant goods and services is civic labour. But, as said, state failure can occur, boosting the level of provision for such needs to an excessive level. How, in principle, do we distinguish between appropriate and excessive levels of provision of such merit goods?

One possible approach has already been suggested in Chapter 2. Recall our discussion there of how we might determine appropriate compensation for handicaps by using the theoretical device of the hypothetical insurance market. The proposal, derived, with some stylization and modification, from the work of Ronald Dworkin, is to ask what level and pattern of compensation for handicaps people would insure themselves for in an insurance market of a very special kind: one in which each prospective insurance purchaser has purchasing power based on her society's average earnings potential and, while knowing population-wide probabilities of having various handicaps, does not know her own, individual probability of having any particular handicap.[8] While it is impossible to know just what level and pattern of insurance each citizen would individually choose in such a situation, we can perhaps venture some claims about the insurance package that the 'average member of the community' would buy.[9] And, as Dworkin suggests, we might then base the level and pattern of public provision for handicaps on this package. Dworkin has himself extended the use of this device to consider public provision for health care, and it is not hard to see how we might use it to think about personal social services and the like.[10] If we can use this device to identify an appropriate level of public provision for various merit goods, or, more plausibly, to identify a range within which an appropriate level of provision would fall, then we will have some benchmark against which to evaluate actual levels of provision as appropriate, inadequate, or excessive. And we can then form a judgement about the extent to which the labour involved in the production of the relevant merit goods is genuine civic labour. (Note that if the overall level of public provision turns out by this benchmark to be clearly inadequate, this may imply that the level of private-sector production of some goods and services is excessive; in which case, it can be argued that the labour involved in producing the excess of private-sector goods and services is not, in fact, genuine civic labour.)

As Miller points out, the notion of merit goods is also sometimes used to refer to a good that ought to be provided for moral reasons other than reasons of distributive justice between citizens. For example, some of us might think that tigers ought to be protected because they are intrinsically valuable, and so we press for public provision of protected tiger habitats. The problem in this sort of case, however, is that in a society characterized by a plurality of conceptions of the good life, citizens are likely to regard different things as having intrinsic value in this way. Or, even if they can and do agree that a given range of activities and/or entities has intrinsic value, they may still disagree about how to rank these various goods when there is a conflict between supplying more of one at the expense of another, e.g. when providing a new tiger sanctuary conflicts with building a new art museum. Miller thinks that provision of such goods only counts as labour worthy of reward (in our terms, as a form of civic labour) to the extent that the supporters of tiger sanctuaries, or art museums, or poetry workshops, manage to persuade their fellow citizens of the intrinsic value of these goods (and, where necessary, on their superior ranking relative to other goods). I am unsure whether Miller thinks it is necessary to achieve unanimity on the issue at hand, or whether it suffices merely to win a majority of one's fellow citizens round to one's point of view. If the relevant criterion is unanimity, then the public provision of any such goods is likely to be hard to justify simply because, given the background plurality of views about the nature of the good life, unanimity is unlikely to be reached. But simple majoritarianism carries with it the usual risks of majority tyranny: specifically, in this context, of a stable, permanent majority raising taxes that are also paid by a stable, permanent minority to fund provision of merit goods that are of sufficient value (worth the tax price) only to members of the majority. On the other hand, the provision of such goods arguably is legitimate if the pattern of provision reflects the preferences of majority and minority in proportion to their respective tax contributions. If, in these circumstances, each community values the goods it receives enough to be willing to pay the relevant taxes, then the labour involved in producing the goods can be regarded as civic labour.[11]

Let us now turn to public goods. Public goods are goods characterized by features of non-excludability and non-rivalry: once such a good is provided, it is not possible (or is prohibitively costly) to exclude anyone from enjoying it; but one person's consumption of the good does not thereby diminish the amount available for consumption by others. There is usually a strong presumption in favour of public provision of such goods because the feature of non-excludability can easily tempt individuals to try to enjoy such goods without contributing to their cost, a strategy that, when widely adopted, results in their undersupply (the lighthouse doesn't get built because each fisher tries to free-ride on the contribution of others). But this still leaves open the question of the appropriate level of public provision of such goods. Defence, for example, may be a desirable public good. But if the level of defence provision is determined by the military, or by the defence industry, then some defence output is likely to be excessive. And some of the labour involved in defence provision should not then be regarded as contributive, for it ultimately serves the private interest of the producers and not a genuine public interest. Once again, therefore, we face the question of how we are to set about assessing whether a given level of tax-financed goods provision is or is not excessive.

Let's begin with the conventional economic analysis of the problem (stated here in very rudimentary terms). According to this analysis, the level of provision of a given public good should be set at the socially efficient level, this being the level of provision at which the marginal valuation of the public good, summed over all individuals in receipt of the public good, equals the marginal cost of providing the public good. So, for example, in a society where there are two possible goods, a public good, and, say, bananas, and the two members of this society value a marginal unit of the public good at three and two bananas respectively, then it is desirable to produce the marginal unit of the public good so long as the marginal cost is five bananas or less. If the marginal cost is, say, four bananas, then it is possible in principle to supply the extra unit of the public good and to give back to both people some of the bananas that they were willing to pay to get this extra unit, thereby making both unambiguously better off than if the extra unit of the public good had not been supplied. Such welfare gains cease only when the marginal cost of the public good equals their combined marginal valuations of the good, so output of the public good should be raised to this point and no further.[12]

Note, however, that even in this extremely simple example each person's marginal valuation of the public good differs: one is willing to give three bananas to get one more unit of the public good, the other only two bananas. As Miller points out, in practice the state is likely to finance public-goods provision from uniform (progressive or flat-rate) taxes; it is usually impractical to tax people according to their different marginal valuations of these goods. In the real world, then, even at the notionally efficient level of public-goods provision, some people will likely pay towards public-goods provision more than their marginal valuations of these goods, incurring thereby a welfare loss, while others will pay less than their marginal valuations, and thereby incur a welfare gain. Thus, even at the efficient level of provision an apparent inequity can arise.

To take account of this, Miller claims that, in specifying an appropriate level of provision of public goods, 'some consideration must be given to the distribution of . . . utility among persons'.[13] If the background distribution of income and wealth is fair, he says, then 'we might think that ideally everyone should gain the same amount from the bundle of public goods that is provided out of state revenues'.[14] At a minimum, we should try to ensure that 'each citizen [is] better off by comparison with a hypothetical situation in which no public goods . . . are provided'.[15] However, there is something paradoxical about what Miller proposes as a response to the alleged equity problem. Miller says that we should give consideration to how different levels of public-goods provision, financed from uniform taxes, affect the distribution of utility. But if we have information on this in the case of specific public goods, then, having attained the efficient level of provision, could we not put a tax on the welfare winners and pay a compensating grant to the welfare losers? And would this not be more or less equivalent to varying the original taxes according to individuals' different marginal valuations of public goods, the proposal that Miller rejects as impractical? That proposal is impractical precisely because the information about the distributional impact of public-goods provision that Miller wants us to take into account is so hard to collect. So I am not sure that Miller is offering us much of a solution to the original problem of how to achieve equity in (notionally efficient) public-goods provision.

Perhaps we can make further progress by trying a different approach to the problem (one which seeks not to supplant the conventional economic analysis, but to supplement it). Economists take individuals' valuations of public goods as given. They do not ask what preferences for public goods people *ought* to have. But perhaps this is a question we should ask: not what an efficient level of public-goods provision is for given preferences, but what a *just* level of public-goods provision is, to which people perhaps ought to adjust their initial, raw preferences. How, though, can we get a handle on the question of what a just level of public-goods provision would be? One possibility that might be worth exploring (I make no greater claim than that here) is to extend the approach I suggested we employ to help assess the appropriate level of provision of merit goods like health care and personal social services.

For illustration, imagine a group of citizens discussing whether or not to go ahead with a proposal for a new street-lighting scheme in their neighbourhood. The scheme is designed to reduce night-time crime. The citizens in this neighbourhood have very different exposures to risk of crime. Consequently, were they to evaluate the proposal in a purely self-interested fashion, they might well value the proposal very differently. Were the proposal to go ahead, financed from uniform taxes, this would then create the kind of equity problem that Miller draws our attention to. However, this particular group of citizens happens to be deeply imbued with the ethos of democratic mutual regard. Accordingly, they each wish to form a valuation of the proposal based, not on simple self-interest, but on taking into account all affected interests equally. To help ensure they do this, they engage in a variation of the thought experiment that I described above. Each imagines herself in a market in which she can choose whether or not to buy the street-lighting scheme, priced at a per capita tax sufficient to cover its cost. Each imagines that she has an equal endowment of purchasing power, based on average earnings potential, but suitably deflated to reflect other, pre-existing public-spending and tax commitments. Each imagines that she knows the population-wide risk of crime, but not her own exposure to risk. Each asks herself: Would I be willing to buy the scheme in this situation?

More generally, we can imagine a market of this kind in which individuals can choose between alternative levels of output of specific public goods, knowing their respective per capita costs, and ask how much of specific goods they would be willing to buy. Perhaps, as Dworkin suggests in the case of provision for handicaps and poor health, we can identify a level of output of public goods that 'the average member of the community' placed in such a market would choose to buy, and then use this as a guide to appropriate levels of provision of these goods. At least, we might be able to identify a range within which an appropriate level of provision of a given good would probably fall. Some individuals' valuations of public goods will still be lower or higher than the average, and so it is likely that some people will still be over- or undertaxed. But it is possible that after undertaking a thought experiment of this kind, citizens' valuations of public goods will be more convergent than they would otherwise be, so alleviating the problem of equity to which Miller points. I do not want to put too much stress on the specific thought experiment I have suggested here.[16] The more basic, and important, idea is that in trying to assess whether existing levels of output of public goods are excessive or not it may help to attend to the question of what level of public-goods production people ought to want, as a matter of justice, and not simply to the question of what an efficient level of production would be for given preferences.

This concludes my discussion of how in principle we might assess whether or not levels of output of merit and public goods are excessive, and thus whether or not the labour involved in their production counts as civic labour (labour that provides goods or services of sufficient value to one's fellow citizens to satisfy one's contributive obligation). It seems clear from the above discussion that there is likely to be some reasonable disagreement about whether or not levels of output of specific merit and public goods are excessive, and thus about the genuinely contributive status of all the labour involved in their production. There should be, in principle, a correct answer to the question of what levels of provision the 'average member of the community' would effectively opt for in the context of a hypothetical insurance market of the kind depicted above;[17] and this corresponds to the package of provision that the community should adopt. But in practice, of course, the conclusions we draw from such a thought experiment are likely to be somewhat speculative; and citizens who share this approach may well disagree as to what the correct answer to the question is. The most we can expect, in practice, is that citizens who employ this approach can agree on plausible, and not too broad, ranges within which the appropriate levels of output probably lie. Provided that actual levels of output fall within these ranges, citizens may then presume that the labour involved in producing the goods in question is genuinely contributive.

Assuming that even this modest hope is not unrealistic, another question now arises: How can we ensure that production of merit and public goods stays within the appropriate ranges? For, as I intimated above, conventional processes of representative democracy offer very imperfect protection against risks of bureaucratic or interest group capture in decisions about levels of merit and public-goods provision. Moreover, aside from this problem, ordinary citizens do not necessarily approach questions of merit and public-goods provision with a view to seeing justice done. Many base their preferences for provision of these goods on pure self-interest, and this can obviously skew levels of provision away from what justice requires or allows. How, then, can we diminish the risk that bureaucrats and lobbyists will push and pull provision to inefficient levels by disregarding ordinary citizens' preferences? And how can we encourage citizens at large to form more public-spirited preferences, and to bring these to bear on decision-makers?

This is, of course, a huge topic, and I will not explore it comprehensively here. But in recent years a number of political theorists have argued that the conventional processes of representative democracy might be usefully supplemented by new deliberative bodies, such as deliberative opinion polls and citizens' juries, that stand outside the normal channels of political representation, and these proposals seem pertinent to the problems at hand.[18] To illustrate the basic idea, imagine that every few years the state convenes a special assembly of randomly selected citizens, large enough to be a representative cross-sample of the citizenry, to discuss the public provision of a specific merit or public good. There might be one assembly for health care, another for education, and so on. We can imagine that such an assembly would meet for a fixed period of time, perhaps a week, during which its members would consider nothing but the issue of health care or education provision. Comprehensive policy briefings would be provided to all assembly members before the assembly convenes. Its members would then listen to expert testimonies and to the viewpoints of representatives of various interest groups, and would discuss relevant issues at length between themselves. At the end of the assembly's week its members would be required to come to some sort of conclusion on what they regard as the desirable level of public provision, or, more realistically perhaps, assuming a background of economic growth, a desirable level of increase in provision. All propositions would be costed and their tax implications made clear before any recommendation is made. The assembly's conclusion would then be publicly announced and forwarded to the legislature and government for consideration.

Assemblies of this type, citizens' commissions, address both of the concerns raised above. Firstly, they encourage citizens themselves to form more expert and public-spirited preferences about merit and public-goods provision. This effect is likely to be strongest for those who actually participate in the commission. Their self-interest and prejudice will be challenged by the direct communication of need by other citizens, by expert witnesses, and, not least, by the need in the course of discussion to offer defences of their views to other citizens that are not obviously merely self-serving. But to the extent that the deliberations and conclusions of the commissions are reported and followed in the media, it is possible that they will also influence the preferences of the citizenry at large. Secondly, the recommendations of such commissions might serve as a useful benchmark against which actual government decisions about the provision of specific goods can be debated. Policy-makers will need to justify to opposing politicians, to the media, and so on, why their decisions differ from the recommendations of the relevant citizens' commission. In many cases, they might have good explanations, such as the fact that they have a responsibility to treat any given question of provision in the context of public spending as a whole, from which perspective some increases proposed by citizens' commissions may look unfeasible or undesirable in the short run. But the mere fact that extra explanation has to be given might serve to discourage policy-makers from pushing levels of provision up to excessive (or, indeed, holding them down at inadequate) levels. And this, in turn, will increase the likelihood that the labour involved in producing the relevant merit and public goods is genuinely contributive.

5.2   *Civic Labour: Care Work*

A frequent criticism of contemporary communitarian thinking about economic citizenship is that it emphasizes paid employment to the exclusion of other forms of work, in particular forms of care work, traditionally performed disproportionately by women, which typically go unpaid. To what extent can such work be regarded as a form of civic labour?

In approaching this question, it may help to note that views about the status of care work, of its relationship to the contributive obligations associated with economic citizenship, have shifted quite substantially over time. Writing in 1911, Leonard Hobhouse was quite clear that a *mother's* care work should be regarded as a form of contribution worthy of reward:

if we take in earnest all that we say of the rights and duties of motherhood, we shall recognise that the mother of young children is often doing better service to the community and one more worthy of pecuniary remuneration when she stays at home and minds her children than when she goes out charing and leaves them to the chances of the street or to the perfunctory care of a neighbour.[19]

Hobhouse's words draw on what one might call the gendered conception of civic labour: men (husbands) satisfy the contributive obligation primarily through paid employment, while women (wives) generally satisfy it primarily through domestic, typically unwaged care work. This conception assumes that people naturally sort themselves into male–female couples through marriage, and that such couples naturally all exhibit the same division of labour between paid work and work in the home. Both types of work then receive some acknowledgement (though not necessarily equal entitlement to public benefit). William Beveridge fought hard to incorporate such an understanding of civic labour and entitlement into his wartime report *Social Insurance and Allied Services*, which exerted a huge influence on the construction of the British post-war welfare state.[20] A similar conception of civic labour has arguably also been a feature of Christian Democratic ideology in continental Europe, and its influence in some of these countries is still reflected in the male-breadwinner assumptions underpinning their welfare states and, relatedly, in their relatively low rates of female labour force participation.[21] Where the breadwinning father-husband disappears, the gendered conception holds, as the quotation from Hobhouse indicates, that the wife-mother ought not to get paid employment but ought to concentrate on the provision of care within the home. The state should assist her in this role, subsidizing her withdrawal from the labour market, while also, perhaps, encouraging her to find another male breadwinner to provide her with support.

As women have increased their participation in paid employment, this gendered conception of civic labour has come to look increasingly anachronistic. In some countries, notably the United States, the result has been a shift in the prevailing conception of civic labour: this conception has at once been degendered and at the same time narrowed so that civic labour is more or less identified with paid employment to the exclusion of unpaid care work. Whether you are a man or a woman, the way you repay society for the income you receive is, on this view, necessarily through paid employment.[22] Accordingly, it becomes harder to explain why those only performing care work should be in receipt of public support. The decision to have a child, or to look after an infirm elderly relative, if it is not seen as a form of civic labour, is naturally seen merely as a personal lifestyle choice on a par with, say, a decision to pursue an interest in bungee-jumping or mountain-climbing. No citizen can credibly claim public subsidy to help her pursue a lively interest in bungee-jumping or mountain-climbing. Thus, following the argument to its logical conclusion, no citizen can legitimately expect public support as a parent or other kind of carer. And so, whereas in 1911 Hobhouse found it obvious that paying single mothers to stay at home and raise their children is fully consistent with the principle that income should follow productive service, by the 1990s, in the United States at least, single mothers doing precisely this had come to be seen as the very model of unproductive, non-reciprocating parasitism. Of course, care work, for children and others, remains essential. And women continue to do a disproportionate share of it, putting them at a disadvantage in the world of paid employment.[23] Aside from contributing in this way to the continuation of gender inequality in the labour market, however, the tendency to identify civic labour with paid employment, to the exclusion of care work, is in itself highly questionable. I think we should integrate care work into our understanding of civic labour, while at the same time avoiding a return to the gendered conception of civic labour embodied in, for example, Beveridge's model of social insurance.

By care work I mean the work of caring for individuals who are unable, or who are not reasonably expected, to meet important needs by themselves, such as the infirm or children. In the case of parental care work, such work might be seen as civic labour because it helps to create the next generation of citizens, and all citizens of the present generation can quite plausibly be said to have a vital interest in the creation and nurturance of this next generation. This interest is, in part, a simple economic interest. All members of a given generation, including those who choose not to have children, will rely on the children of the next generation to support them as they age and their own productive capacity diminishes. But this interest also runs somewhat deeper, having to do with citizens' ambitions as ethical agents. Across a wide range of conceptions of the good, the meaning of one's life and projects, one's sense of their import, will depend on the emergence of subsequent generations who can appreciate one's achievements and, perhaps, carry on the work that one has begun. Many people, even those who choose not to have children, will have conceptions of the good that have this sort of intergenerational import. In these respects, at least, those members of a given generation who choose to raise children are providing a service of value to their fellow citizens, and this establishes a presumption that parental care work is to some extent civic labour. In the respects described, the raising of children has some features in common with public-goods provision. By treating some quantity of parental care as a form of civic labour, and thus allowing it to ground claims to the social product, we help ensure that the work involved in providing this particular public good is reciprocated, that other citizens do not free-ride on the efforts of those who provide it. However, much will depend here on what view the community has (assuming it has a settled view) as to the desirable future size of its population. Where citizens want their community to grow, parental care work will count as civic labour to a greater extent (i.e. a given amount of such labour will ground a claim to a larger share of the social product) than where citizens want their community to remain stable in size, or to shrink. And, in view of environmental constraints, there may be some limitations on what preferences it is legitimate, as a matter of justice, for citizens to have about the size of their community. Depending on what view the community has, having and raising children does become, beyond a point, a purely private good, and the care work involved in raising children beyond this point should not be regarded as civic labour. This work is then part of the price which the parents have to pay for enjoying more of this particular good.[24] Moreover, if we do include parenting in our account of civic labour, then it is important that as citizens we understand and appreciate the reasons for regarding it as such, and that parenting itself be informed by a commitment to produce these wider public benefits. Certainly if the state, on behalf of the wider community, supports parenting in view of the contribution it can make to specific public ends, then it is appropriate to expect those receiving such support to commit themselves to these ends.[25] Parents should see themselves, in part, as trustees for the wider community, who, in return for public support, are responsible for raising children in ways that serve the public good, e.g. to help nurture the virtues and capacities relevant to effective citizenship.[26] Parents should be seen as accountable to the wider community for responsible trusteeship, and it will be appropriate for the state to take measures to encourage and nurture parental capacities to this end.[27]

What about care work towards, say, elderly infirm relatives? This can be seen as a form of civic labour on the assumption that there is a community-wide obligation to help ensure that the basic needs of the infirm are met. Primary carers who look after infirm individuals on a day-to-day basis are, in effect, taking the full burden of this community-wide obligation upon their own shoulders. They are individually discharging what is in fact a collective obligation. For this reason they may be said to be providing a significant service to the wider citizenry, as civic labour requires, even though the immediate beneficiaries of their labours may well be within their own home or family. Primary carers can be seen as unofficial providers of a particular merit good, and as having a claim to share in the social product based on this fact. Of course, this leaves the question why we should assume that such care is a merit good which there is a community-wide obligation to help provide. In the previous section I argued that we should approach the question of appropriate merit-goods provision by applying a variant of Dworkin's hypothetical insurance market approach. To clinch the argument that this kind of care work is civic labour, then, I think we would have to show that the services provided by primary carers are services of a kind that people would agree to insure themselves for in a hypothetical insurance market of this kind. I think we can assume, however, that an averagely prudent individual would insure themselves for some level of such care. It can thus be regarded at least to some extent as providing a genuine merit good, and, therefore, as genuinely civic labour.

Note that we can expand our conception of civic labour to include these forms of care work without granting similar status to any and all unpaid labour performed within the household. Indeed, this is a move that should be resisted. To see this, consider the example of Anne and Bob. Anne and Bob share a house together. They perform no work in the world outside the house, but they work very arduously within their home. Anne washes their clothes, and does various DIY jobs about the place. Bob does the cooking and cleans the floors and washes the dishes. Each works, and each of them generates something that is of benefit not only to him- or herself, but to at least one other person. But it is still hard to see how this work could be seen as reciprocating those citizens beyond their home who, we may assume, provide them with the resources that underwrite their active domestic life (the food they eat, the pots and pans they use to cook it, the tools used for their DIY, etc.). As a matter of purely domestic justice, each may be said to reciprocate the other through the work each performs, but taken as individuals or as a household, they cannot plausibly be said to be making a productive contribution to the wider community through such work, and thus to be reciprocating members of the wider community for the economic benefits they provide. Housework per se is not contributive, therefore, in the sense that is relevant here (and the demand of 'Wages for Housework' is to this extent misguided). The wider community owes people like Anne and Bob absolutely nothing in return for the routine housework they perform, any more than it would owe me anything for cooking a meal which I proceeded to consume myself.[28]

Note, however, that if we combine a simple, unqualified claim that paid employment is a form of civic labour with the claim that housework of this kind is not, we can easily generate a paradoxical result. Imagine that, in addition to Anne and Bob depicted above, we have a second couple, Chris and Denise. Chris and Denise both perform identical amounts of housework to Anne and Bob. One day Anne, Bob, Chris, and Denise decide on the following exchange: Anne and Bob will do all of Chris's and Denise's housework for a sum of £x; Chris and Denise will do all of Anne's and Bob's housework for the same sum of £x. These two households are now in paid employment. So they seem to be performing civic labour. But they are also both performing exactly the same amount and kind of work as they were before. Since that labour was not civic labour, how can the labour they are now doing be civic labour? I think this case (a variant on the familiar adage about housewives taking in each other's washing) underscores the need, already emphasized above, for caution in assuming that work counts as civic labour simply because it is paid employment. Clearly, we need to adjust our account of when paid employment counts as civic labour to deal with such an apparently paradoxical case. The obvious route to take is to stipulate that for any person or household there is some amount of work that is typically necessary for personal and household reproduction, which is a normal part of personal and domestic life. Civic labour is labour over and above this personal and domestic labour; and for paid employment to count as civic labour, it must therefore amount to more than a symmetrical monetization of personal and domestic labour of the kind practised by Anne, Bob, Chris, and Denise. It must provide a significant service to one's fellow citizens after netting out, so to speak, substitute personal and domestic labour of this kind.[29] Still, it must be acknowledged that there is likely to be some disagreement among citizens about what kinds and amounts of work are necessary features of personal and domestic life, and, to this extent, we will have yet another source of disagreement at the margin about when labour is civic labour.

5.3   *The Basic Work Expectation*

Following the discussion of the previous two sections, we are now in a position to see how the citizen's contributive obligation might be elaborated in practice. At the outset I should emphasize that this elaboration is to an extent properly a *political* practice. In a society regulated by justice as fair reciprocity, it is necessary that citizens share a clear, public conception of what they can do to meet their contributive obligations. In certain respects, which I shall try to indicate below, the process by which this conception is elaborated should be receptive to citizens' context-specific preferences and judgements. At the same time, considerations of the kind discussed above can and should help frame the way in which citizens approach the problem of giving content to their contributive obligation.

In approaching their work of elaboration, citizens might usefully take as their starting point the idea of a *basic work expectation*.[30] In satisfaction of her contributive obligation, each citizen is expected to perform at least some minimum quantity of civic labour. In the first instance, following the analysis laid out above, and bearing in mind the various qualifications introduced in the course of this analysis, this can be understood to refer to a socially defined minimum number of hours of paid employment per week or year. The community should also stipulate, I think, that citizens ought to take jobs at or above some minimum percentage of their peak-ability wage rate. The thought here is that higher pay may be indicative of more socially valuable employment, and that individuals who are capable of more valuable employment ought to realize this capacity at least to some moderate extent. They shouldn't hide their talents too much under the proverbial bushel. Of course, in any contemporary real-world capitalist economy, relative wage rates are affected by all kinds of institutional and social forces, making it very difficult to say whether, in a given individual case, a higher-paid job really would represent a more socially valuable employment. The higher pay attached to a given job may reflect some market imperfection, or an effect of the maldistribution of income and wealth. For the informational reasons discussed in Section 4.3, it would in any case be very difficult to enforce a rule requiring people to work at some minimum proportion of their earnings potential. But these problems do not necessarily imply that we should give up on the underlying idea entirely. One can imagine a strong social expectation that individuals will, over the course of their working lives as a whole, avoid types of employment that are obviously out of line with their talents. Such an expectation may not be directly enforceable, but adherence to it could be encouraged through various labour market institutions such as benefits and training agencies, trade unions and employee mutuals, as well as through the secondary education system. It might be objected that this proposal smacks of 'slavery of the talented'. But such an objection is misplaced. It is quite likely, for reasons I will explain in Chapter 6, that the institutional and policy mix necessary to satisfy fair reciprocity (in its non-ideal form) will include a minimum-wage law. The effect of such a law is to limit how far less talented workers can work below their maximum earnings potential. They will thus be constrained on the whole to make good use of their talents. In this context, at least, it would be inequitable not to expect the talented also to make good use of their more productive talents.

Exactly how many hours of paid employment per week or year should citizens be expected, as a norm, to do? The answer to this sort of question is, I think, properly a matter for political determination, taking into account local circumstances. Factors that will be relevant to this decision will include things like the existing level of technological development, the demographic features of the economy, and the level of income and wealth to which all citizens are to be guaranteed access. Another aspect of the basic work expectation, to be determined in the same way, concerns the expectation about length of working life: how many years citizens should be expected, as a norm, to meet the work expectation. And some degree of flexibility over the course of a normal working life, allowing citizens to vary work effort around the normal weekly or yearly expectation, should of course be allowed.

Once this initial expectation, relating wholly to paid employment, has been specified, it can (and usually should) be adjusted to take account of care work. Thus, if the community expects a single adult with no children to perform an average of, say, thirty-five hours per week of paid employment, for a given number of years, then we may adjust the immediate expectation of paid employment down to, say, fifteen hours for a single parent who has childcare responsibilities. In the case of those who care full-time for elderly or sick relatives, or for newborns, we might adjust our immediate expectation of paid employment to zero, treating the individual's care work as sufficient in itself to satisfy her immediate obligation to perform a decent minimum of civic labour. These figures are, of course, purely illustrative. The same adjustments should be made for all citizens in the same circumstances, according to general rules that are, again, determined through the political process. Decision-makers should take into account the factors identified in the previous section as relevant to assessing how far care work should be regarded as a form of civic labour. And, to prevent the decision-making being distorted by ignorance and self-interest, I think we should insist particularly strongly here on giving a role to citizens' commissions and the like in guiding these decisions, and to ensuring that carers' groups are adequately represented in the deliberations of such commissions.

Individuals who suffer significant productive handicaps should be altogether exempted from the work expectation. The precise rules governing exemption can also be determined through appropriately representative and deliberative citizens' commissions. It is also important, to anticipate a point I shall make in Chapter 6, that individuals have strong rights of appeal against decisions to refuse exemption.[31] Finally, in the case of those who are capable of working but who are involuntarily unemployed, we can stipulate, as a further aspect of the work expectation, an obligation to make a conscientious effort to prepare for and find appropriate employment. The citizen's contributive obligation can be understood, then, as an obligation to satisfy a work expectation of this kind, clarified through the political process in accordance with local circumstances.

Let me now enter a new, complicating consideration. Thus far I have assumed that in some essential respects the basic work expectation will not differ according to the marketable talent of the citizen. In particular, the baseline expectations regarding hours or years of paid employment, and the adjustments from this baseline for care work responsibilities, I have assumed to be the same for low- and high-earners (with the qualification that those with severe work-related disability, who will typically have very low earnings ability, should be altogether exempted from the expectation). Now, in a society that satisfies the demands of fair reciprocity in its non-ideal form, some inequality in economic opportunity and outcome due to brute luck inequalities in marketable talent will remain. Bearing this in mind, it might be argued that we should try to compensate for this by varying the basic work expectation in inverse proportion to talent. We should expect the less talented to do less work, to work fewer hours or years, than the talented, in return for the high minimum share of the social product accessible in such a society.[32]

The proposal to vary work expectations in this way, according to level of marketable talent, defines a variant of non-ideal fair reciprocity that one might call *semi-ideal fair reciprocity*. Under this form of fair reciprocity, brute luck inequality in marketable talent is not corrected for in anything like a perfect manner (as it is, for example, under ESS as described in Section 4.1). But while the talented, with sufficient effort, might still be better placed to acquire resources over and above the minimum available to all, the less talented would have a somewhat offsetting advantage in terms of the effort needed to get to the minimum. The talented would not, other things being equal, dominate the less talented in access to all levels of the social product; over some range the less talented would dominate the talented. The proposal obviously runs up against the informational problems that afflict efforts to make discriminations in formal rights and obligations according to individuals' levels of marketable talent. But in principle it seems to follow from the egalitarian ambitions of justice as fair reciprocity, and some of the policy proposals discussed in Part II will address this form of fair reciprocity (see especially the discussion of targeted basic income in Section 7.5.2).

What if it proves unfeasible to vary the basic work expectation in the suggested fashion? Some might argue that unless the background economic system is fully just in other respects, i.e. comprehensively egalitarian, then the obligations people notionally have as a matter of fair-dues reciprocation simply do not apply. We should simply give up the effort to define and implement a basic work expectation. But this view seems implausible. If society is substantially just in other respects—as it is when fair reciprocity is satisfied in its non-ideal form—then it seems more plausible to say that everyone has an obligation to contribute that is at least close to that they would have in a fully just society. Morally speaking, the obligation of those disadvantaged by society's residual injustice may be less, relative to this baseline, than that of those who are advantaged by this injustice. But it is still a non-negligible obligation. The policy issue becomes one of deciding whether the work expectation should be harmonized at the level that would apply to all in the fully just society,[33] or whether it should be harmonized down to the level of those who are unjustly disadvantaged in a substantially (but not fully) just society. Either policy will result in some injustice. If we harmonize at the higher level, then we demand more contribution of the disadvantaged (less talented) than is strictly required of them. If we harmonize at the lower level, then we demand less contribution of the advantaged (talented) than is strictly required of them. And if members of the advantaged class do contribute less than is strictly required of them, this, too, could harm some members of the disadvantaged class. They could end up helping to bear the costs created by undercontributing members of the advantaged class (e.g. paying more in tax to finance the public health service because the talented do less work and pay less tax than they should). What is certainly true, however, is that the unjustly advantaged (talented) citizens cannot demand, as of right, that the disadvantaged (less talented) contribute at the same level as they would have to in a fully just society. The issue is justly settled by attending to the interests of the disadvantaged, though, as suggested, these may not point unambiguously in one direction.

I conclude, then, that in a society which satisfies the demands of fair reciprocity in its non-ideal form, it is acceptable to apply a uniform work expectation where it is not possible to vary the expectation according to degree of marketable talent; that this work expectation ought to be set at a level that is close to the level that would apply in a fully just (comprehensively egalitarian) society, though not necessarily at exactly this level—a modest downward adjustment of the work expectation, relative to that which would prevail in a fully just society, may be justified. I should emphasize that throughout the discussion in this section I have assumed that, if society is not fully just, it is at least substantially just in the sense that it meets the demands of fair reciprocity in its non-ideal form (see Section 4.2). If society does not even meet this lower threshold of justice, then, as I noted in Chapter 4, those who are unjustly disadvantaged by this have a reduced obligation to contribute—reduced, that is, relative to the obligation they would have in a society that is substantially, though not fully, just. We are then confronted with another, repeat set of questions as to how this should be acknowledged at the policy level. Ideally, we should seek some way of lowering the work expectation, relative to that we think should obtain in a substantially just society, specifically for those disadvantaged by their society's failure to achieve substantial justice. Failing this, we will need, once again, to give serious consideration to whether the interests of the disadvantaged might be best served by a general downward revision of the work expectation (in this case, a downward revision relative to the expectation we think should apply in a substantially, but not fully, just society).

5.4   *Capital, Contribution, and Sacrifice*

If people enjoy returns on capital they are likely to be under less pressure to satisfy the basic work expectation in order to enjoy a given share of the social product. Does this mean that, from the standpoint of fair reciprocity, such income is illegitimate? Or can such income be justified as payment for a particular kind of productive contribution, or on some similar basis? This is the question I shall try to give at least a preliminary answer to in this section.

To begin with, I should make clear that my concern is with income received by owners of capital, not with payments in return for managerial or entrepreneurial activity. In practice, managerial, entrepreneurial, and purely capitalistic roles may all be performed by one individual. But they are conceptually distinct and, in practice, they are often also performed by different people. Indeed, it is a commonplace of much commentary on the development of modern capitalism that the roles have tended to become more separate.[34] Management is, I think, fairly clearly a particular form of civic labour, one which concerns the supervision and direction of workers in the production process (the ends of the process being provisionally given). Entrepreneurship can also be regarded as a form of civic labour. It is the labour of trying to identify and then organize productive resources to meet currently unmet consumer preferences. As we noted above, there are some moral limitations on the kind of consumer preferences that it is legitimate, and should be legally permissible, to cater for. But within these boundaries entrepreneurial activity is plausibly seen as contributive. Note also that entrepreneurial activity is not necessarily motivated solely or even primarily for pecuniary reasons. One could conceivably be motivated as an entrepreneur by the simple challenge of identifying and organizing the production of something that others value enough to pay for, and by the self-esteem that comes from succeeding in this challenge. This point is important, from an egalitarian point of view, because it suggests that maintenance of the entrepreneurial spirit is in principle compatible with tax transfers that redistribute monetary gains from entrepreneurial activity.[35]

Let us turn, then, to the mere capital-owner, the person who, let us imagine, owns a factory or some other productive asset and who receives a monetary return on this. Is the return received by the capitalist consistent with the reciprocity-based demand that income should follow productive contribution? One might argue as follows: the capitalist, *qua* capitalist, provides capital; capital contributes to production (in the sense that the amount produced would be lower in its absence); therefore, the capitalist contributes to production; therefore, the return on capital is fundamentally consistent with the idea that income should follow productive contribution. There is, however, an obvious flaw in this reasoning. From the fact that an asset, x, contributes to production, it does not necessarily follow that the x-owner, who grants permission for x to be used for production, thereby makes a personal contribution to production and so meets the demands of reciprocity. This point is clearly brought out in the following imagined conversation between a socialist critic and a defender of the capitalist economy:

SOCIALIST CRITIC. You capitalists are free-riders. There you sit, enjoying a high level of consumption without making any contribution to production; it is we poor proletarians who do all the work.

CAPITALIST DEFENDER. But you proletarians only produce as much as you do because of these machines. (The capitalist gestures agitatedly, waving a cigar, in the direction of the factory he owns.) I supply the machines. *That* is my contribution.

SOCIALIST CRITIC. No one denies that the *machines* are contributive in the sense that much less could be produced in their absence. But it does not follow from this that *you*, who happen to own the machines, and allow them to be used, are therefore contributing anything. To see this, consider what would happen if you and all the other capitalists were to mysteriously disappear overnight. What would change? The machines would still be here, and we would operate them as we do now, producing just as much as we do now, but consuming somewhat more of what we produce. Forgive the rhetorical question, but how can you and your fellow capitalists be making any personal contribution to production when your disappearance need make absolutely no difference to the amount that is produced? And, if you are not making such a contribution, doesn't my original objection stand?

A very similar (indeed, essentially the same) objection to the claim that capitalists are contributive has been put forward by David Schweickart.[36] According to Schweickart, someone makes a personal contribution to production when he or she engages in some form of 'productive activity'. When someone 'provides capital', however, all they are doing is 'allowing capital to be used', and, in and of itself, this does not constitute productive activity. Consequently, Schweickart continues, 'providing capital' does not constitute a personal contribution to production and, if income is supposed to be grounded in contribution, the return to capital is unjustified. The capitalist is a gatekeeper to a productive asset. The return on capital is, as it were, the price others pay for him to open the gate and let them use the asset. The socialist point is that to exercise this gatekeeper function alone is not to make a personal contribution to production.[37] Note that, in pressing this point, the socialist need not deny that capital itself is productive, nor that it is a scarce 'factor of production' which, in the interests of achieving economic efficiency, should be paid for at a competitive price by those who use it. But accepting this is quite compatible with a scenario in which the state itself owns capital, leases it out at a market price, and uses the returns to finance spending on, say, public services.[38] It does not explain why, as a matter of justice, the prices paid for the use of this good should translate into income in the pockets or bank accounts of specific individuals, rather than revert to the community of worker-citizens as a whole.

I think one can accept the basic socialist criticism of capitalist income, however, without throwing out altogether the idea that returns to capital-holding and the like can be legitimate. Firstly, there are cases where the asset that the capitalist gatekeeps is an asset that she has directly created through her own labour. Imagine that Harriet spends her Saturday afternoons building a machine in her backyard; when it is finished, she leases it out to another group of workers to use for productive purposes. Now in this case it is not true that 'providing capital' consists merely in 'allowing capital to be used'. Providing capital has two distinct aspects here: (*a*) a gatekeeping aspect, in which the individual permits the capital she holds to be used for productive purposes; and (*b*) a generative aspect, in which the capital is generated by the capital provider's own labour, expanding production possibilities beyond what they would be in her absence. In this case, one of *direct production of a productive asset*, provision of capital can plausibly be seen as a productive contribution by the capital-provider. Thus, in this kind of case, income from capital is not necessarily at odds with the reciprocity-based idea that income should be linked to productive contribution.[39] On similar grounds, R. H. Tawney argues that copyrights and patents, held by the original writers and inventors, are in principle a form of 'functional property': property rights which secure rewards for the performance of productive services, rather than enabling their holder to extract social product without the performance of productive services.[40] Note, however, that there is an important difference between saying that incomes from these sources are of an essentially legitimate kind, and saying that people are entitled in full to the market-determined levels of these incomes. As with the income from the sale of labour services, the egalitarian considerations that inform justice as fair reciprocity may well imply that Harriet is entitled only to a portion of the market return on the asset she produces, and that writers and inventors are entitled only to a portion of what they could secure in a free market through copyrights and patents. Differences in market returns may in part reflect differences in degrees of risk, however, and I do not think it in principle illegitimate for riskier forms of productive investment (including investments like those considered in the next paragraph) to receive higher rewards should they succeed.[41]

A second kind of case where claims to income from capital seem to me to have some legitimacy concerns what we may call *earnings-derived saving*. Imagine, for example, that I establish a legitimate claim to a share of the social product through some form of civic labour. I then save a portion of the income earned, and use the savings to make a loan to someone, who pays me interest on the loan. Describing this situation slightly differently: I have a legitimate claim over a portion of the social product and instead of pressing this claim in full immediately myself, I agree, for a price, to let another person press part of my claim. Now we certainly cannot say in all such cases that the return the lender receives is a return for a particular kind of productive contribution. That way of describing what happens may have some intuitive credibility if the loan is used in a way that expands the community's production possibilities (e.g. if the loan is to an entrepreneur who uses the funds to buy a new productive asset). But the loan need not be used in this way. It might be used by another simply to boost her consumption above her present income. However, in both cases, it might be argued that I have nevertheless made a *sacrifice*, by forgoing immediate consumption, and that this justifies some kind of return. Such, at any rate, has been a long-standing defence of interest, the return on savings, a defence that can be traced back at least as far as Alfred Marshall's *Principles of Economics*.[42]

To see why the defence has some force, consider the case of Milly and Billy. Milly desperately wants a new bike. She has worked for some months to save up the money to get the bike she wants and she has now just finished the paper round that will see her accumulated savings reach the level necessary to get the bike. However, returning home with the week's wages in her hand, she encounters Billy. Billy is crying on the pavement, having just accidentally dropped and smashed his mother's favourite vase. Billy asks Milly if she will lend him her week's wages to get a replacement for the vase. Although it means going one more frustrating week without the bike, she sympathizes with Billy and agrees to lend him the money. Now in this case the sacrifice argument for interest on her 'saving' (in the form of the loan to Billy) seems very plausible. There is a real loss to her from having to wait one more week to get the bike, and Billy should surely at least make good that loss by returning not only the original sum but a little extra too.

However, following the logic of the sacrifice argument, the level of return should be proportional to the loss genuinely incurred.[43] This sets a limit on the level of interest Milly can legitimately expect from Billy. And, in other cases, where no genuine sacrifice is in fact made, it casts doubt on the appropriateness of there being a positive level of interest at all.[44] Would a very rich person, for example, really miss the sum that Milly advances to Billy? What urgent acts of personal consumption would this rich person have to postpone to make such a loan? Probably none. In which case, he surely has a right only to his original sum back (assuming, of course, he was originally entitled to this sum). An argument of this sort is the one that socialists have traditionally made in reply to Marshall-like defences of interest on capital. J. A. Hobson sympathetically describes the reply as follows:

The working-class socialist will recognise that the savings he may make out of his wages 'cost' him something in the sense of sacrifice of present satisfaction. . . . What he recognises in his own case will he apply to capital in general? Probably not. Though there is a personal cost or sacrifice in the case of his savings, he finds none in the case of the savings of the rich.[45]

Hobson indicates his agreement with the viewpoint of this 'working-class socialist' when he writes elsewhere that

A great deal of saving is regardless of the rate of interest, consisting of the almost automatic accumulation of the unspent surplus of the rich—unspent because all their felt wants have been fully satisfied.[46]

In practice, of course, capital markets do not discriminate between savers making genuine sacrifices and those not: in a perfectly competitive market, all get the same rate of interest. Thus, while some interest to some people might be justified in Marshall's terms, some interest will be unjustified.[47]

Some capitalist incomes seem justifiable then. On the other hand, other kinds of capitalist income look particularly questionable. Inherited wealth, for example, seems particularly vulnerable to the kind of socialist criticism that I outlined, and gave a qualified endorsement of, above. Inheritors can function purely as gatekeepers of capital, imposing a straightforward burden on their fellow, productive citizens. (Note that the defence of interest as a reward for saving presupposes the right to consume what is saved. This right is doubtful here, I think, precisely because the consumption needn't be matched by any contributive activity.)[48] The foregoing discussion also suggests that the justifiability of interest income, from saved earnings, depends on how far it tracks genuine sacrifice. Since the discrepancy between interest and sacrifice is likely to be greatest for high-income, wealthy savers, we can assume that as a general matter people are entitled to a greater proportion of the interest income they receive, the less income and wealth they have. Finally, there is a compelling tradition of scepticism concerning the justice of certain kinds of capital gains. Imagine that someone has an asset and that we are satisfied she is receiving an income from it that tracks a productive contribution on her part. But over time the value of the asset increases owing to factors that have nothing at all to do with her own effort. Is she really entitled to this 'unearned increment'? Historically, critics have pressed this question with particular vehemence against landlords enjoying increases in land value that are entirely owing to the productive efforts of other citizens (e.g. the development of industry and railways in the vicinity of their land).[49] Going back to the case of Harriet, imagine that having produced her machine there is a catastrophe of some kind that destroys all other machines of this kind and the raw materials necessary to build new ones. Her machine is now an extremely scarce good, and one that consequently commands a much greater market value than it did originally. It does not seem fair that she should benefit from this by receiving the full increase in the machine's market value, for the extra claim on the social product she would obtain in this way does not reflect any additional productive contribution that she has made. This underscores the point made earlier that even if the receipt of income from a given asset is essentially legitimate, this does not mean that the asset-holder is entitled to whatever return on the asset the market currently secures for her.

5.5   *Conclusion: The Politics of Contribution*

In a society where the institutions governing economic life satisfy the various conditions set out in Section 4.2, those who claim the high minimum share of the social product available to them under these institutions have an obligation to make a decent productive contribution to the community in return. This is the citizen's contributive obligation. In this chapter I have argued that this obligation should be understood primarily in terms of the citizen's duty to meet a basic work expectation: a minimum number of hours and years of paid employment, adjusted for specific care work responsibilities. The supply of capital can also be a form of productive contribution, and thus may necessitate some adjustment of the citizen's work expectation. On the other hand, I have argued that some forms of capitalist income are inconsistent with the reciprocity-based demand that income entitlement track productive contribution. It is, I suggest, unjust to allow citizens to use these incomes to reduce their work effort and thereby escape the basic work expectation.

In closing, I want to acknowledge, indeed emphasize, the great difficulty of the task that I have set about in this chapter, namely, giving an account of 'what counts as contributive'. I have tried to show how we might plausibly construct an account of contributive activity as part of a public understanding of what fair-dues reciprocation requires. But I have also noted, repeatedly, how the process of construction is likely to be subject to dispute: dispute, for example, over what kinds of goods and services it is legitimate to produce for the market; dispute over appropriate levels of provision of merit and public goods; dispute over the justifiable (and, within the limits of the justifiable, desirable) size of future generations; even dispute over how much domestic work an individual or household should be assumed to do for themselves. To this extent, I agree with Lawrence Becker that any account of contributive activity, or civic labour as I have called it, is going to be 'fuzzy'.[50] (And this, of course, is before we even get to the questions concerning the contributive standing of capitalist incomes briefly discussed in the penultimate section of this chapter.) And yet I am not so distressed by this—the fact of fuzziness, if you like—as to think that we should abandon the project of constructing an account of contributive activity as part of a public understanding of what justice requires. The basic demand for reciprocity is too important, I think, for us to do so. (Moreover, I suspect that if the effort to construct an account of contributive activity is not explicitly considered, society will evolve an understanding anyway, and one that may not be altogether desirable.[51]) In this area, as in many others, citizens inevitably have to live with some degree of reasonable disagreement over the content of their rights and obligations. The challenge is to ensure that the current, provisional resolution of the disagreement has a legitimacy that all citizens can acknowledge. To this end, it is first of all vitally important that the prevailing public definition of contributive activity—centrally, the prevailing basic work expectation and the rules for adjusting it—be clear and well publicized. It is essential, secondly, that the prevailing work expectation, and rules associated with it, be ones that citizens who accept the basic ideas of justice as fair reciprocity can accept as reasonable: they must be capable of reasoned defence in terms of the considerations that I have identified as relevant to the task in this chapter.[52] And, thirdly, it is essential that disputes over the boundaries of the contributive be resolved, always provisionally, through a political process that is inclusive and contestable; all citizens must feel that they can get a fair hearing for any revisions they may wish to make to their community's provisionally authoritative account of what fair-dues reciprocation requires and permits.

PART II

———

The Civic Minimum

CHAPTER 6

———

Welfare Contractualism

> If citizenship is invoked in the defence of rights, the corresponding
> duties of citizenship cannot be ignored.
>
> (T. H. Marshall, *Citizenship and Social Class*)

Introduction: The Challenge of Welfare Contractualism

What are the institutional and policy implications of justice as fair
reciprocity? This is the question I shall address in Part II of this volume.
My aim is to offer an account of the civic minimum: of the kind of
policies and institutions that are necessary to realize the demands of
fair reciprocity in its non-ideal form. Identifying the civic minimum
is of course no straightforward matter. There is, I think, a limit to
how far one can simply read a specific set of policies off from the
basic commitments of fair reciprocity. The best package of policies and
institutions will likely depend on answers to a wide range of empirical
questions, and may well differ according to local circumstance. Indeed,
at any given place and moment in time there may be no single correct
package of policies and supporting institutions but a range of possible
packages that can each plausibly claim to offer a way of satisfying
the demands of fair reciprocity in its non-ideal form. However, some
packages are clearly more attractive than others when judged against
this standard. Reference to the commitments of fair reciprocity can aid
our efforts to identify the range of reasonable policy options, even if
it cannot always pick out very specific sets of policies and institutions
as uniquely just.

To make our discussion manageable, I shall focus here on the
issues raised by the controversial practice of welfare contractualism.
As noted in Chapter 1, there has been a perceptible shift towards

welfare contractualism in many advanced capitalist countries (certainly in Britain and the United States) in recent years,[1] and the legitimacy of welfare contractualism is one of the main points of contention between communitarian and real libertarian philosophies of economic citizenship. In this chapter I consider welfare contractualism from the standpoint of justice as fair reciprocity. I concentrate specifically on the practice of work-testing or work enforcement: making eligibility for welfare benefits more tightly conditional on employment-related activity, such as job search, training, or work itself. Chapter 7 then evaluates arguments for an unconditional basic income (UBI), while Chapter 8 considers related proposals for 'asset-based welfare', and, in particular, a universal basic capital grant. I argue that welfare contractualism is legitimate provided that certain conditions are met, and that if these conditions are to be met, then basic income or basic capital policies may well be needed as a complement to contractualist welfare. In Chapter 9 I sketch a reform programme suggested by discussion of the civic minimum in Chapters 6–8, and I discuss the political feasibility of a politics, grounded in the philosophy of fair reciprocity, oriented to such a reform programme.

In this chapter I begin my analysis, in Section 6.1, with an explanation of why fair reciprocity requires the institution of a right to a decent minimum of income, and why, from the standpoint of this same conception of justice, incorporation of a work-test into a welfare system intended to secure this right seems legitimate in principle. However, under fair reciprocity, equal application of the work-test to all citizens is unfair unless other demands of justice are satisfied to a sufficient extent, and the demands of reciprocity are themselves applied in an equitable fashion. Accordingly, Section 6.2 identifies four basic requirements for the fair application of the work-test. In Sections 6.3–6.5 I consider three objections to work-testing. These include the objection that work-testing is necessarily incompatible with a Marshallian conception of social rights; that work-testing reinforces market vulnerability; and that work-testing imposes unjust costs on the dependants of welfare recipients. I consider how these objections can be met, and in doing so identify further qualifying requirements for a fair work-test.

In the contemporary policy literature, arguments for the work-test, and other kinds of welfare contractualism, are not made only in terms of what justice to others, on the part of the welfare recipient, demands. Emphasis is also placed on paternalistic considerations. Therefore, in Section 6.6 I consider paternalist arguments for the work-test, including the 'New Paternalist' philosophy of welfare defended by Lawrence

Mead. I argue that paternalistic considerations do indeed strengthen the case for the work-test, but that these considerations are unlikely to be decisive if citizens lack the opportunities and protections that fair reciprocity demands. Paternalism does not justify indifference to the considerations of justice discussed in Sections 6.2–6.5 (and further explored in Chapters 7 and 8).

6.1   *The Right of Reasonable Access to a Decent Income*

There is a widespread intuition that in a just society citizens must have access on reasonable terms to the resources necessary to meet their basic needs.[2] Basic needs include needs for food, housing, clothing, and effective social participation. Health care should also be added to this list. Justice as fair reciprocity affirms this intuition. In order to satisfy the demands of fair reciprocity, in its non-ideal form, a society must arrange the distribution of the social product so as to recognize and effectively institute for its members a right of reasonable access to the resource package standardly necessary to meet these needs—a right of reasonable access, as I shall say, to a decent income. (I do not say that this is all fair reciprocity, in its non-ideal form, demands as regards the distribution of income; only that this clearly is demanded by fair reciprocity.)

There are at least two independent reasons why fair reciprocity demands the institution of such a right. Firstly, fair reciprocity, in its non-ideal form, requires that citizens be protected from brute luck deficiency in core well-being and/or in holding a decent minimum of resources to support ethical agency. Nobody should suffer poverty through no fault of their own (this is of course the non-immiseration condition I identified in Section 4.2 as a requirement of the non-ideal form of fair reciprocity). Determining exactly what amount of income is standardly necessary for someone to have a minimum capability for ethical agency is, of course, by no means a straightforward matter. But I shall assume that it is possible to establish legitimate, provisional determinations of this through a suitably open and contestable political process. This minimum should be understood to include, however, not only a level of income sufficient for the basic needs of a healthy, fully able-bodied citizen, but a package of health-care and disability benefits consistent with the theory of compensation for handicaps sketched out above (see Section 2.4). Given realistic assumptions about distributions of ability, handicaps, and the likelihood of market failure, it is unlikely that all citizens will have reasonable access to this minimum under a laissez-faire regime. Some libertarian theorists might dispute this, pointing to the possibilities for individuals to protect themselves against brute luck poverty through personal saving and/or insurance. But those with low earnings potential may have little realistic opportunity to save; and citizens may be effectively excluded from insurance coverage due to the level of premiums or because certain contingencies are simply uninsurable.[3] Thus, securing universal reasonable access to a decent income will almost certainly require the institution of some sort of positive claim-right to income against the community; that is, the institution of some sort of formal income support system that by correcting distributions thrown up spontaneously in the marketplace maintains the incomes of unfortunate citizens who would otherwise fall below the relevant decency threshold because of bad brute luck (e.g. owing to congenital disability or involuntary unemployment).

Secondly, fair reciprocity requires that citizens be protected against market vulnerability and the risks of dependent exchange (exploitation and abuse). As Robert E. Goodin has argued, this concern also seems to demand the institution of a right of reasonable access to a decent income.[4] Vulnerability arises from the pressing need to sell one's labour-power. If, however, individuals have a source of income that is independent of the immediate sale of their labour-power, as they do (or can have) under an income support system of the kind just described, they will feel less pressure to sell their labour-power and thus should be less vulnerable and at risk of exploitation or abuse. They need not suffer the acute dependency, and corresponding loss of freedom, characteristic of the proletarian condition.

The two concerns—protection from brute luck poverty and protection from market vulnerability—obviously overlap to a considerable extent because brute luck poverty is itself a cause of market vulnerability. But the one concern is not reducible to the other. On the one hand, a citizen can certainly become market-vulnerable in ways that are not attributable to bad brute luck. An individual could be very poor and vulnerable because of bad option luck: she invested all her assets and earnings in a risky investment which crashed. Although this perhaps requires a greater stretch of the imagination, it is also conceivable that someone could suffer brute luck poverty without thereby being vulnerable to dependent exchange. Imagine, for example, someone who, through no fault of his own, has no assets or personal marketable qualities. In a laissez-faire regime he consequently suffers extreme brute luck poverty. But precisely because he has no marketable qualities, nobody is interested in employing him and he is thus invulnerable to dependent exchange (at least within the labour market). Moreover, even when the situations of brute luck poverty and market vulnerability do overlap, there is a clear difference between claiming assistance on grounds of bad brute luck ('It's not my fault I ended up in this mess—so help me out!'), and claiming it on grounds of vulnerability ('However I got into this mess, now I'm in it others will take unfair advantage of me unless you help me out').

In saying that fair reciprocity requires the institution of a right of reasonable access to a decent income, I am for the moment leaving many policy design questions open. As already noted, I do not intend to say anything here about the precise level of income decency, though it is perhaps worth emphasizing that we should not necessarily think only in terms of existing official poverty lines which in some cases (notably the United States) are quite arbitrary and, I think, implausibly ungenerous. Another policy design issue concerns the mix of means-tested and universal benefits in the income support system. Again, for the moment I shall bracket this issue.[5] Which model, or hybrid, we adopt is a highly contextual matter that we need not consider in detail at the present level of abstraction, though much of the discussion in Part II of this volume speaks indirectly to this issue.

One design issue must be confronted, however. According to justice as fair reciprocity, citizens who share to a sufficiently generous extent in the social product, and who enjoy sufficiently generous opportunities for productive participation, have an obligation to make a decent productive contribution to the community in return. In a context of otherwise sufficiently fair economic arrangements, each should do his bit in terms of productive contribution. Failure to meet this contributive obligation constitutes a form of exploitation of one's fellow citizens. Given the concern to prevent this form of exploitation, it seems advisable to structure the right of reasonable access to a decent income so that the receipt of income support is conditional on willingness to make a reciprocal productive contribution. In the language of Chapter 5, eligibility for the relevant income transfers should be conditional on the individual satisfying, or demonstrating a willingness to satisfy, a suitably defined basic work expectation. The income support system which assures citizens their reasonable access to a decent income should, in other words, incorporate some form of *work-test*. This could in principle take many forms. It might take the form of requiring recipients of income support actually to do work in return for their benefits, i.e. 'workfare' in the strict sense of the term. But if the aim is to ensure due reciprocation over time, rather than exact reciprocation at every single moment in time, then participation in educational or training programmes or active job search are possible alternatives to workfare.[6] (Nor need the work-test apply to each and every element of the decent income package taken in isolation; to prevent serious violations of the reciprocity principle, it suffices, I think, that the work-test be incorporated at a strategic point within the welfare system as a whole.[7])

In principle, therefore, fair reciprocity appears to support the institution of a system of generous, but work-tested, income support. To this extent, welfare contractualism seems perfectly consistent with a philosophy of economic citizenship grounded in the conception of justice as fair reciprocity.

6.2   *A Fair Work-Test: Four Basic Requirements*

Does this mean, then, that the moves towards welfare contractualism that we have recently seen in advanced capitalist countries like Britain and the United States are consistent with, indeed required by, justice as fair reciprocity? Not necessarily. As explained in Part I, and as intimated immediately above, there is more to fair reciprocity than mere reciprocity. Fair-dues reciprocation, the specific form of reciprocity defended in Part I, holds that when the institutions governing economic life satisfy other key demands of justice to a sufficient extent, the citizens who actually claim the high minimum share of the social product available to them under these institutions have an obligation to make a decent productive contribution to the community in return. Where the institutions do not meet these demands to the relevant extent, those citizens who are disadvantaged by this have proportionately diminished contributive obligations. The fairness of applying the work-test equally to all citizens depends in part, therefore, on how far existing institutions and policies satisfy other relevant demands of justice. Bearing in mind the account I gave of these demands in Chapter 4 (I am thinking particularly of the account I gave in Section 4.2 of what fair reciprocity demands in its non-ideal form), and bearing in mind too that the demand for reciprocity must itself be applied to citizens in a consistent manner, the four following, intuitive conditions for a fair work-test can be identified:

1. *Income adequacy.* Economic institutions must be structured to ensure that citizens who are required to satisfy a publicly defined work obligation have access to a share of the social product sufficient to escape brute luck poverty.

2. *Participation adequacy*. Economic institutions must be structured so that citizens who are required to satisfy a publicly defined
   work obligation have adequate opportunities for work.
3. *Participation equity*. Economic institutions must be structured
   so that, in specifying what citizens need to do to meet their contributive obligations, different forms of productive participation
   in the community are treated equitably.
4. *Contribution equity*. Economic institutions must be structured
   so as to ensure that contributive obligations apply equally to all
   citizens who claim (at least) the high minimum share of the social
   product available under otherwise just arrangements.

This first requirement for a fair work-test (income adequacy) may
seem so obvious as to be hardly worth mentioning. Its importance
can be readily appreciated, however, by looking at the record of
the welfare-to-work schemes introduced in many parts of the United
States in the 1980s. The best available empirical research on the impact
of these schemes indicates that they did have the intended effect of
moving recipients of income support off welfare and into work more
rapidly than they would otherwise have moved.[8] But this research also
reveals that many of those who left welfare for work as a result of
these programmes ended up in low-paid jobs with final incomes that
placed them and their dependants below the official (and hardly generous) US poverty line. This problem was addressed during the 1990s
by increases in the national minimum wage and by increases in the
Earned Income Tax Credit which provides extra income for low-paid
workers (a combination which has provided a model for governments
elsewhere, including the 1997–2001 Labour government in Britain).
However, the problem remains. More recent research indicates that,
in the wake of the 1996 Personal Responsibility and Work Opportunity Reconciliation Act, welfare rolls and poverty rates in the United
States have fallen. However, many who have left welfare for work continue to have incomes below the official poverty line, and many also
lack affordable access to a decent package of health-care insurance.[9]
   Let us now turn to the second requirement for a fair work-test
(participation adequacy). What does this involve? Assume provisionally (I will relax the assumption in a moment) that productive
contribution is made through paid employment. If citizens are told
that they have a reciprocity-based obligation to do work of this kind,
conscientiously internalize this obligation, but then find themselves
without opportunity to work, they will suffer a noxious form of brute
luck disadvantage: the frustration and disappointment of fruitless job

search, and the loss of self-respect, as, erroneously but perhaps inevitably, they start to blame themselves for their situation. As a result, they may be poor in capability even if they are not strictly poor in terms of income. Given the commitment to prevent brute luck poverty, or immiseration, it is therefore essential that citizens are not excluded from the employment necessary to meet their reciprocity-based obligations in a self-respecting manner. The duty to contribute implies a right to work. More than this, however, fair reciprocity demands that citizens have a tolerably wide range of choice as to the kind of employment they do. One of the main bads of the proletarian condition (see Section 4.2) is the lack of opportunity for self-realization in work. If citizens are to be free of the proletarian condition, as I have argued they should be, then citizens must have real opportunity, over the course of a whole working life, to relate to their employment as a site of intrinsically valuable challenge. If they do not, then the burdens of reciprocity will clearly fall with inequitable heaviness on the shoulders of those who lack prospects for self-realization in work.

The importance of the third requirement for a fair work-test (participation equity) can be appreciated if we recall my argument, in Chapter 5, that care workers, whose care work is not necessarily remunerated in the market, may nevertheless be providing productive services of sufficiently significant benefit to the wider community as to justify public recognition and support. This also needs to be factored into our account of who is obliged to satisfy a work-test, and of what different categories of citizen are obliged to do to satisfy such a test. If we do not factor this consideration in, then we may arbitrarily penalize some individuals for meeting their contributive obligations in one way rather than another.

Fourthly, if we are going to insist that any one citizen makes at least some minimum productive contribution in return for sharing in the social product, then the most elementary consideration of equity requires that we make the same demand of all other citizens (contribution equity). It is patently unfair if I have to contribute for my living while you do not (assuming, of course, that you are not disabled from contributing). As simple as it sounds, this is in fact a very demanding condition; just how demanding it is is hardly appreciated. In capitalist societies like our own, one major worry here must be that asset-rich citizens, who are more able to dispense with the benefits of the welfare state, will be able to escape contributive obligations while the asset-poor find themselves, as a condition of receiving these benefits, compelled to work. In the case of inherited capital it is, as I argued in Chapter 5, particularly hard to see how the asset-rich individual, living off his inheritance, is making any personal productive contribution to the community as the fair-dues conception of reciprocity requires. A second possible problem concerns those with high earnings potentials who may be able to achieve a minimally decent living standard without much productive contribution (relative to their capacity to contribute). Equity in the implementation of contributive obligations requires that the community also attend to this potential problem.[10]

So here we have four initial requirements for a fair work-test. Work-testing, and related measures of welfare contractualism, will not be legitimate, from the standpoint of justice as fair reciprocity, unless these four requirements are met. In evaluating contemporary moves towards welfare contractualism, therefore, we must ask ourselves to what extent these requirements are already satisfied or are accompanied by other policy initiatives which can be expected to meet the requirements.[11] I have not said much here about how they might be met for I shall return to this in later chapters. Moreover, while these four requirements may be individually necessary for a fair work-test, I do not think they are jointly sufficient. There are further requirements that must be met, and we can identify some of these by considering how a proponent of the work-test might respond to the chief objections to work-testing. It is to these objections, therefore, that I shall now turn.

6.3   *The Objection from Social Rights*

I shall deal first with what I think is the weakest objection to the work-test. Some critics argue that work-testing and related measures of welfare contractualism are incompatible with the idea of a decent income being the focus of a universal, Marshallian social right.[12] For rights necessarily have a quality of unconditionality, it is said, and if we make the payment of welfare benefits notionally covered by a social right conditional on doing x or y, such as passing a work-test, this violates this necessary quality of unconditionality. Of course, this observation in itself does not discredit the work-test. But if we take the commitment to social rights as a given, then, following the logic of this argument, it appears that we must relax any commitment we might have to the work-test or to similar measures of welfare contractualism. This argument is implicit, I think, in much of the recent commentary on welfare contractualism in Britain and elsewhere in which it is commonly asserted that contractualist 'welfare to work' reforms necessarily (and, it is implied, regretfully) break with 'Marshall's concept of citizenship based on universal and unconditional entitlement'.[13] Contractualism is said to represent 'a fundamental challenge to the dominant intellectual tradition in British social policy and administration, that of the social rights of citizenship formulated by T. H. Marshall'.[14]

There is, however, no intrinsic incompatibility between work-testing or related measures of welfare contractualism and the idea of a decent income being the focus of a social right. The crucial distinction to which we must pay attention here is the distinction between: (i) a right to be *given* some resource, *x*, unconditionally; and, (ii) an unconditional right of *reasonable access* to a given resource, *x*, where reasonable access means that the resource in question can be acquired and enjoyed by the individual concerned without unreasonable effort. A person can obviously have reasonable access to something, in this sense, without necessarily being directly given this thing.[15] The notion of a social right can quite intelligibly be understood in the second of the above senses as well as in the first: as an unconditional right of reasonable access to a given resource, rather than as a right to be given this same resource unconditionally. This is, of course, exactly how I earlier defined the right citizens have in relation to a decent income. This distinction is important for our immediate purposes because while the work-test does seem incompatible with a social right of the first kind it is by no means necessarily incompatible with a social right of the second. If, for example, Smith is perfectly capable of working, then it is not clear that making Smith's eligibility for welfare benefits conditional on, say, active job search necessarily violates Smith's unconditional right of reasonable access to a decent income.

It might be objected that I am revising the traditional conception of a social right here; that, under the cloak of an apparently innocent analytical point, I am in fact proposing a fundamental substantive revision of the notion of a social right. But this is not the case. If we first consider theorists who preceded T. H. Marshall, we can see a similar distinction being made, and, at least in the case of some areas of economic citizenship, a clear statement of preference for social rights of the second kind. Consider, for example, the following passage from L. T. Hobhouse's *Liberalism*:

the function of the State is to secure conditions upon which its citizens are able to win by their own efforts all that is necessary to a full civic efficiency. It is not for the State to feed, house, or clothe them. It is for the State to take care that the economic conditions are such that the normal man who is not defective in mind or body or will can by useful labour feed, house, and clothe himself and his family. ... [In this sense t]he 'right to work' and the right to a 'living wage' are just as valid as the rights of person or property.[16]

What Hobhouse says here seems in fact to be fairly representative of New Liberal and early Fabian thinking about what we now term social rights.[17] These early social democrats recognized that in a market economy many citizens will lack reasonable access to certain vital resources, to a decent level of income. The state, on their view, has a responsibility to ensure that all citizens do have reasonable access to these resources. In some cases it may be appropriate for the state simply to give citizens the relevant resources. But this need not, and probably ought not, always to be the case. In the quoted passage Hobhouse proposes that this right take the form of being given adequate opportunity to acquire the relevant resources through one's own efforts. As said, work-testing eligibility for unemployment or other welfare benefits is by no means incompatible with this.

But what about Marshall himself? Did he perhaps break with what might today be dismissed as merely the Victorian prejudices of these earlier theorists and offer a more radical conception of social rights? The first thing to say here is that the two general definitions of social rights that Marshall gives are each sufficiently abstract to accommodate both understandings of a social right distinguished above.[18] Secondly, as the epigraph to this chapter indicates, Marshall explicitly affirms the importance of the duties of social citizenship as well as the rights. Moreover, thirdly, he elaborates this point by saying that the duty 'most obviously and immediately' implied by our social rights is 'the duty to pay taxes and insurance contributions'.[19] Clearly implicit in this duty, however, is the duty to work (to earn the money to pay the relevant taxes and insurance contributions); indeed, fourthly, Marshall explicitly says that the duty to work is of 'paramount importance'.[20] The work-test does not follow ineluctably from this, of course; but it would seem to be quite consistent with Marshall's emphasis on the citizen's duty to work as a corollary of his social rights. Turning finally to more indirect evidence of Marshall's position, it is clear that Marshall's thinking about social rights was heavily influenced by the Beveridgean model of social insurance which dominated policy discussions in Britain in the 1940s. In this model eligibility for welfare benefits is typically conditional on past productive contribution and, in the case of some benefits (notably Beveridge's proposed Unemployment Benefit), also on a willingness to cooperate with the community's efforts to maintain one's readiness for future employment.[21] Marshall does not explicitly endorse the work-test incorporated within the Beveridgean model; but nor does he explicitly—or as far as I can see implicitly—reject it. All in all, then, I can see no warrant, textual or contextual, for attributing to

Marshall a conception of social rights that is intrinsically exclusive of work-testing.

The choice between the work-test and social rights (or, more exactly, the idea of a decent income being the focus of a social right) is, therefore, a choice that we do not really face. It is forced upon us only by an arbitrarily narrow definition of what a social right is—one, moreover, that we should be wary of reading back into Marshall's text or into the broader intellectual tradition in which he worked. Of course, the critic of the work-test can still make the case that it is preferable, on moral grounds, to understand certain social rights in a way that is exclusive of work-testing. But he or she will then be making a case against the work-test on independent moral grounds, rather than trying to pre-empt ethical discussion by means of arbitrary definitional fiat.

6.4 *The Objection from Market Vulnerability*

On what independent moral grounds, then, might the critic challenge the practice of work-testing? One of the requirements of fair reciprocity, as outlined in Chapters 2 and 4, is that the institutions governing economic life protect citizens from the dangers of market vulnerability (one of the main bads of the proletarian condition). As we saw above, this provides one of the main reasons for instituting an income support system. It might be argued, however, that rigorous work-testing will prevent the income support system from performing this protective role. If eligibility for income support is made conditional on some sort of work-test, such that citizens lose eligibility for the relevant income transfers if they fail to look arduously for jobs and to take any job offered to them, then the income support system will not significantly increase the freedom of asset-poor individuals to refrain from accepting exploitative or abusive job offers. There is, the critic argues, a deep tension between the aim of enforcing citizens' contributive obligations, via the work-test, and the aim of protecting individuals from market vulnerability. We have to make a choice between the two aims, and the choice should be to protect citizens from vulnerability, and thus to relax the work-test.

One response to this objection is to point out that if the community did what was necessary to satisfy the requirements of a fair work-test already enumerated above, then the problem of market vulnerability would probably be less severe than it currently is in capitalist societies like Britain and the United States. In particular, satisfying these requirements almost certainly requires a much more egalitarian distribution of assets than currently obtains (see Chapter 8), and this should reduce the extent of market vulnerability. However, even if this is true, there is no reason to think that the problem would in these circumstances become negligible. Even if all citizens have very generous initial endowments of educational resources and working capital, some may squander their endowments and end up vulnerable to dependent exchange. To defuse the objection, therefore, we need to think of ways in which we might structure the process of work-testing, and further complement the work-test, so as to protect citizens effectively from market vulnerability. Pursuing this line of enquiry will extend our understanding of the requirements of a fair work-test.

The central point to make here is that under a fair work-test unemployed welfare recipients are bearers not only of obligations but also of procedural rights—of what I shall call *claimants' rights*. Firstly, fair reciprocity requires that the unemployed have what we may call a right of reasonable refusal. Under a fair work-test, the unemployed welfare recipient is not obliged to accept *any* offer of employment on pain of a loss of his benefit, but is obliged only to accept a *reasonable* offer. What, one might ask, would constitute a reasonable offer? First and foremost, a job offer is reasonable only if it pays a sufficient amount, in combination with extant in-work benefits, to guarantee a citizen who meets his basic work expectation the decent minimum of income discussed above.[22] No welfare recipient may be sanctioned for refusing a job that pays below this limit. Depending on the structure of in-work benefits for the low-paid, even a rather modest right of reasonable refusal will help put an effective floor under wages and will thus help limit the extent to which employers can take advantage of market vulnerability to pay exploitative wages. However, we can and probably should expand our account of the claimant's right of reasonable refusal. For example, welfare recipients might be allowed to refuse up to a specified number of apparently satisfactory job offers before being subject to sanction. Or they may be allowed, at least for some period of time, to refuse any job that pays less than some specified percentage of their previous wage or the wage that they could plausibly be expected to command given their current skills.[23] They should have the freedom to refuse jobs that would make it difficult for them to discharge parental and other care work responsibilities. And so on. Within the framework of supervised job search, it is surely possible, and desirable, to give unemployed welfare recipients a degree of freedom over job applications and acceptances, rather than requiring them, as we initially imagined, to apply for and accept any job that is available and for which they are qualified. And this freedom will help protect them from the risk of taking an exploitative or abusive job.

However, individuals may still feel pressured to accept exploitative or abusive job offers if the terms and conditions of eligibility for welfare transfers are made sufficiently unattractive. If, for example, I have to wear a convict's uniform and break rocks for forty hours a week as a condition of receiving these transfers, then I may well enthusiastically agree to an exploitative or abusive job even though I would not suffer any cut in transfers were I to refuse the offer of this job. Parallel to the claimant's right of reasonable refusal, therefore, is a second claimant's right: a right of dignified treatment. Respect for the right of dignified treatment requires that the terms and content of the work-test, or any related measure of welfare contractualism, avoid humiliation of the welfare recipient. To this end, task assignments under the work-test may not be punitive: that is, tasks may not be of a kind that a typical citizen would regard as especially arduous or otherwise unpleasant, and they must have some genuinely productive end in view (at least the production of some socially valued output and preferably also the acquisition of new skills). Similarly, welfare recipients may not be required to live in special 'labour colonies' or workhouses where their compliance with the work-test can be more effectively enforced. More generally, respect for the privacy interests of welfare recipients will set limits on the methods by which officials can monitor their behaviour.[24] Another crucially important element of the welfare claimant's right to dignified treatment is her right to due process in decisions to terminate welfare benefits. A very suggestive discussion of the welfare claimant's right to due process can be found in Justice William Brennan's opinion in the US Supreme Court case *Goldberg v. Kelly*, decided in 1970. In this case the court decided by a 7–2 majority that a state law allowing administrators to terminate a welfare recipient's benefits subject but prior to a subsequent written appeal violated welfare recipients' constitutional rights of due process. Brennan, writing for the majority, argued that termination of benefits could not constitutionally occur until after the recipient's appeal had been heard, and that in making an appeal the recipient must have the right to a full oral hearing with counsel before an impartial adjudicator and the opportunity to cross-examine adverse witnesses.[25]

Thus, from the standpoint of fair reciprocity, welfare recipients have rights of reasonable refusal and dignified treatment which limit the form that the work-test can take. Note that these rights may be desirable on a number of grounds, though here I have chosen to focus specifically on the argument that they will protect unemployed citizens from market vulnerability. I have, of course, only described the rights in very broad terms. In practice, communities would need to design more detailed 'bills of rights' for unemployed welfare recipients in line with the general ideas of reasonable refusal and dignified treatment, as well as procedures for securing these rights against the encroachments of officialdom. Responsibility for these design questions could—and probably should—be devolved to special forums in which various affected parties (employers, welfare officials, the unemployed, and members of the general public) have fair representation. It should be noted that the shift to welfare contractualism has coincided in some countries with efforts to introduce a purchaser–provider split and/or new forms of performance management into the delivery of welfare programmes.[26] One interesting and important issue that I lack space to consider here concerns the possible implications of a decent welfare recipient bill of rights for the legitimacy and design of these innovative forms of programme delivery. It seems plausible, for example, that performance management systems that link payment of welfare officials too narrowly to targeted reductions in the welfare caseload will encourage violations of these rights and, for this reason, should be avoided.[27]

However, some proponents of the work-test might begin to have doubts at this point. Is there not a likelihood that strong due-process rights will be abused by some welfare recipients? There is surely something of a trade-off between a system with a lengthy appeals process that prioritizes the interests of the welfare recipient, and a system in which officials can sanction recipients speedily for non-compliance. If the work-test is not to be undermined, we cannot, in making this trade-off, tip the balance wholly in favour of the welfare recipient. The more we tip the balance in favour of the officials seeking to enforce work norms, however, the more risk there will be of an injustice towards any given welfare recipient. And even if there is no injustice, in the sense that everybody who is sanctioned is genuinely non-compliant, there is still the undeniable risk that those who are justly sanctioned nevertheless end up vulnerable in the labour market. And that fact of vulnerability remains a legitimate moral concern in its own right. So while a strong bill of rights for welfare recipients can certainly mitigate the problem of market vulnerability, some residual, and worrying, vulnerability is likely to remain.

6.5   *The Objection from Innocent Third Parties*

I have left the toughest objection to the work-test until last. A citizen who refuses to comply with the demands of a work-test thereby loses entitlement to income support. So far as this particular individual is concerned, this would seem fair enough (provided, of course, that the various conditions for a fair work-test are satisfied). But what if this individual has dependants, such as children? Will they not also suffer from the resulting fall in household income? Does the work-test not threaten, therefore, to penalize children and other dependants for decisions over which they have no control? And if we are committed to protecting citizens from brute luck poverty, does this not mean that the work-test is unjust (at least for those with dependants)? Do the claims of reciprocity not have to give way in this case to the urgent claims of this other consideration of justice? This objection is particularly tough precisely because of the way it points to a conflict between two of the most important commitments of justice as fair reciprocity.

How might the proponent of the work-test respond to this objection? A first point is that it is possible to structure benefit entitlements so as to soften the blow to innocent third parties of financial penalties imposed on others for their non-compliance with the work-test. A portion of the welfare benefits paid to a given household can be earmarked specifically for children's (and other dependants') needs, and these benefits can be ring-fenced from financial penalties for non-compliance with the work-test. A related idea, of course, is to provide certain benefits for children (or other dependants) in kind, effectively taking them out of the household economy, i.e. to directly socialize some costs of child-rearing. Examples include the direct public provision of primary and secondary education and health care to all children as of right. Many of the basic needs of children (and other dependants) can be secured in this way. These two ideas of ring-fencing dependants' cash benefits and publicly providing basic goods for dependants in kind[28] are thus vitally important additions to our understanding of a fair work-test. One of the more alarming features of the recent shift towards welfare contractualism in the United States is the extent to which ring-fencing and related ideas have been abandoned, most notably in the so-called 'family cap' policy, now widespread in many states, which denies mothers extra benefits to cover the living costs of children born while they are on welfare.[29] Institutionally speaking, there is a need here for something like a bill of rights for children and other dependants, analogous to the bill of rights for unemployed welfare claimants discussed above, setting out the basic welfare and related resource rights of dependants, and which trustee associations can enforce on their behalf should the state seek to punish welfare claimants by abrogating the rights of their dependants.

Two other responses to the problem are worth considering. One, of course, is to moderate the financial penalty imposed on the non-compliant welfare recipient. Non-compliance may be sanctioned not with full loss of benefit (by which I mean the portion of benefits paid to the household that is not ring-fenced to protect dependants' interests), but with a reduction in benefit. The cut may be for a specified period, after which normal benefit payments will resume, giving individuals a chance to reconsider their position and move into compliance. An ingenious suggestion is to postpone the financial penalty until such time as the non-compliant welfare recipient no longer has dependants, though this move would create an incentive for people to reacquire dependants and may also leave people with hefty welfare fines at a point in their life when they are much less able to meet them.[30]

What about non-financial penalties for non-compliance? One possibility, defended by Amy Gutmann and Dennis Thompson, is a system of direct labour penalties—court-enjoined compulsory community labour.[31] There is something intuitively fitting about sanctioning non-compliant parents with a labour penalty given that the wrong they allegedly commit consists in a failure to make a productive contribution to the community. But is such a policy compatible with respect for the basic liberties and securities that fair reciprocity is committed to uphold? One can readily imagine critics arguing that the proposal amounts to a policy of forced labour, thus violating the basic liberty of the citizen to choose whether or not to work.

A persuasive response to this objection is to point out that on becoming a parent one thereby acquires a set of role-related responsibilities that temporarily qualify one's rightful basic liberties in specific respects, including one's basic liberty in relation to work. To begin with, if one brings a child into the world, then one surely has a moral responsibility to nurture this child, where nurturing includes provision for its basic material needs. Biological parents may transfer this responsibility to others at the point of the child's birth, but keeping the child from birth ought to be conditional on assuming such responsibility. Moreover, parents must surely meet this duty to provide for their child's basic material needs in a manner that is consistent with the principles of distributive justice which properly govern the acquisition of income and wealth in general, which include fair-dues reciprocity. It would seem, then, that parents have a moral duty to work (to make a productive contribution to the community) in order to acquire the income necessary to provide for the basic material needs of their children. Finally, it seems perfectly proper to regard the moral duties that parents have to secure the basic needs of their children as legally enforceable duties. A parent who just ignores the health of his child, so that the child dies or suffers severe physical impairment due to lack of medical attention, is surely guilty of something that not only is morally wrong but which ought to be subject to legal penalty. Parents have a duty to work to provide for the basic material needs of their children, therefore, and the state may rightfully enforce this duty. The proposed labour penalty would therefore seem perfectly consistent with what the state is entitled to demand of citizens. John Stuart Mill expresses a similar view in *On Liberty*, where he writes that

idleness . . . cannot without tyranny be made a subject of legal punishment; but if, either from idleness or from any other avoidable cause, a man fails to perform his legal duties to others, as for instance to support his children, it is no tyranny to force him to fulfil that obligation by compulsory labour if no other means are available.[32]

However, there is a second worry: that the labour-penalty proposal may be impractical. If some citizens have refused to comply with the demands of a fair work-test and the state responds by imposing a direct labour penalty, why should we expect them to respect this second demand to work given that they ignored the first? The proposal clearly rests on an assumption that citizens will regard the demand to perform a labour penalty, presumably issued by a court, as more authoritative than the demand to comply with the work-test made by administrators of the income support system. The assumption is that their sense of public obligation is more likely to motivate in the first case than in the second. In general, this is probably a valid assumption. But it is not obviously correct and there may be individual cases in which it does not apply. One can imagine a hard core of individuals who tear their court orders up and refuse the labour penalty. At this point we are almost certainly led back to financial penalties in the form of fines for non-compliance with the labour penalty, with qualifications and caveats of the kind we have already noted.[33]

Thus, through a combination of ring-fencing dependants' cash benefits, in-kind public provision to dependants of a range of basic goods, moderation of financial penalties imposed on non-compliant welfare recipients, and perhaps partial substitution of cash penalties with labour penalties, a community can sanction individuals for non-compliance with a fair work-test while at the same time minimizing the risk of harm to innocent third parties. Nevertheless, even this moderated sanctions regime will leave the children and other dependants of welfare recipients at risk of serious brute luck disadvantage. Of course, the force of this point should not be exaggerated. No welfare system can provide absolutely foolproof protection against such disadvant-age. Even if welfare benefits are not subject to a work-test, parental irresponsibility as to how the benefits are spent could plunge children into poverty. But the expectations of responsible behaviour in a work-tested system are ordinarily higher than in a non-work-tested system and, for this reason, the risk of harm to innocent third parties is also that much higher.

6.6   *Paternalism and the Work-Test*

6.6.1   *Liberal Paternalism*

Thus far I have considered the case for the work-test only from the standpoint of distributive justice: the suggested rationale for the work-test is to protect citizens from being unfairly burdened by the resource claims of other citizens who are unwilling to make due reciprocation for the share of the social product they receive. But the work-test is often defended on quite different, paternalistic grounds: as a means of forcing welfare recipients to do what is in their own best interests. To what extent do paternalistic considerations require us to modify what has been said about the conditions under which the work-test is legitimate? We will find it useful to break this question down into two questions: (i) Can paternalist considerations ever justify the work-test? (ii) Can paternalist considerations justify the work-test even when the background distribution of economic opportunity is sig-nificantly unjust (i.e. fails to satisfy requirements of the kind described in Section 6.2)?

I assume that the commitment to respect and protect citizens' integ-rity interests establishes a general presumption against paternalist restrictions on individual liberty: respect for the citizen's expressive integrity generally requires that she be left free to determine how far she will expose herself to various kinds of risk, for such decisions are integral to the citizen's ability to live a life that is an authentic expression of her own values and priorities. Something like this, at any rate, is the standard liberal view of paternalism, and I do not intend to dissent from this view here. However, even within liberal theory, paternalism is acknowledged as potentially legitimate where the individual in question lacks the capacities of self-government—of rationality and self-discipline—that citizens are assumed in general to have. Moreover, as Gerald Dworkin has pointed out, even if most citizens are rational and self-disciplined most of the time, the vast majority of us are nonetheless vulnerable to periods of irrationality and/or weakness of will. At these times we may choose to do things that have tragic and irreversible consequences. Aware of these two facts, a citizen looking ahead in a spirit of reflective prudence might rationally choose to limit her own liberty in specific ways so as to forestall action, undertaken in moments of irrationality or weakness of will, that risks these consequences. This suggests a possible criterion for justified liberal paternalism: paternalistic intervention is justifiable if the restrictions it involves are restrictions that citizens would individually consent to, in a state of sober reflection, as a way of insuring themselves against individual weaknesses of rationality and/or will that might have significantly bad and irreversible consequences for their own welfare or freedom.[34]

This conception of paternalism has obvious application in the welfare context. We know, for instance, that the experience of long-term unemployment can be profoundly debilitating. Skills and motivation can both atrophy so that the individual who has been out of work for a long time runs the risk of never getting back into work. If this is so, then it is by no means absurd to suggest that a prudent citizen, concerned to protect himself against these adverse effects of long-term unemployment, would agree on reflection to a system of eligibility rules for welfare benefits that will require him to continue looking for work, or to enrol in a training or public-works programme, should he suffer unemployment lasting more than a short length of time. So work-related eligibility rules do perhaps have a paternalistic justification when they can be seen as rational self-insurance devices of this kind: as policies which track the hypothetical, self-insuring choices of the reflectively prudent citizen.

However, even if some measures of welfare contractualism are potentially legitimate for these paternalistic reasons, are such measures still justifiable if there are significant inequalities of economic opportunity in society? The worry must be that enforcement of the relevant measures in these circumstances could expose more vulnerable citizens to harms and unfair burdens that they might be more readily able to avoid under a more permissive welfare system.

In the case of some rather weak types of paternalism, this worry seems misplaced. Imagine, for example, a rule requiring the welfare recipient simply to turn up periodically to a meeting at which she will be provided with information about work and educational opportunities without any additional requirement that she pursue any of these opportunities.[35] No welfare recipient is going to be required by this specific measure to search for a job and expose themselves thereby to the risk of exploitation or abuse. Indeed, such a measure could conceivably help reduce this risk by making welfare recipients even more aware of how poor their immediate prospects are.

What about stronger forms of paternalism which require welfare recipients to seek work? Here it is tempting to say that the paternalistic intervention is justified if the gains to the disadvantaged welfare recipient from such intervention outweigh the possible costs to this same person in terms of increased pressure to take poor-quality jobs, increased exposure to exploitation, and so forth. If this is our criterion for judging the legitimacy of paternalism in circumstances of grave inequality, however, then we face a problem. The relevant gains and losses could well be very unevenly distributed among the class of disadvantaged and vulnerable people with whom we are concerned. On just about any credible metric of cost and benefit, there will usually be a net gain for some and a net loss for others. Empirical assessment of the relative magnitude of these effects is likely to be extremely difficult, and I can see no uncontroversial way in which we might weigh the respective gains and losses even if we knew them with perfect accuracy.

It would seem, then, that paternalistic considerations do add something to the case for the work-test. However, in view of this last point, it seems unlikely that they can provide a justification for the work-test that will hold irrespectively of how distributively just our society is. They do not, apparently, justify disregard for the fair work-test requirements set out above.[36]

6.6.2 *Lawrence Mead's 'New Paternalism'*

Any evaluation of paternalist arguments for the work-test would be incomplete without considering Lawrence Mead's 'New Paternalist' theory of welfare contractualism.[37] Mead advances his theory in the US context, but he thinks it has some applicability to other advanced capitalist countries, including Britain. As I noted in Chapter 1, this theory has contributed to the emerging communitarian philosophy of economic citizenship that has informed the policy of recent governments of the centre-left.[38] Does Mead give us any reason to moderate the conclusions we seem to have reached concerning the limits of paternalistic justifications for the work-test?

In its mature form, Mead's New Paternalist theory has three main elements which can be set out as follows:

1. There is a problem of non-work among the long-term poor which is the primary cause of their poverty.

2. The primary cause of non-work among the long-term poor is their lack of 'competence'.
3. Work should be enforced in the immediate and long-term interests of the poor; work is in their immediate interests because (*a*) it is the route out of poverty; and it is in their long-term interests because (*b*) it builds psychological health and (*c*) it makes them 'deserving' and thereby gives legitimacy to other claims the poor might make.

A striking feature of Mead's theory is his explanation of non-work in terms of the limited 'competence' of the non-working poor and his characterization of work enforcement as a means of substituting for and restoring the competence that they allegedly lack. The 'competence assumption', says Mead, is the 'assumption that the individual is willing and able to advance his or her own economic interests. . . . the ordinary citizen is a maximizer, seeking not just survival, but advancement in material terms—supporting one's family and propelling oneself to a higher station in life'.[39] But, argues Mead, many citizens, particularly among the long-term poor, no longer exhibit competence in this sense. How, then, do we 'cope with people who seem unable to advance their own interests, let alone society's?'[40] The answer: society must force the incompetent to act as if they were competent. In this way, over time, they may come to acquire the competence they lack.

Mead's argument appears to rely, however, on confusing (at least) two quite distinct notions of competence. The first, 'thin' notion of competence is the notion of advancing one's economic interests in a rational way (optimizing for a given set of preferences and constraints); this, at least, is how one might interpret the idea that the competent individual 'is able and willing to advance his or her own economic interests'. The second, 'thick' notion adds to this stipulation that the competent individual necessarily has *a very specific set of preferences* focused on 'maximizing' his or her success in materialist terms: such is the import of saying that the competent seek 'advancement in material terms . . . to [propel themselves] to a higher station in life'. Now to call someone who cannot advance their economic interests in a rational way incompetent is fair enough; and it is plausible to assume that everyone has an interest in being competent in this sense. But to call someone incompetent because they are not interested in 'getting on' in a materialistic sense is highly tendentious; and it is by no means as plausible to assume that everyone has an interest in being, and ought to be, competent in this sense. Consider people whose aim in life is to write great poetry. To this end, they work just enough to get a subsistence income so that they can spend the rest of their time trying to write poetry. Mead would have to say that these people are incompetent because they are not motivated to seek success in material terms. But I find it hard to see what such people are doing that is irrational. The competence argument might still be persuasive if the non-working poor were clearly incompetent in the first, thin sense (rather than the second). But their non-work might well reflect a perfectly competent, welfare-maximizing response to a labour market which offers them only poor-quality jobs at low wages.[41] In short: the non-working poor with whom Mead is concerned are not clearly incompetent in the sense of 'incompetent' that clearly does matter; and even if they are incompetent in Mead's thicker sense, it is not clear why this in itself does matter and demands correction.

However, Mead's policy recommendations are not necessarily invalidated by this weakness in the competence argument. If we cast our eye back over the three main elements of Mead's theory as I summarized these above, we see that element 3, which expresses Mead's policy recommendations, contains its own rationale for work enforcement which appeals to specific interests of the welfare poor rather than to Mead's somewhat confused notion of 'competence'. This is (again) a paternalistic rationale and, as such, I think it is ultimately subject to the same caveats, identified above, that apply to paternalistic arguments for the work-test identified above. The New Paternalist must make a persuasive case that the restrictions on welfare recipients' freedom that he or she proposes, firstly, are restrictions that would be chosen by a citizen of moderate prudence concerned to insure him- or herself against the possible consequences of future irrationality and/or weakness of will; and, secondly, will produce a net benefit for welfare recipients even under circumstances of limited economic opportunity and (hence) distributive injustice.

In at least one respect, however, Mead does give the paternalist defence of the work-test a distinctive and interesting twist. He emphasizes how work affects the perceived legitimacy of the poor's claims on society. Claims to assistance, or for the expansion of opportunity, acquire a new legitimacy once the poor are in work. This argument links the paternalist defence of welfare contractualism with the justice based defence reviewed above. It may be true that, morally speaking, the rights of economic citizenship must be in place before we can fairly enforce reciprocation for benefits received. But politically, in some societies at some times, the logic may work in the other direction. It may be necessary to enforce the notional claims of reciprocity, through work, before (more affluent) citizens will consider the redistribution necessary to secure the rights of the disadvantaged. This perhaps explains what Mead is really getting at when he appeals to the notion of 'competence': poor citizens must prove *through actual work* that they have a specific *civic* competence, namely, the effective capacity to satisfy the demands of reciprocity, before their claims for assistance and increased opportunity will receive political attention.[42] As Mead puts it, 'When work competence is no longer at issue, then justice can be.'[43] If the political prognosis underlying this argument is correct, then it would offer a plausible justification for applying the work-test even if the requirements for a fair work-test are not in place. The possible long-term pay-off to such a strategy must, however, be set against the danger that the envisaged reform process gets blocked half-way, so that the welfare poor end up with tougher new responsibilities and little or no additional assistance.

6.7   *Conclusion*

From the standpoint of fair reciprocity, welfare contractualism seems, at first sight, and in principle, a wholly legitimate practice. The work-test can be defended as a necessary device for protecting citizens against the unfair resource claims of those who are unwilling to meet the contributive obligations they have to the community. This is one message of this chapter. But this message comes with important qualifications. I have stressed that, from the standpoint of fair reciprocity, the work-test is just only if certain conditions are met. Some of these conditions have to do with the background distribution of assets and opportunities in the economy. Others have to do with the structure and design of the work enforcement regime itself. Paternalistic considerations add something to the case for the work-test, but do not justify disregard for these distributional and structural conditions. Moreover, there are forceful objections to work-testing, and, while I have replied to these objections, I do not claim to have wholly defused them here. In later chapters I will give thought to how the community might complement work-tested welfare with other policies so as to address these remaining concerns. This will enable me to be more specific about some of the distributional conditions for a fair work-test. Keeping these concerns in mind, I now turn to consider the merits of a radical policy proposal that is often advanced as an alternative to contractualist, work-tested welfare: the proposal for an unconditional basic income.

CHAPTER 7

Basic Income

...property is moral and healthy only when it is used as a condition, not of idleness, but of activity, and when it involves the discharge of definite personal obligations.

(R. H. Tawney, *The Acquisitive Society*)

As I noted in Chapter 1, the contemporary shift towards welfare contractualism has not gone uncontested. In many countries of the advanced capitalist world there is at present growing interest in and support for the idea of unconditional basic income (UBI): an income paid to each citizen (i) on an individual basis, (ii) irrespective of income from other sources, and, perhaps most controversially, (iii) without regard to past or present work performance or willingness to accept a job if offered.[1] Supporters of this idea disagree over the size of the UBI which should be aimed at, but many argue that the long-term goal should be an UBI set at or close to a level sufficient to cover a standard set of basic needs, or what we may call a substantial UBI.

Given the problems I identified in the previous chapter with contractualist, work-tested forms of income support, there is obviously something attractive about UBI. On the other hand, there is a reason for the practice of work-testing. According to the fair-dues conception of reciprocity presented in Part I, where the institutions governing economic life provide citizens with sufficiently egalitarian and otherwise just access to the social product, those who claim the high minimum share of the social product available to them under these institutions have an obligation to make a decent productive contribution to the community in return. An injustice occurs if the citizen does not make this reciprocal productive contribution. By disconnecting income entitlement from productive contribution, however, an UBI makes it that much easier for citizens to enjoy a high minimum share of the social product without making such a contribution. It may help provide (more) egalitarian access to the social product, but on terms that also allow citizens to violate their contributive obligations. This is one way of starting of a common objection to UBI, that 'it would amount to an institutionalization of free-riding, to the exploitation of hard workers by those able-bodied people who would choose to live on their [UBI]'.[2] My aim in this chapter is to consider in more depth the philosophical arguments for UBI, particularly as they bear on this exploitation objection, and to consider what place an UBI might therefore have in the civic minimum.

Some supporters of UBI claim that, as a matter of what justice fundamentally requires, citizens have a right to an UBI. Sections 7.1 to 7.3 consider three arguments in support of this claim. My main focus, in Section 7.1, is on the job assets argument for UBI set out by Philippe Van Parijs.[3] This argument holds that people have a right to an UBI as an expression of their right to an equal, tradeable share of their society's jobs. The main problem with the argument is the idea that individuals have a right to equal, tradeable shares of society's job assets regardless of their work preferences. I argue that, since one's share of job assets directly affects the share of the social product one can claim, the demand for a share of such assets should be respected only if its maker has work preferences consistent with the contributive obligation which, so I have argued, applies to all citizens in a just society who are able to work. Section 7.2 considers and rejects the argument that individuals have a right to an UBI as an expression of their rightful share of their society's technological inheritance. In Section 7.3 I consider the argument that a right to an UBI can be derived from each citizen's alleged right of exclusive access to a share of her society's land (meaning, the surface area of a territory and the fruits growing on this territory without the assistance of human labour). I argue that citizens do indeed have such a right (it is what I referred to in Section 4.3 as a primitive resource right). However, an UBI, understood as a periodic cash grant, is only one way of implementing this resource right. Moreover, even this resource right arguably carries with it specific obligations, and enforcement of these obligations will reduce the level of UBI that can justifiably be claimed as of right on these grounds.

Turning from these rights-based arguments for UBI, I next consider, in Section 7.4, whether a more persuasive case for UBI might be made on consequentialist terms, i.e. by reference to the beneficial effects that an UBI might have. Specifically, I consider how someone might defend an UBI as an instrument for achieving or advancing the various distributive goals associated with fair reciprocity (in its non-ideal form), such as market security and adequate opportunity for self-realization in work. An UBI can be expected to have many positive effects of this kind. A proponent of UBI might argue that these effects in some sense outweigh the undesirable free-riding that an UBI makes possible, and that an UBI is therefore justified in spite of this free-riding. I think there is much force to this argument. However, this consequentialist argument can not only be advanced in support of UBI in its standard, pure form. It can also be advanced in support of a number of variants on the UBI proposal, variants that modify the original proposal in a way that explicitly addresses the reciprocity-based concern about economic free-riding. Section 7.5 outlines and considers the respective strengths and weaknesses of a number of these variants: republican basic income (which links UBI to some form of public-service requirement); targeted basic income (which restricts UBI, or pays it at a higher level, to those most disadvantaged in the labour market); and time-limited basic income (which restricts the proportion of a normal working life over which an UBI can be received). While all of these variants of UBI have their own weaknesses, they should be included in the prospective mix of policies geared to achieving the demands of fair reciprocity in its non-ideal form, and may be preferable to UBI in its pure form.

7.1   *The Job Assets Argument*

As said, some proponents of UBI claim that citizens have a fundamental right to an UBI. This claim is defended in a number of ways. This section focuses on one recent defence developed by Philippe Van Parijs: the job assets argument for UBI. Van Parijs's starting point is the claim that justice fundamentally requires citizens to have equal, or at least maximin, 'real freedom'.[4] Real freedom is 'formal freedom', i.e. formal, legal permission, to do things—'whatever one might want to do'—combined with the 'opportunity' to do them that is conferred by command over resources, where resources include both external assets of various kinds, and the individual's internal resources, i.e. talents, handicaps, and the like. Now, if we make the simplifying assumption that individuals have equal endowments of internal resources, real freedom would be equalized by assuring each citizen of an equal share of their society's external assets. (Just what counts as an external asset for purposes of the argument is a matter I shall return to in a moment.) Rather than literally cutting up these assets and distributing them to each person, however, we could instead give each person an unconditional income grant equal to the market value of a per capita share of the relevant assets. This is equivalent to cutting the relevant assets up, and giving equal, tradeable shares of the assets to each citizen. So, according to Van Parijs, once we have specified the external assets that ought properly to be available in this way, the state should tax their value to the revenue-maximizing extent, and redistribute the proceeds as a uniform, unconditional income grant to all. Van Parijs claims that, in the circumstances of at least some advanced capitalist countries today, such a policy would yield a substantial income grant, i.e. an UBI set at, or close to, a level sufficient to cover a standard set of basic needs.[5] Thus, Van Parijs concludes that in at least some advanced capitalist countries today, each citizen is entitled to an UBI set at or close to a level sufficient to cover a standard set of basic needs, an UBI financed from the revenue-maximizing taxation of the value of specific external assets.

Exactly what counts as a relevant kind of external asset for purposes of this argument? According to Van Parijs, relevant assets include, first, our common inheritance of what we may call pure natural resources.[6] In addition, Van Parijs argues, they include transfers (gifts, bequests, inheritances) of non-natural wealth.[7] Van Parijs thinks that the UBI which could be financed by revenue-maximizing taxation of these assets would not be substantial, probably well below the level necessary to cover a standard set of basic needs. However, Van Parijs argues, there is at least one other kind of asset that is important to individuals' real freedom: *jobs*. Clearly, in societies like our own, jobs are vitally important determinants of life chances, both because of the intrinsic benefits that employment confers, e.g. opportunities to develop and display various skills, or to socialize purposively with others; and because of the access which a wage provides to the social product. However, citizens are, of course, frequently unable to obtain employment though they have the requisite skills for a given type of work, and are willing to work at, or slightly below, the prevailing real wage for work of this kind. Van Parijs argues that even under competitive conditions such involuntary unemployment is likely to arise because certain of the assumptions underpinning the influential Walrasian model of the economy, in which there are no frustrated buyers and sellers in equilibrium, do not in fact hold in the real world.[8] In such a non-Walrasian world, where involuntary unemployment persists in competitive equilibrium, there will be a significant and morally arbitrary inequality in opportunity between those insiders fortunate enough to be in employment, and the involuntarily unemployed, the outsiders, who are excluded, at least for some period of time, from desired employment.

An important corollary of this equilibrium involuntary unemployment is the existence of substantial employment rents enjoyed by
those fortunate enough to be in employment, which are given by the
difference between the wage they receive and the hypothetical market-
clearing wage. Van Parijs's innovative proposal is that we address the
inequality between employment insiders and outsiders by including
these employment rents in the tax base for financing an UBI. Van
Parijs argues that we should regard the citizens of a non-Walrasian
society as having rights to equal tradeable shares of available jobs, or
equivalently, to an unconditional income equal to the value of a per
capita share of available jobs. And this amounts, Van Parijs tells us, to
giving each person an equal share in the employment rents arising from
job scarcity.[9] These rents will be particularly large when involuntary
unemployment is high, but may still be considerable even if everybody
has a job, because some of those with relatively poor jobs may want
and be able to do more attractive jobs at, or slightly below, the relevant prevailing wage for these jobs. Van Parijs argues that once the UBI
tax base is accordingly expanded to include these employment rents,
it becomes large enough to finance a substantial UBI.[10]

One potential difficulty for this argument arises when we relax
the assumption that citizens have identical skills and handicaps. For
if these endowments differ, the underlying commitment to equalize,
or maximin, real freedom would require that we make specially targeted payments out of the external assets fund to compensate those
with relatively poor endowments, using only the residual to finance
an UBI. We may then be unable to finance a substantial UBI even
after employment rents have been added to the fund. For present purposes, however, I propose to set this possible difficulty aside.[11] This
leaves us free to focus on a second and, I think, more fundamental
issue: the nature of the citizen's right to a share of her society's job
assets.

Why might we think that citizens have rights to things like job assets?
The basic consideration, as Van Parijs's own discussion suggests, is the
injustice of involuntary exclusion from the opportunity for full economic participation in one's society.[12] The appropriate image, bringing
the underlying moral concern into focus, is of a citizen standing at the
'factory gates' of her society clamouring to be let in and to be given the
opportunity to go to work and enjoy the benefits that this brings. In
demanding a share of job assets, the citizen is, as it were, demanding
the right to enter this factory. The question we have to consider, then,
is whether or not the wider community is entitled to set some conditions on this right of entry. Specifically, should entry be conditional

on the citizen's willingness to put the opportunity it affords to good use by making a productive contribution?

If, as we have supposed, involuntary exclusion from full economic participation is the main consideration behind the putative right of entry, then there seems no reason in principle why the community shouldn't impose such a condition. The aim is to provide access to work for all those who wish to work; making access to the social factory, i.e. a share of society's job assets, conditional on willingness to work is obviously not in contradiction with this aim. But there may also be good reason why the community should impose such a condition. Imagine a citizen, I will call him the lifestyle non-worker, who wishes to claim a decent minimum share of the social product (enough to underwrite his basic projects), but who wishes to minimize his productive contribution to the community in return. He demands a right to enter the social factory for equal time to others, explaining his demand as follows: 'I would like to be given an equal allotment of time in the social factory. It is not that I wish to make a productive contribution. But if I have an allotment of this time I can sell it to others who are more enthusiastic about making a productive contribution and so enjoy a given share of the social product for less contribution'. Were someone with the imagined preferences challenged to explain his motivation for claiming an equal allotment of time in the factory, an honest answer would, I think, have to go something like this. But, dropping the metaphor, there is surely something objectionable about this demand for a share of job assets, once its motivation is made clear. Recall the contributive obligation explained in Chapters 3 and 4: roughly stated, an obligation to make a decent productive contribution to the community in the context of economic institutions that secure access to the social product for one on sufficiently egalitarian terms. It is objectionable to demand a share of job assets with a view to evading this obligation. And this is what the imagined lifestyle non-worker would seem to be trying to do.[13] The demand for a 'right to work' is somehow transmogrified here into a demand for the right not to work—while still sharing in the social product.

The key issue is whether or not people's work preferences are themselves a matter of, or relevant to, justice. According to one view, articulated by Van Parijs, work preferences are no different in this sort of case from, say, people's musical or religious preferences. It would be arbitrary, so the argument runs, to allot external assets differentially between people on the basis that some like Mozart and others don't, or that some are Catholic and others Protestant. It is no less arbitrary, no less a violation of 'liberal neutrality', to discriminate on the basis of work preferences. But it is a commonplace observation that liberal neutrality is not absolute neutrality: some preferences can only be satisfied by violating the demands of justice, and it is not objectionable to define rights in ways that disadvantage people with such preferences. According to justice as fair reciprocity, however, work preferences are implicated in the demands of justice. As said, according to fair reciprocity in its non-ideal form, where the institutions governing economic life meet the threshold conditions defined in Section 4.2, so that access to the social product is on substantially egalitarian and otherwise just terms, citizens who actually claim the high minimum of the social product available to them under these institutions ought to satisfy a basic work expectation in return. To the extent that sharing in one's society's stock of job assets helps provide one with access to the social product on these terms, one should have work preferences consistent with meeting the corresponding work expectation. On this view, then, it is perfectly appropriate, in principle, to condition the right to job assets on the citizen's having work preferences of the required, reciprocity-respecting kind. Job assets should not go, therefore, to the lifestyle non-workers who wish to use their command over these assets to evade their basic work expectation. The corollary of this is that it is inappropriate, as a matter of basic principle, to redistribute the employment rents attached to job assets indiscriminately in the form of an UBI. The funds should rather be redistributed in a form that specifically compensates those who are frustrated in their desire to work: concretely, the funds might be spent on wage subsidies, unemployment benefits, public works programmes, or retraining schemes, rather than UBI.

In claiming that the right to a share of job assets depends on work preferences, my argument here has strong affinities with that developed by Gijs van Donselaar.[14] In van Donselaar's illuminating analysis, the fundamental source of the problem is that Van Parijs insists on our distributing resources, including job assets, to individuals without any regard to their 'independent interests' in using them, so allowing those with weak independent interests to extract 'parasitic' rents from those with stronger interests. Van Donselaar offers the following example to illustrate the problem. There are two people, Lazy and Crazy, and four identical units of land. In Crazy's absence, Lazy would appropriate and work one unit of land. In Lazy's absence, Crazy would appropriate and work three units of land. In van Donselaar's terms, Lazy thus has an independent interest in one unit, and Crazy an independent interest in three units, of land. Say that we now give Lazy and Crazy each two units of the land and allow trade. Lazy will likely lease some of his land to Crazy in return for a share of what Crazy produces on the land; and Lazy thereby ends up better off, and Crazy worse off, than each would respectively be in the absence of the other. The fair division, van Donselaar argues, is to apportion land in accordance with the underlying pattern of independent interests (adjusting the apportionment if these interests change). By insisting on strictly equal division regardless of the underlying pattern of independent interests we can, as in this example, create a scarcity that is not inherent in the situation, a scarcity that Lazy can then exploit to enjoy the benefits of Crazy's work. What applies to land in this case applies no less to job assets, and to the parasitic rents that an equal division of tradeable job assets would allow the lifestyle non-worker to extract from harder-working citizens. Job assets should be distributed in proportion to citizens' willingness to work.[15]

Van Donselaar's analysis not only concurs on this point with that based on the conception of reciprocity set out in Part I. In important respects, it extends and deepens this analysis. For one thing, it offers a way of tackling some issues of distributive justice that are not obviously tractable in terms of the reciprocity principle introduced in Part I.[16] Relatedly, it promises to help us get a firmer hand on the nature and limits of what I referred to in Section 4.3 as citizens' primitive resource rights. Van Donselaar's analysis has the implication that where non-productive citizens do have a genuine independent interest in some manna-like asset, e.g. land, but are excluded from it, then some transfer of social product to them may be justified by way of compensation for the frustration of this interest. This is an implication I shall return to when I discuss the land right argument for UBI in Section 7.3 below. Returning, however, to the job assets argument, van Donselaar's critique of this argument is also particularly helpful in revealing the way in which a simple equal division of job (or other) assets among citizens, as proposed by Van Parijs, may in fact run counter to the animating spirit of an egalitarian society. An egalitarian society should be characterized by a spirit of solidarity between citizens. But citizens who claim a share of their society's job assets, not with a view to working, but with a view to gatekeeping the assets,[17] allowing others access to them for a price, arguably do not stand in a relationship of solidarity with their fellow citizens. Their stance is essentially manipulative. The spirit of solidarity seems much more alive where institutions ensure *equal access to work for those with equal willingness to work*, and citizens with little enthusiasm for work accordingly allow those with more enthusiasm a higher share of job assets, rather than insisting on an equal share and then trying to extract rents in return for their essentially unwanted surplus.[18]

7.2   *The Technological Inheritance Argument*

A second, more widespread argument that we have a right to an UBI appeals to the idea that as citizens we have a common right to our society's technological inheritance. The productivity of those who work is, it is said, only as high as it is because of the technology embodied in the means of production. Morally speaking, this technology is a common inheritance of all citizens. Accordingly, the increment to total output attributable to this technology should be regarded as the common property of the citizenry. This common property may be used for public-spending projects of benefit to all, or else distributed to all citizens as an UBI. As one UBI proponent, Gar Alperovitz, puts it: 'If we agree that today's technology is akin to a pebble resting on a mountain of previous achievements, then a substantial portion of society's current income should go as a matter of equal right to each individual, apart from the amount he or she earns from current work or risk, or to the entire community.'[19] When one thinks about it, this argument really implies that almost all the social product should in principle be distributed as an UBI (or as equivalent goods in kind). For the difference between our society's hypothetical pre-technological social product and the actual, technologically enhanced social product is surely huge, accounting for virtually all of the social product. I shall not discuss all the problems with this argument here, but the following story serves, I think, to explain why the argument is essentially flawed.

Imagine two people, Alf and Betty, who, following a shipwreck, find themselves treading water in a becalmed sea. Each spends a frantic hungry day in the water, splashing about, trying with their bare hands to catch the fish swimming around them to eat. But the fish are too quick and the output of caught fish of each at the end of the day is consequently zero. The following day the tides carry them to a beach. On the beach they find a large pool full of fish and, as luck would have it, two sets of excellent fishing rods and nets left by previous inhabitants of the beach. After a sleep Betty sits down at the pool's edge and starts fishing. By the end of the day she has a sizeable catch. Alf, who has spent the day lounging in the sun in the expectation that Betty would be busy catching fish, now sidles over. Somewhat airily, he demands an equal share of Betty's catch. First he recalls how low Betty's fish productivity was the day before when they splashed about in mutual frustration. Then he makes the argument that since Betty only has a positive output of fish today because of the beach inheritance (the pool, rods, and nets), and the beach inheritance is their common property, the fish output is also their common property. As such, he should have an equal share of it. How plausible is Alf's argument? It is, I think, entirely unpersuasive. It is surely sufficient for Betty to reply that Alf had the same opportunity to fish (the same access to the pool, and to equivalent rods and nets), that this option was his fair (equal) share of their beach inheritance, and that it is Alf's lookout if he has chosen not to make good use of it.

Now the technological inheritance argument for UBI, in the simple form presented above, seems to be on a par with Alf's rather implausible beach inheritance argument that he is entitled to receive an equal share of the fish that Betty catches. It has the same essential structure and the same essential flaw. If there were some technological inheritance which you wished to use and my use of this technological inheritance somehow precluded your use of it, then you could have a plausible case for compensation against me and anyone else who is responsible for excluding you from use of this technology. But in general, as Van Parijs points out in rejecting the technological inheritance argument,[20] my decision to deploy a given inherited technology productively need not deprive you of the option of also deploying this technology. If, for example, I build a cart with wheels instead of dragging things along the ground, I do not, ordinarily, thereby preclude you from acting on the same idea. Of course, some people may be endowed with more intelligence or strength which enables them to get more out of a given technological inheritance and their raw labour-power. Or they may have larger initial endowments of external wealth, making it easier for them to harness society's technological inheritance. We should indeed be concerned with these inequalities. But at this point we are clearly passing from an argument about common property in society's technological inheritance to an argument about the need to redress inequality in inheritances of skill and external wealth. Addressing these inequalities is a key demand of justice as fair reciprocity, one I consider elsewhere in this volume, and one that does not necessarily call for an UBI.[21]

7.3   *The Land Right Argument*

In Section 4.3 I imagined a society in which there are two groups occupying a previously uninhabited territory: the Lockeans, who wish to use the territory's available land for productive purposes; and the Hermitians, who wish to use land for non-productive, largely contemplative purposes. Now, in accessing and using a portion of the territory's land for their contemplative purposes, the Hermitians obviously do not lay claim to a share of what the Lockeans produce. They do not free-ride on the Lockeans' productive efforts merely by meditating on a portion of the territory's land. Moreover, they do have a genuine wish to make direct use of the land, albeit for non-productive purposes: their desire for land is not strategic, made with a view to gatekeeping the resource, and extracting an income from the Lockeans in return for allowing them to use it. In these circumstances, as I argued in Chapter 4, it seems quite arbitrary to deny the Hermitians rights of access and use with respect to a portion of the territory, even though they do not wish to participate in the productive endeavour which the Lockeans intend to initiate. The Hermitians have what I have called in Chapter 4 a primitive resource right to a portion of their society's land, a right that the Lockeans, in setting up their scheme of productive endeavour, must respect. The thought I wish to explore here is, first, whether it is plausible in general to see land—understood as the surface area of a territory and the fruits growing on this territory without the assistance of human labour—as the focus of such a right; and, second, whether an UBI might be a legitimate way of implementing this primitive resource right in practice.

The case for regarding land in general as the focus of a primitive resource right rests first on the fact that it is not a product of human industry. Thus, in directly using it, individuals cannot be said to be claiming a share of the current social product (or using a share of the product of past generations of workers that the current generation has a duty to replace). The second, vitally important consideration is that all people, regardless of their willingness to be productive, can quite plausibly be said to have a direct interest in access to, and use of, at least some minimum quantity of land. All people, regardless of their particular philosophies of life, can be said to have a genuine *need* for some non-trivial, minimum quantity of land. (In van Donselaar's terms, everyone, regardless of how important work and production are to them, has an independent interest in at least some non-trivial, minimum quantity of land.[22]) It would be objectionable for productively inclined citizens to frustrate this genuine need on the part of less productively inclined citizens, by excluding them from an initial share-out of use-rights to land, given that the needed resource in this case is not itself part of the social product and that it is indeed genuinely needed, rather than being desired for strategic, gatekeeping purposes.

Why do all citizens need some minimum of land? The main reason is that command over a minimum quantity of land is essential to personal liberty, and all citizens, as ethical agents (Section 2.2), have a vital interest in personal liberty. In order to live as an independent ethical agent, one first needs a space from which one cannot legally be excluded by others. If someone lacks access to such a space, then any action they perform is putatively illegal: whatever they do, some property owner somewhere is legally empowered to make them desist and move on.[23] Meaningful ethical agency also requires that we have a predictable relationship to the basic physical infrastructure of our existence; and one's psychological integrity depends on being able to obtain and enforce some degree of privacy. These things require, so to speak, a space to call one's own. It is not enough merely to have access to a common space, like a public park, from which one cannot be excluded, but from which one cannot exclude others. One must have access to a space from which one can legally exclude others.

Let us accept, then, that land is the focus of a primitive resource right. This is an important point to accept. For it implies that all citizens, regardless of their willingness to make a productive contribution to the community, have some legitimate resource claim against their society. On a very general definition of UBI, all citizens may be said to have an UBI that corresponds to this primitive resource right. However, the issue still arises as to the form this UBI should take. If we can agree on the minimum quantity of land that anyone needs (perhaps a big 'if'), we might then look at the current market value of this amount of land and give every citizen an income grant equal to this sum. This might be financed from a tax on large private landholdings. In effect, those with large landholdings would be required to redistribute some of their claim on land to those who would otherwise lack direct access to it by paying some form of land tax into a compensation fund that would then be used to finance an UBI set at the suggested level. However, there may be other ways of implementing the primitive resource right to land. The community could perhaps hold specific tracts of land in common and allow citizens use-rights over a fixed period.[24] Or the community might introduce a scheme of vouchers or subsidies for low-cost housing as a rough simulation of the primitive resource right to land. Or policies of these kinds might be combined.[25] So while this argument does appear to justify an UBI in one sense, at the policy level the logic of the argument does not necessarily support an open-ended cash benefit over more purpose-targeted and/or in-kind benefits.

Moreover, we should note some complications that arise in thinking about the enactment of the universal primitive resource right in land.

Firstly, a legal and political system will be necessary to define and enforce citizens' primitive resource rights. Such a system is not costless. So an issue arises as to whether all citizens, including people like our Hermitians, are obliged to contribute to these costs. The answer we give to this question depends, I think, on what theory of political obligation we endorse. According to one influential theory, we acquire an obligation to contribute to the cost of our society's basic legal and political framework only if we consent to the benefits of protection that this framework provides (knowing the likely cost). If we follow this theory, then it may be that some of the Hermitians, those who are conscientious anarchists and who therefore will not consent to any governmental system on principle, would not have an obligation to contribute to the cost of the legal and political framework within which they enjoy their primitive resource rights. According to another influential theory, however, the concern for reciprocity itself grounds political obligation. Those who receive the undeniable benefits of protection have an enforceable obligation to contribute to the cost of the legal and political framework which provides this protection. This is because some citizens would otherwise enjoy these benefits without sharing the costs, thereby free-riding on the efforts of their fellow citizens. I do not intend to try to resolve this dispute over the basis and limits of political obligation here.[26] I merely wish to indicate how different theories will have different implications for how we enact the primitive resource right to land. The latter theory suggests, for example, that the government may be justified in claiming back a portion of the relevant resource entitlement as a contribution to the costs of defining and enforcing primitive resource rights (implying a correspondingly lower UBI).

Another complication arises when we consider who is liable for contributing to a scheme of just compensation for handicaps. I discussed the issue of just compensation for handicaps in Section 2.4. Even if one is unconvinced by the specific, Dworkinian approach to determining just levels of compensation explained there, there is no reason to suppose that the tax liabilities corresponding to just compensation payments should be borne exclusively by those who wish to participate in their society's productive system, i.e. by citizens with Lockean rather than Hermitian preferences. It seems quite appropriate that citizens with Lockean preferences should bear additional tax liabilities to cover the additional risks of injury specifically due to their collective productive endeavour. But some handicaps arise quite independently of this and it is arguably quite arbitrary to place the burden of compensating for these handicaps solely on the shoulders of citizens with

Lockean preferences. Perhaps one could argue that concerns for personal liberty rule out any encroachment on primitive resource rights intended to recoup these compensation payments. But the case for an UBI based on primitive resource rights will remain incomplete, and uncertain in its full implications, until this issue is resolved.

7.4   *A Consequentialist Argument for Basic Income*

Let us now turn to a somewhat different strategy for defending UBI. The general form of the strategy is consequentialist. It involves identifying desirable consequences that the introduction of an UBI can be expected to have, and arguing that these justify its introduction, notwithstanding other, undesirable effects an UBI might have. A wide range of consequentialist arguments for UBI can be found in recent literature, appealing to goods such as efficiency,[27] community,[28] and democracy.[29] I shall not explore all these arguments here, but will instead focus on a variant of the consequentialist strategy which incorporates some of the insights contained in these arguments, but which appeals explicitly to the conception of justice as fair reciprocity. The argument proceeds from the claim that the introduction of an UBI can be expected to have a range of effects that are highly desirable from the standpoint of fair reciprocity. Some of the more important possible effects are the following:

1. *Employment opportunity.* Fair reciprocity requires that citizens have adequate opportunity to work so as to satisfy their contributive obligation in a psychologically fulfilling manner. It is sometimes suggested that UBI will affect the level and/or flexibility of wage rates in a way that conduces to higher and more stable levels of employment. If this is so, then an UBI will help create the circumstances in which citizens do have the opportunity to work and meet their contributive obligation in a psychologically fulfilling manner.

One version of this argument focuses on the complementarity between UBI and revenue-sharing within productive enterprises. Under revenue-sharing arrangements, workers are paid at least part of their pay as a share in the firm's profits or net revenues rather than as a fixed wage. Some economists argue that this mode of labour remuneration, if adopted by enough firms, will make for a higher and more stable level of employment than will arise under an otherwise equivalent fixed wage economy.[30] From the worker's point of view, however, the diminished risk of unemployment comes at the price of greater variability of income while in employment. It is sometimes argued, therefore, that in order to offset the increased variability in employment income, citizens in an economy with revenue-sharing firms must receive a sizeable slice of income that is independent of their employment status. And this is just what an UBI does.[31] An UBI, in other words, may be the precondition of an institution, revenue-sharing, that itself may be essential for a high and stable level of employment, which is, in turn, a precondition for citizens being able to meet their contributive obligation in a psychologically fulfilling manner.

2. *A guaranteed social wage*. Fair reciprocity requires that all those making a productive contribution in satisfaction of the basic work expectation receive a high minimum of the social product in return. But how can we ensure that those whose productive contribution to the community largely takes the form of care work receive some remuneration in return for this contribution? And how can we supplement the pay of low-wage workers, who have satisfied their basic work expectation, so as to bring their final incomes up to a decent level? One answer is: UBI. Payment of an UBI, set at an appropriate level, will help to ensure that those who make productive contributions that are not adequately acknowledged with monetary reward in the marketplace are nevertheless at least moderately well remunerated.

3. *Reduced domestic exploitation and abuse*. Where one party within a household bears a disproportionate share of the household's total labour, relative to the cash or in-kind income she consumes, then one might argue that there is exploitation at the domestic, household level. From the standpoint of justice as fair reciprocity, this possibility raises an awkward problem. It seems undesirable, firstly, that the state should formally require households to respect an anti-exploitation norm in their internal arrangements if only because of the huge invasion of privacy that would be necessary to secure compliance with, and punish transgression of, the norm. Some might argue that it is even undesirable for the state to encourage households to respect such a norm, to propagandize for it, because this would pit the state against conceptions of family life that some citizens hold on religious or similar convictions.[32] However, it is appropriate for a state committed to freedom of association to ensure that individuals are not pressured into domestic relations that are exploitative because of financial dependency.[33] Such dependency is additionally worrying because it may lead to physical and psychological abuse. By reducing the costs of leaving the household, an UBI could serve to empower otherwise

vulnerable partners, enabling them to press for non-exploitative and non-abusive domestic relations.

4. *Opportunity for self-realization in work*. Fair reciprocity requires that citizens have not merely opportunity to work, but opportunity for self-realization in work, i.e. to treat work, over the course of a normal working life (if not at every moment of one's working life), as a site of intrinsically valuable challenge. Contemporary capitalist societies, such as Britain and the United States, almost certainly fall short of providing this opportunity for all workers, especially for unskilled workers. UBI offers one way to attack this problem. By disconnecting income from employment, UBI obviously enhances the citizen's ability to refuse unchallenging jobs. In consequence, as Philippe Van Parijs and Robert van der Veen have argued,[34] it puts employers under pressure to improve job quality. As wages for unpleasant (typically low-skilled) jobs are bid up in the effort to attract people to them, technological development should become geared towards the creation of labour processes and workplaces that offer greater intrinsic job satisfaction. An UBI can thus help ensure that the burdens of productive contribution do not fall with inequitable heaviness on the shoulders of some (typically low-skilled) citizens.

5. *Residual safeguard against significant brute luck disadvantage and market vulnerability*. Fair reciprocity requires that we enforce citizens' contributive obligations in a manner that does not expose individuals to significant brute luck disadvantage or to the risks of dependent exchange. As we saw in Chapter 6, however, it is difficult to calibrate work-tests in a conventional welfare system so as to ensure this. There is, of course, the innocent-third-parties problem: if we discipline adult non-workers by cutting their income, this is likely to harm any third parties who are dependants of these adults. Work-tests can also have the unintended effect of consolidating market vulnerability, or of disadvantaging someone who is, contrary to appearances, unemployed through no fault of his own. There are a number of ways we can grapple with these problems, some of which I discussed in Chapter 6. But UBI can make a contribution here. Even a modest UBI would provide a critically important residual safeguard against vulnerability and brute luck disadvantage that might unintentionally creep through the net of an income support system that ties every penny of support to work or willingness to work.

Acknowledging these various possible effects of an UBI, one might now advance the following argument in defence of UBI: 'While UBI has one effect that is a bad from the standpoint of fair reciprocity—the free-riding it permits—it nevertheless has other effects that are good from the standpoint of fair reciprocity; thus, on balance, a contemporary capitalist society might get closer to satisfying the overall demands of fair reciprocity with a substantial UBI than without one.' We try to defuse the standard exploitation objection to UBI by showing how it points only to the debit side of the moral ledger, ignoring the sizeable credits which must be entered on the other side of the ledger's page. This is a forceful argument, and one that seems particularly effective as a reply to the standard exploitation objection to UBI. The proponent of this argument need not deny that an UBI will allow for some degree of objectionable free-riding by lifestyle non-workers on the efforts of more productive citizens. But, while accepting that this is a *valid* objection to UBI, she can question whether it is a *decisive* objection, given the other effects an UBI can be expected to have. Having said that, however, I do not think this consequentialist argument represents a decisive rejoinder to the standard exploitation objection to UBI.

The first reason for this is that the alleged effects of UBI in the areas discussed above are in fact uncertain. There are grounds for thinking that the impact of UBI in some of these areas could be a negative, rather than a positive, one. For example, while we can tell one plausible story about how UBI will expand employment opportunity, we can tell another about how it will increase equilibrium unemployment (and so make it harder for some citizens to meet their contributive obligation in a psychologically fulfilling manner). An UBI could cause some workers to look less hard for jobs, and the consequent fall in the intensity with which people look for work may mean that a higher rate of involuntary unemployment is necessary to contain inflationary pressures. Some argue that the introduction of a sizeable UBI would not only lead many people to participate much less actively in the labour force but would also encourage them to invest less in human capital.[35] The results of this may be to exacerbate financial dependencies in the household context, particularly if, owing to the continuing gendered division of household labour, the negative impact on participation and human capital is stronger for women. Low participation and limited human capital investment may also create the very 'poor-quality job trap' that UBI is supposed to spring. It is not just that each individual who chooses not to work much or to train may be diminishing their own long-term options for good-quality jobs. The aggregate effect of many people doing this might well be to drag job quality down in general as employers, constrained by a dearth of skilled and committed labour, adopt product market strategies based on keeping costs and prices low rather than on improving product quality.

A second problem with the foregoing consequentialist defence of UBI is that other policies might produce the same effects, but do so in a way that is less vulnerable to the exploitation objection. One can hardly appeal to the positive effects of an UBI to defuse this objection if there are other, perfectly feasible ways of achieving these effects that are not subject to this objection (or, one should add, to some other, equally weighty objection). Particularly interesting here, I think, are some proposals which have much in common with UBI, but which modify the original proposal in ways that address directly the concern for reciprocity that motivates the exploitation objection. These variants of UBI will be the focus of the next section.

7.5   *Variants of Basic Income*

I shall consider three variants of UBI here: republican basic income; targeted basic income; and time-limited basic income.

7.5.1   *Republican Basic Income*

One idea is to link UBI to some form of public-service requirement. One version of this idea that has acquired some salience in recent policy debates is the participation income outlined by Anthony Atkinson.[36] A participation income is identical to a pure UBI except that eligibility for the income grant is conditional, in the case of all working-age, productively capable adults, on satisfying a broadly defined participation requirement. Atkinson defines participation to include paid employment or self-employment; certain forms of care work; participation in education and training; job search; and various approved forms of voluntary work. A participation income could empower disadvantaged and vulnerable workers in the same way as a pure UBI, but, because of the participation requirement that limits eligibility, also addresses the concern that citizens do something to reciprocate their claim on the social product.

A second version of the idea is what one might term a service dividend. There has been some interest in recent years, in Britain and in the United States, in the establishment of so-called citizens' service schemes. On leaving school, individuals would be eligible to participate in a national community service programme. Work assignments might include environmental task forces, help with urban renovation, school assistance and refurbishment, and help with delivery of health care or personal social services. Aside from the concrete goods that participants would produce, Mickey Kaus argues that the shared experience of participating in a nationwide citizens' service scheme would help break down class and racial barriers and so contribute to the creation of a more egalitarian public culture.[37] Interestingly, Philippe Van Parijs also floats the idea of such a scheme as a possible way of cultivating the spirit of 'solidaristic patriotism' without which, he thinks, it will be impossible to build and maintain political support for a generous UBI scheme.[38]

Citizens' service might be introduced as a complement to UBI. One possibility, suggested by Ronald Dore, is to run a compulsory system of citizens' service alongside an UBI.[39] An unconditional income right in one domain would be matched by an enforceable (though time-limited) obligation to perform productive service for the community in another.[40] Another possibility is to make participation in citizens' service strictly voluntary, but to condition eligibility for UBI on participation in such a scheme. Those who do not participate will get no UBI or a reduced level of UBI.[41] A particularly radical version of this proposal was advanced by the eco-socialist André Gorz in the 1980s. Gorz proposed guaranteeing each citizen a minimum income for life in return for an agreement to perform 20,000 hours of socially necessary public labour.[42] Similar ideas were set out in the 1930s by philosophers of the Personalist movement, Alexandre Marc and Arnaud Dandieu.[43] Finally, UBI might be left in its original form, but complemented by a concerted programme of civic education, from primary schools on up, to emphasize the importance of productive service to the community, with some of the funds that would otherwise be used for UBI being used instead to finance this educational programme.

7.5.2 *Targeted Basic Income*

Another variant, or family of variants, on UBI is what we may call targeted basic income. The idea behind targeted basic income is not to qualify the unconditionality of UBI in relation to work, but, as Andrew Williams has suggested,[44] to qualify its universality. An UBI is not paid to all citizens, or to all citizens at the same rate. Instead, it is targeted at those who are most disadvantaged in some way, e.g. in their opportunities in the labour market.[45]

There are at least two reasons why a targeted basic income should be of interest to policy-makers concerned to achieve justice as fair reciprocity. Firstly, where fair reciprocity is satisfied in its non-ideal form, the institutions governing economic life do not correct fully for talent-based inequality in income and wealth. One form of non-ideal fair reciprocity, which I referred to in Section 5.4 as semi-ideal fair reciprocity, tries to compensate for this by setting the less talented a lower basic work expectation: they are expected to work fewer hours than more talented workers in return for a high minimum share of the social product. One way of expressing the lower work expectation in policy terms would be to give all citizens with earnings potential below some specified level a modest UBI.

A second important consideration is that, in its non-ideal form, fair reciprocity requires that all citizens (with significant contributive obligations) have opportunity for self-realization in work, i.e. to relate to their work, over the course of a working life, though not necessarily at every moment of this working life, as a site of intrinsically valuable challenge. However, as I noted above, some citizens in contemporary capitalist societies may have job options which offer little realistic prospect for any degree of self-realization. To the extent that this situation is beyond their control (i.e. not something that can be redressed through education or training), these citizens should be regarded as having a lower work expectation than citizens who can find self-realization in work. And, again, one way we might express this idea in policy terms is by giving this group of disadvantaged workers in particular an UBI that enables them to work less for a given minimum share of the social product than others. These two considerations pick out two different groups for targeted basic income: those with low earnings potential and those with little or no realistic prospect of self-realization in their working life. In practice, however, there may well be a fair bit of overlap between the two groups.

In principle, then, there is much to be said for the targeted basic income proposal. However, there is the obvious difficulty of identifying who ought to receive the targeted basic income. I have already stressed, in Section 4.1, the difficulty of formally differentiating people according to their earnings potential. The challenge of identifying specifically those workers with poor prospects for self-realization in work is probably no less considerable. I am not sure that this problem amounts to a decisive objection to targeted basic income. But it certainly is a problem that the designers of a targeted basic income programme will have to grapple with, which they will almost certainly fail to solve fully, and which, in consequence, is likely to exert an ongoing, downward pull on the perceived legitimacy of such a programme.

One approach to the problem is to base eligibility for a targeted basic income on some personal characteristic that is an acceptably close proxy for labour market disadvantage. Adopting this approach, a tentative link might be made with an idea recently explored by

Bruce Ackerman and Anne Alstott, the idea of a childhood privilege tax.[46] Ackerman and Alstott argue that individuals enter adult life on unequal terms in part because of unequal degrees of 'childhood privilege': inequality in how nurturing family environments are due to unequal resources and unequal parental capacities. As a partial corrective for this, they propose to phase in, over a number of years, a tax which varies according to an individual's estimated degree of childhood privilege. Their suggested measure of childhood privilege is the level and consistency of parental income in one's childhood years. A variant on the proposal would be to pay special subsidies or tax credits specifically to children who come from underprivileged family backgrounds. From the standpoint of fair reciprocity, the proposal has clear merits. A policy of this kind can be defended in terms of one of the main requirements of fair reciprocity in its non-ideal form: the requirement that the institutions governing economic life reduce class inequality and division to a reasonable minimum. But, in addition, to the extent that childhood underprivilege and lifetime labour market disadvantage do correlate (and there is evidence, cited by Ackerman and Alstott, to show that they do), a tax credit scheme targeted at the underprivileged would perhaps be a tolerable approximation of a targeted basic income aimed at those with poor earnings potential and/or poor prospects for self-realization in work.[47]

7.5.3   *Time-Limited Basic Income*

One idea that came to dominate debates over welfare reform in the United States in the 1990s, and which was eventually enacted in the 1996 Personal Responsibility and Work Opportunity Reconciliation Act, is that of time-limited welfare. Individuals should only be able to claim welfare, it was argued, up to some fixed period of years over the entire course of their working lives and only for limited durations over shorter periods.[48] Judged by the standards of fair reciprocity, such a policy has little to recommend it. A citizen could conceivably make a good-faith effort to find work and yet still find herself unemployed at the end of the specified time period. Cutting her off welfare at this point, with no further support, violates in a very marked way the commitment to protect citizens from significant brute luck disadvantage.

However, imagine that we have a system of income support in place which is not time-limited, but which is work-tested along the lines set out in Chapter 6. A proposal is now made to introduce a non-work-tested income grant as a complement to this system of work-tested income support. This income grant is, however, to be time-limited. Citizens will not be able to claim it indefinitely, but will only be able to claim it for a maximum number of years over the course of their whole working lives (e.g. up to a maximum of three years in total). There might also be limitations on how long the grant can be used within shorter time periods (e.g. not for more than six months within any given year). Subject to these time limitations, however, citizens would be free to claim this grant whenever they want. We would then in effect have a two-tier system of income support: a first tier of conventional income support for the unemployed that is work-tested but not time-limited; and a second tier of universal basic income that is not work-tested, but which is time-limited. Is there much to be said for this proposal?

I think so. A time-limited basic income of this kind would provide a substantial residual safeguard against the brute luck disadvantage and market vulnerability that, as we noted above, could conceivably slip through the cracks of a single-tier work-tested system of income support. If people get into difficulty, and the first tier of the income support system somehow fails to pick this up, then they can activate this second tier of protection as an emergency measure, giving them-selves time to sort their position out.[49] At the same time, because this basic income is time-limited it does not allow citizens who wish to maintain a decent standard of living to withdraw from productive par-ticipation in their community over the long term. The obligations of reciprocity should be satisfied, more or less, over the course of the individual's entire working life. Thus, from the standpoint of fair reci-procity, time-limited basic income looks like an especially good bet. We would seem to get an important additional safeguard against brute luck disadvantage and market vulnerability without allowing lifestyle non-workers much of a free ride on the labour of their fellow citizens. In policy terms, it would be very easy to integrate a time-limited basic income into a universal capital-grant scheme of the kind I will discuss in the next chapter.

7.6   *Conclusion: The Merits of Two-Tiered Income Support*

Contemporary debate over welfare reform is excessively polarized between (communitarian) advocates of welfare contractualism and (real libertarian) supporters of UBI. In this and the previous chapter I have shown that, judged against the standards of fair reciprocity in its non-ideal form, there is good reason to be wary of both types of policy taken on their own. Rather than setting welfare contractualism and UBI in opposition to each other, a policy-maker guided by the distributive aims of fair reciprocity, and by legitimate paternalistic considerations, should think about how constructively to combine them. Such combinations seem to offer the most promising way of addressing the range of fair reciprocity's commitments, including the commitments to protect citizens from significant brute luck disadvantage, to market security, and, of course, to reciprocity. Interestingly, some social-policy specialists have in the last few years begun to outline proposals for the reform of income support that draw on elements of both contractualist and UBI models. Anthony Atkinson, for instance, proposes combining a range of benefits targeted at specific contingencies like unemployment, underemployment, sickness, disability, and so on ('modernized social insurance'), some of which may be work-tested, with a modest participation income set somewhat below the poverty line.[50] In the language of this volume, the basic vision is one of work-tested income support underpinned by a form of republican basic income. In the United States a similar policy vision can be found in some recent work by Robert Haveman. He has proposed combining (i) a modest 'credit income tax', basic income, or participation income with (ii) a scheme of employment subsidies targeted at the low-paid, and (iii) a system of work-tested benefits, supplementary to the credit income tax, for the unemployed.[51] As noted above, one can also imagine a system that combines a work-tested first tier of income support with a time-limited basic income as a second tier. I will take up and develop this proposal in the next chapter, which looks at the idea of universal basic capital.

CHAPTER 8

Basic Capital

When a young couple begin the world, the difference is exceedingly great whether they begin with nothing or with fifteen pounds apiece. With this aid they could buy a cow, and implements to cultivate a few acres of land; and instead of becoming burdens upon society . . . would be put in the way of becoming useful and profitable citizens.

(Thomas Paine, *Agrarian Justice*)

Justice as fair reciprocity emphasizes the obligation of the citizen to make a productive contribution to the community in return for sharing in the social product. But for significant reciprocity-based obligations to be held by all, the institutions governing economic life must be sufficiently just in other respects. This is one of the main reasons why, as explained in Chapter 6, fair reciprocity does not offer unequivocal support for welfare contractualism, or, more specifically, for work enforcement in the welfare system. Work enforcement is justifiable, as a general practice applied equally to all, only against a background of institutions and policies that protect citizens against objectionable kinds of brute luck disadvantage and against market vulnerability and the related risks of exploitation and abuse. In Chapter 6 I identified some of the requirements for fair contractualism, and in Chapter 7 I discussed some policies which might help to meet these requirements. In this chapter I aim to develop a fuller account of these policies, paying particularly close attention to the idea of basic capital: the idea that the state endow each citizen on maturity with a generous capital grant. I shall seek to elaborate and defend a right to basic capital as the centrepiece of a new, reformed model of inheritance ('social inheritance').

I begin the discussion in Section 8.1 with the question 'What's wrong with inheritance?' In its conventional form the institution of inheritance violates some of the core demands of fair reciprocity. It is a source of significant brute luck inequality, apparently enables citizens to share in the social product in violation of reciprocity, and, not least, may contribute to the creation of a class-based culture that is at odds with the ethos of democratic mutual regard. On the other hand, as I explain in Section 8.2, there are powerful objections to the abolition of inheritance. It is argued, for example, that such a policy would place an intolerable burden on the liberty of the citizen, and that it will severely impair economic efficiency. However, while these objections do suggest that the outright abolition of inheritance or full confiscatory taxation of wealth transfers is undesirable, I argue that they by no means defeat the case for high taxation of wealth transfers. Moreover, the perceived legitimacy of such taxation can arguably be enhanced, and thus potential problems of implementation diminished, if such a tax is explicitly linked or hypothecated, as I argue it should be, to the institution of a right to basic capital.

In Section 8.3 I turn to the right to basic capital. The essential idea is that every citizen should receive on maturity a generous capital grant or drawing account that she would then be able to use to facilitate productive participation in the community. There has been a notable growth of interest in basic capital and related proposals in recent years, whether as 'stakeholder' grants or 'baby bonds' in the United States and Britain, or as 'social drawing rights' in continental Europe. While avoiding detailed policy prescriptions, I review some of these proposals and offer my own account of how the idea of a right to basic capital might be developed. A key issue in the design of a capital-grant scheme concerns what kind of restrictions, if any, ought to apply to the use of such a capital grant. Should use of the funds be restricted to allegedly responsible uses, such as education and training, or the establishment of a new business? Or should individuals be free to use the funds in whatever way they like? I argue that there are strong reasons, on grounds of reciprocity and paternalism, for placing some such restrictions on use of the grants. However, building on the argument of Chapter 7, I argue that it would also be desirable to incorporate a time-limited basic income into the basic capital grant, i.e. to allow citizens the freedom to use a portion of such a grant to supplement income at their discretion. In Section 8.4 I explain how the institution of a right to basic capital, in something like this form, is supported by a wide range of considerations internal to justice as fair reciprocity (in its non-ideal form). Instituting such a right can be expected to do a lot to help society meet the requirements for a fair work-test.

How would such a right be financed? One obvious and appropriate source of funds is, as intimated, a tax on wealth transfers. However, there can be no guarantee that such a tax will raise sufficient revenue to finance an adequate system of capital grants. In Section 8.5 I therefore offer some thoughts on other possible sources of revenue. One possibility I think worth consideration is the establishment of a community fund, based on collective asset ownership, as a way of supplementing tax revenues for purposes of financing the right to basic capital. Section 8.6 concludes.

8.1   What's Wrong with Inheritance?

As I noted at the beginning of Chapter 1, contemporary capitalist societies such as Britain and the United States exhibit very substantial inequalities of wealth. In the United States close to 50 per cent of the nation's financial wealth is owned by the richest 1 per cent of the population. The asset-poorest 40 per cent of the population own less than 1 per cent of the nation's financial wealth.[1] Moreover, wealth inequality has increased rapidly in the United States in recent years. In the 1980s (1983–9) real mean wealth grew at 3.4 per cent annually, but this increase in wealth was almost exclusively concentrated in the richest 20 per cent of households.[2] Britain exhibits a similar, though less extreme pattern. In Britain the wealthiest 5 per cent of the population in 1992 owned 37 per cent of all personal wealth; the wealthiest 10 per cent, some 49 per cent of all personal wealth.[3] As in the United States, wealth inequality is considerably greater than income inequality, the income-richest 10 per cent of the population claiming only 26 per cent of total income as compared with the aforementioned 49 per cent of total marketable wealth claimed by the asset-richest 10 per cent of the population.[4] The level of wealth inequality has been quite stable in Britain in recent years rising a little in the second half of the 1990s, having previously been on a steady downward course from the 1920s to the mid-1970s.[5]

The causes of wealth inequality continue to be a source of debate among economists. But few specialists would deny that one major source of the inequality we see is the conventional institution of inheritance. In a 1978 study John Brittain estimated that around 67 per cent of the fortunes of the very rich in the United States could be attributed to inheritance rather than to original accumulation. This result is qualitatively similar to the results of studies of the British case.[6] Lisa Keister, while stressing how uncertain we are about the quantitative importance of inheritance in generating wealth inequality, cites more recent studies which suggest a significant role for inheritance in generating wealth inequality in the United States: 'as little as 20 and as much as 80 per cent of wealth could be inherited'.[7] Racial inequalities in wealth in the United States 'may result to a large extent from racial differences in inheritance'.[8] Inheritance is able to play such a role in determining the distribution of wealth because of the low rate of effective taxation of wealth transfers in most capitalist countries. The tax systems of some countries do exhibit high nominal rates of taxation, but actual levels of taxation nevertheless remain very low, in large part because of exemptions and loopholes in the relevant tax laws.[9]

From the standpoint of justice as fair reciprocity, this situation appears to be straightforwardly unjust. Inequality in wealth directly attributable to unequal inheritance is to a very considerable extent simply a reflection of differential brute luck. Moreover, this initial brute luck inequality in resources may produce or exacerbate other brute luck inequalities. For example, initial inequality in endowments of external wealth will swiftly translate into unequal access to credit markets and, in turn, to education and training, thereby exacerbating the initial brute luck inequality in wealth, and, perhaps, widening brute luck inequality in marketable talent. Recent research has underscored how asset poverty makes the lives of the asset-poor more insecure with profound effects across a range of areas including employment, health, and personal relationships.[10] In its non-ideal form, fair reciprocity does not require that we eliminate all significant brute luck disadvantage. But it does require, among other things, that we reduce class inequality, as embodied in inequality of educational opportunity and initial wealth endowments, to a reasonable minimum. The conventional institution of inheritance is clearly one major source of class inequality, in this sense.

Secondly, the conventional institution of inheritance apparently facilitates violation of reciprocity. If someone receives a substantial inheritance, then she is to this extent more able to share generously in the social product without making a productive contribution in return. If inheritances are unequal, then, as I explained in Section 6.2, this may result in a failure to apply the demands of reciprocity to all citizens equally, casting doubt on the fairness of work-tests in the welfare system. As Leonard Hobhouse wryly remarked, 'it seems sometimes to be regarded as quite a providential arrangement that some should be born without the necessity of working for their own living so that they have leisure to impose this fundamental duty on others'.[11]

Thirdly, we must consider the possible impact of conventional inheritance on citizens' attitudes towards one another. I have taken as a starting point for purposes of this book the idea that the good society is one animated by an ethos of democratic mutual regard: in determining the institutions that are to regulate their lives together in a fundamental way, citizens ought to regard one another as equals, and manifest this regard in the design of their common institutions. Precisely because it produces class inequality, the conventional institution of inheritance could undermine the sentiments involved in this kind of mutual regard. Conventional inheritance could encourage the view that some people are superior, and others inferior, by birth, simply because it allows so much to be determined by accident of birth. These cultural effects of inheritance were probably at the forefront of R. H. Tawney's mind when, echoing Hobhouse's remark on inheritance, he wrote tellingly that

One of the regrettable…effects of extreme inequality is its tendency to weaken the capacity for impartial judgement. It pads the lives of its beneficiaries with a soft down of consideration…and secures that, if they fall, they fall on cushions. It disposes them, on the one hand, to take for granted themselves and their own advantages, as though there were nothing in the latter which could possibly need explanation, and, on the other hand, to be critical of claims to similar advantages advanced by their neighbours who do not yet possess them. It causes them, in short, to apply different standards to different sections of the community, as if it were uncertain whether all of them are human in the same sense as themselves.[12]

This cultural dynamic is something that a society aspiring to fair reciprocity must make strenuous efforts to avoid.

8.2   *Should we Abolish Inheritance?*

Given the injustice of conventional inheritance, what are we to do? One thing we might do is simply to abolish inheritance in its conventional form. To be more precise, we could tax all wealth transfers (inheritances, bequests, and *inter vivos* gifts) at the rate of 100 per cent and then distribute the relevant resources back to citizens, in cash or kind, in some appropriately opportunity-spreading and reciprocity-friendly way.[13] In the course of this chapter I shall argue that a policy not too far removed from this is indeed appropriate. Before we draw any policy conclusions, however, we must first examine some familiar and powerful objections to wealth transfer taxation. Critics variously object that such taxation is: (i) an objectionable infringement of the citizen's liberty; (ii) likely to impair economic performance; and/or

(iii) subject to deficits of popular legitimacy and, therefore, problems of avoidance in design and implementation. These are serious objections. I shall argue that they do not justify a retreat from a policy of heavy taxation of wealth transfers, but that they do have implications for exactly how we structure a system of wealth transfer taxation. Philosophically speaking, the most radical of these objections is the first, liberty-based objection, and it is with this objection that I shall therefore begin.

It is obviously true that the taxation of wealth transfers limits the freedom of individuals to transfer wealth to each other. That is the point. But all kinds of policies and institutions restrict individual freedom. Merely pointing to the coercive feature of a policy or institution is not, as it stands, necessarily to point out anything very interesting. What has to be shown is that the restriction of individual freedom in question is in some way objectionable. A restriction of freedom can plausibly be seen as objectionable in at least two cases: firstly, if the restriction is simply arbitrary, i.e. serves no clear justice-related objective or other legitimate public objective (such as compelling paternalist objectives); secondly, if the restriction, while non-arbitrary, burdens a morally significant interest, and this burden can plausibly be said to outweigh the good achieved through the restriction. Interests like the integrity interests discussed in Chapter 2 will be particularly important in evaluating whether a given restriction on individual liberty is objectionable in this second sense. Now, taxation of wealth transfers is clearly not objectionable in the first sense: the proposed policy does serve an important justice-related objective. This leaves us with the question of whether the proposed policy is objectionable in the second sense. Does the freedom to transfer wealth serve some interests that are so important, morally speaking, as to make it inappropriate to restrict the freedom even though such restriction would serve a justice-related objective?

There are, I think, two interests connected with the transfer of wealth that are sufficiently important as to justify some freedom to make wealth transfers. The first interest relates to what we can term *expressive* transfers. As ethical agents, individuals typically develop strong attachments and commitments to particular associations and causes, and, as an expression of their commitment to these associations and causes, they may wish to donate wealth to them. Given how important such transfers can be to the expression of an individual's religious and political beliefs, the liberty to make such transfers must be to some extent protected.[14] Secondly, the giving of valuable items, including money wealth, obviously represents an important means by which individuals express love and affection for one another. Such transfers are also often very important in creating and maintaining a sense of intergenerational continuity within a family, a continuity that is itself important to personal identity. Many cases of intergenerational wealth transfer may have both qualities. For example, a grandmother may transfer her wedding ring to her granddaughter, and, by means of this act, both express love for her granddaughter and help sustain a sense of intergenerational continuity within her family. As long as friendship and family remain central to human life, such activity is likely to remain profoundly important to many people; it will be at the heart of what they regard as a life lived in authentic accordance with their deepest values. It seems necessary, then, to regard the freedom to practise some degree of such *affective* transfer as a freedom that should not be restricted. Some freedom of expressive and affective giving is justifiably seen as included in the basic liberties and securities that fair reciprocity is committed to uphold.

However, citizens' interests in expressive and affective giving can surely be respected without retreating too far from the policy of full taxation of wealth transfers. We can accommodate these interests by means of specific, targeted tax exemptions. To secure the citizen's interest in expressive giving, there should undoubtedly be an exemption for transfers of a strictly charitable nature. To protect liberty of affective giving, there should also probably be a large, probably blanket, exemption for transfers between spouses, reflecting the familiar idea that married individuals 'live as one'. But what about intergenerational transfers like the transfer between grandparent and grandchild that I pictured above? The most obvious way to accommodate the interest in affective giving (and receiving) at stake here is to allow all individuals a modest lifetime accessions quota. Each citizen is allowed to receive gifts of wealth from others up to some total, lifetime ceiling without being subject to tax on any wealth she receives. But once this ceiling is reached, further transfers will be subject to tax.[15] How far this would compromise the stringent position on wealth transfers suggested above obviously depends on how high the ceiling is set. A low ceiling will not add up to much of a compromise; and my guess is that the citizen's interest in affective giving can be adequately protected with quite a low ceiling. While people should be at liberty to express their parental love and maintain intergenerational continuity by leaving their children certain items of deep personal significance, such love can ordinarily be expressed, and continuity maintained, within the confines of a modest lifetime accessions ceiling, without leaving them stately homes or large portfolios of shares.[16] If this policy is felt to give insufficient weight to this interest, however, the state could also provide generous credit arrangements to enable individuals to pay the taxes that fall on transfers in excess of the ceiling. People would in effect be able to pay the state, in instalments, for the extra wealth they receive.[17]

Let us now turn to the argument that wealth transfer taxation will depress economic performance. A familiar argument is that if wealth transfers are taxed heavily individuals will be less motivated to work hard and be enterprising since, so it is claimed, a primary motivation for hard work and enterprise is to build up a fortune that one can transfer to others. A second, related argument is that such taxation will lead to a net reduction in saving and investment by undermining an important motive for saving, the bequest motive. These concerns are important and should be taken into account in considering the level at which to set taxes on wealth transfers. In particular, we ought not to want to set tax rates at levels that are counter-productive in terms of increasing the resources available to the most asset-disadvantaged. The critical question is how high rates of taxation on wealth transfers can be pushed before they become counter-productive in this way; and this in turn depends on how significant the alleged disincentive effects of wealth transfer taxation really are.

There are a number of standard but nonetheless important points which caution against an exaggerated view of these effects.[18] As far as work incentives are concerned, it is rightly pointed out that there are many motivations for hard work, of which leaving one's children (or others) a fortune is only one, and probably not the most important motivation for most people. It is also plausibly pointed out that the heavy taxation of wealth transfers could actually serve to improve the work motivation of some people—namely, those who might otherwise have lived idly on inherited wealth. Turning to asset accumulation, bequest considerations are not the only or even the primary motivation for saving, even among retired and elderly households. We do see a low rate of dissaving among retired households. However, in Britain at least, there is some evidence that retirees without children have very similar saving behaviour to those with children, which implies that late-life saving is not entirely, or even primarily, motivated by bequest considerations.[19] Moreover, even if the savings ratio does fall in response to the taxation of wealth transfers, there are other policy levers which governments can pull to compensate for this.[20] One possibility would be for the state to hypothecate some fraction of tax revenues to public investment funds, a practice the Swedish government has relied upon for many years to help underwrite the long-term commitments of the Swedish state pension system. (I shall discuss public investment funds a little more in Section 8.5.)

Two further points should be made. Firstly, we should recall the point that the incentive effects of wealth transfer taxation will depend to some degree on the social norms that inform individuals' economic decisions. These norms ought not to be taken as a given, but ought to be taken as part of the institutional framework to which the demands of justice as fair reciprocity apply. Of course, in the short run a government acting to realize justice as fair reciprocity does have to take existing norms as given, and it is in this context that the responses reviewed in the foregoing paragraph are especially pertinent. But over the long run a government committed to justice as fair reciprocity should seek to shift social norms so that they permit more substantial reduction of brute luck inequality in inherited wealth (consistent with respect for the qualified freedoms of expressive and affective giving acknowledged above). Citizens who have really internalized the commitment to equality of opportunity should not begrudge the taxation necessary to prevent inequality in inherited wealth, and should not allow this to impact significantly on their investment decisions. They should, in other words, see the very long-term benefit of their investment as something that properly belongs to a future generation as a whole, and not just to their own children or favoured individuals. They should take pride and pleasure in being general benefactors of this generation, rather than in transferring wealth to their own children, which they should see as potentially giving their own children an unfair advantage over some of their children's peers.

Secondly, in considering the net impact of wealth transfer taxation on economic performance, particularly in a world where social norms remain highly imperfect, we should take into account the possible effects of how the funds so raised are spent. For these funds may be used to finance projects that have a positive effect on economic performance. One possibility, which I shall discuss at length in the next section, is to use the funds from wealth transfer taxation to finance a system of basic capital grants. Each citizen would receive a capital grant on maturity. Uses of the grant might be restricted, at least in part, to projects that are broadly related to productive participation in the economy, such as courses of higher education, vocational training, or the establishment of a new business. As I shall explain below, institution of such a right can be expected to have a number of desirable economic effects.[21] Alternatively, funds from wealth transfer taxation might be used for investments in infrastructure, subsidies for research and development of new products, and so on, with potentially positive effects on economic performance. Of course, such effects may not out-weigh the negative effects of wealth transfer taxation; and, even if they do, an even bigger positive net effect on economic performance might be achieved by funding such initiatives from a different tax base. But failure to take these effects into account can all too easily lead to an overly pessimistic view of the net impact of wealth transfer taxes on economic performance.

A third objection to wealth transfer taxation focuses on the alleged deficit of the policy in terms of popular legitimacy and the related problem of tax avoidance. Where people regard a tax as essentially legit-imate, they will feel a greater obligation to comply with the relevant tax rule. They will be less likely to push politically for new exemptions so that they can engage in avoidance legally, or be tempted to avoid the tax in other ways. If at present wealth transfer taxation is not widely seen as legitimate—and recent research in Britain shows that it is cer-tainly not popular[22]—this may be because citizens see such taxation as merely a levelling-down policy instrument and, rightly or wrongly, people in advanced capitalist societies tend to dislike egalitarianism of a purely levelling-down variety. Assuming this speculation is correct, the obvious response is to make very explicit the connection between wealth transfer taxation and other, levelling-*up* measures. How are we to do this? Here, again, the basic capital proposal is relevant. Wealth transfer taxation can be explicitly linked to the establishment of a basic capital scheme of the sort I shall discuss in the next section. This would make clear that the point of such taxation is not simply to deny a group of citizens opportunities they would otherwise have enjoyed, but to ensure a high initial level of opportunity for all.[23] Citizens would be more likely to associate the tax with a concrete benefit that they have enjoyed and/or that their children will enjoy. This would presumably enhance the perceived legitimacy of the tax, and, as a result of this, problems of avoidance might become more manageable.

I have now considered three objections to wealth transfer taxation based on considerations of liberty, economic performance, and pop-ular legitimacy and avoidance. None of these objections, I have argued, provides strong grounds for eschewing a high level of wealth transfer taxation. These objections do have some implications, however, for how we structure such taxation and, in closing this section, I should like to draw these implications out more fully.

In designing a scheme of the wealth transfer taxation, the first choice is whether to tax donors or recipients of wealth. Respond-ing to the liberty objection above, I suggested that the state adopt a recipient-based tax system in which each individual has a lifetime accessions quota (with additional exemptions for transfers to charities and between spouses). The simplest system would then impose a flat tax of 100 per cent on all transfers of wealth to individuals above the basic lifetime quota. Less radically, we could impose a progressive tax structure on transfers in excess of the lifetime quota.[24] For example, to pluck some purely illustrative figures out of the air, we could tax transfers up to double the lifetime quota at a rate of 50 per cent, transfers up to triple the quota at 70 per cent, and so on, perhaps eventually hitting a marginal tax rate on further wealth transfers of 100 per cent. The revenues yielded by such a tax can be used, of course, to help limit inequality in individuals' initial holdings of wealth, and in the next section I shall consider one way in which this might be done. In closing, however, I should acknowledge a point frequently made by supporters of this 'accessions tax'. Under such a tax an asset-rich person has a strong incentive to transfer her wealth to a large number of individuals, and particularly to those who have not yet received any wealth from others, in order to minimize the overall amount of tax paid on the wealth she transfers. This will help to promote a more equal distribution of wealth even before we take into account the potentially redistributive effects of the uses of the revenues gained from the tax.[25]

8.3   *The Basic Capital Proposal*

I have suggested that wealth transfer taxation should be linked to the introduction of a basic-capital scheme. In this section I want to take up this idea in more detail. The essential idea can be elaborated in a number of ways, and what follows is just one: On maturity each citizen will be eligible for a sizeable capital grant. The individual will be free to use this endowment to finance a range of activities broadly related to productive participation in the community, e.g. to finance courses of higher education or vocational training, to establish a new business, to finance the costs of moving to a new area in search of employment, or, perhaps, to subsidize time off from employment to care for dependants. A portion of the endowment might also be available to spend more widely, as a supplement to income. Such a capital endowment need not be drawn down all at once (indeed, this may be inadvisable), and the balance would remain for future use. Citizens would of course be free to add to their account through private saving. Trade unions or other employee organizations could negotiate employer contributions to supplement individual accounts. On retirement, citizens could use the funds remaining in their accounts to supplement their pension income.

This proposal should be put in the context of a growing interest in 'asset-based egalitarianism' and 'asset-based welfare' in recent years, signs of which were already evident in the policy literature in the late 1980s and early 1990s. In the United States in the late 1980s Robert Haveman proposed a 'universal personal capital account for youths'.[26]

The proposal is for a universal capital grant of, say, $20,000 to be given to all youths at age eighteen, to be used for human capital investments of their choice. . . . They could draw on this account at any time for approved purchases of education and medical care services . . . and an annual statement of the value of the account would be sent to each youth. . . . The account would earn interest, and to the extent that it was not drawn down prior to the normal age of retirement, it would be available to supplement other income sources at that time.[27]

In its essential structure this is like the basic-capital proposal sketched above. A few years later, in Britain, the policy analyst Michael White proposed a system of 'flexible lifetime credits' as a means of tackling unemployment. Under this proposal each citizen would receive on maturity an allocation of credits, the value of which would be linked to average earnings. As White says,

Credits [could then] be drawn for a specific purpose—such as job search, retraining, or beginning a business—rather than for unemployment as such. They could not be drawn solely to create or supplement income, but would be tied to what one might call a *labour market need*—that is, the need to *do something* in relation to the labour market. For example, someone wishing to use credits for job search . . . might have to join a . . . job agency and draw up a professionally backed plan of job seeking.[28]

White conceives of the credits, I think, primarily as a means of supplementing income during periods in which the individual is engaged in some sort of investment activity, e.g. training, rather than as contributing to the costs of the investment itself, e.g. the costs of the training programme. But there is no reason why the idea could not be extended to help meet the costs of the relevant investments themselves. In this case, White's system of flexible credits looks very similar to the basic-capital proposal set out at the beginning of this section. Yet another variant of the idea appeared in the 1994 report of the Commission on Social Justice, set up in Britain by the then opposition Labour Party. Among its many policy recommendations the Commission advocated the establishment of a national 'Learning Bank' at which each citizen would in principle have an 'Individual Learning Account'[29] on which she could draw to finance the equivalent of three years of full-time higher education.[30] The Learning Bank proposal is obviously more narrowly tied to participation in education and training than the basic-capital proposal set out above, but there is an obvious similarity.

More recently, Bruce Ackerman and Anne Alstott have proposed that each citizen of the United States receive an $80,000 (1996 prices) grant on maturity.[31] This would be financed from a tax on wealth and, over the longer term, by a tax on estates at death and *inter vivos* gifts. The capital grant would be supplemented by a universal citizen's pension of some $670 per month (financed from a tax on 'childhood privilege').[32] In contrast to the basic-capital proposal described above, Ackerman and Alstott propose that no restrictions be placed on the uses to which the grant may be put. However, they do wish to restrict access to the capital to those who have completed high school and to those who lack a criminal record; and, in addition, they would not allow citizens to capitalize their future citizen's pension entitlement.

Closer to the basic-capital proposal described at the beginning of this section, David Nissan and Julian Le Grand have recently argued that all citizens should be endowed on maturity with a grant of some £10,000 which would go into an individual Accumulation of Capital and Education (ACE) account (financed from a revamped inheritance tax).[33] Each ACE account 'would be handled by a set of trustees, whose purpose would be to approve the spending plans of individuals before releasing any capital'.[34] Nissan and Le Grand mention education, training, business start-up costs, and housing down-payments as possible approved uses for the grant. More modestly, Gavin Kelly and Rachel Lissauer have proposed that the government provide each child at birth with a capital grant of £1,000 (with additions for those with parents on low incomes).[35] This grant would be invested and held in trust as the child matures, providing him or her with a capital sum on maturity. Like Nissan and Le Grand, they would restrict the range of uses to which the resulting funds could be put on maturity. This 'baby bonds' idea has, in turn, been picked up by the British government. In its consultation paper *Saving and Assets for All* the government proposes to introduce a Child Trust Fund for every child.[36] At birth 'every baby would receive an endowment', though 'those with families on lower incomes would receive a larger sum'.[37] The endowment would grow over time so that on maturity each citizen would have at least a modest amount of financial assets with which to enter working life. The consultation paper expresses sympathy for restricting the uses to which these funds can be put, but also frankly acknowledges the 'regulatory and implementation issues' raised by restricting the way citizens might use these funds.[38] Interest in Child Savings Accounts of this kind has also been voiced in the United States.[39] In continental Europe there is growing interest in the idea of so-called 'social drawing rights': personal accounts linked to specific contingencies, such as education, training, or parental leave. These suggestions also have much in common with the basic-capital proposal outlined above.

As this brief review indicates, one of the controversial design questions in thinking about the structure of basic-capital schemes concerns whether or how far use of the relevant capital funds should be restricted to certain purposes, in particular to purposes that are connected, albeit quite broadly, with productive contribution to the community. As my initial sketch of the basic-capital proposal suggests, I think there is much to be said for a basic-capital scheme with a restrictive element of this kind. Connecting the capital grant to productive contribution can be defended on two grounds. Firstly, of course, it can be defended on reciprocity-based grounds. Giving citizens a large unconditional cash lump sum on maturity would be similar to giving them an UBI and would thus be subject to the same objection that it could be used to subsidize self-indulgent withdrawal from productive contribution to the community. By contrast, if use of the capital grant is linked to productive participation, and/or to activities that facilitate such participation, then it is more likely to be used in ways that satisfy the reciprocity principle. Secondly, restrictions on use of the capital grant can be defended on paternalistic grounds. If, for example, one of the underlying aims of the scheme is to reduce market vulnerability (see below, Section 8.4), then this aim might well be more readily achieved if people are required to use at least a portion of their grants for purposes like education and training, purposes that develop their skills and thus widen the range of market opportunities they face. In the same way that people's interest in personal freedom is protected by prohibiting voluntary enslavement,[40] it might be argued that some restrictions on how capital grants can be used are justified as a way of protecting individuals from the vulnerability and dependency that would come from a reckless 'blowing' of their stakes; a way, as it were, of forcing citizens to be free.

Of course, a real libertarian might object that an appeal to paternalistic considerations fails to respect individual liberty sufficiently. In response, one can invoke the argument for liberal paternalism outlined in Section 6.6.1: paternalistic measures are justified if they correspond to restrictions that prudent individuals would typically choose to place on themselves in order to prevent themselves from doing things in moments of weakness or irrationality that significantly compromise their long-term interests. Restrictions on the use of capital grants which prevent citizens from imprudently consuming their capital, and which encourage them to use the grants in ways that will increase their employability, seem at least consistent with this general principle of justified paternalism. The real libertarian might simply reject this principle. But here it may be important to note that something like this principle is in fact accepted and employed by some leading real libertarian thinkers themselves. Philippe Van Parijs, for example, appeals to paternalistic considerations to justify paying an UBI as opposed to a lump-sum capital grant of the kind that Ackerman and Alstott propose.[41] And Ackerman and Alstott, in their turn, appeal to such paternalistic considerations to justify their insistence that citizens not be allowed to capitalize their future citizen's pension entitlements when young.[42] If the real libertarian accepts the principle of justified paternalism in these contexts, she obviously cannot consistently object to paternalism on principle. She must find fault with the particular application of the principle suggested here, and explain what it is about the specific form of paternalism suggested here that makes it objectionable.

Having laid out the two main considerations which support a use-restricted form of basic-capital scheme, however, one must acknowledge that there are other considerations which support making the basic capital grant open for a wider range of uses. Here I refer the reader back to the proposal made in the previous chapter for a time-limited basic income. This is an unconditional income grant that a citizen may draw on up to some maximum amount of time over the course of a normal working life (e.g. up to one, two, or three years). A time-limited basic income can't be used to finance indefinite withdrawal from productive participation in the community. But, managed prudently, it could be used to help cope with periods of transition and crisis in the individual's life that might otherwise carry grave risks of market vulnerability and dependency. Thus, a time-limited basic income appears to give us one of the key benefits of an UBI, but without the same risk to reciprocity as a more conventional UBI. Rather than being an alternative to conventional, contractualist welfare policies, it would serve as a complement, offering a second tier of income support that citizens could fall back on should they choose or if they slip through the net of the first, contractualist tier. Given its attractive qualities, there is a strong case, from the standpoint of fair reciprocity, for incorporating something akin to a time-limited basic income into the proposed basic-capital scheme.

If we now bring these various considerations together, what overall picture emerges of the proposed basic-capital scheme? Taken together, these considerations seem to point towards a scheme with something like the following structure: On maturity all citizens receive a sizeable capital endowment. This endowment consists of at least two basic accounts which we may term a Participation Account and a Life Account.[43] The Participation Account provides the citizen with funds that can be used specifically for purposes that are linked in a broad way with productive contribution to the community. These purposes might include education, training, setting up a new business, and, perhaps, leave from paid employment to undertake parental duties (bearing in mind that care work can also count as a form of productive contribution to the community in satisfaction of reciprocity). The Life Account would provide the citizen with additional funds that she could use to supplement income at her discretion, though there might be ceilings on how much of the funds can be accessed within a given time period. This Life Account would thus be more or less equivalent to what I have described as a time-limited basic income. Thus, if we were to introduce a basic capital grant set at the sort of level that Ackerman and Alstott envisage—say, £50,000—then perhaps 60 per cent of this could be allocated to an individual Participation Account, and 40 per cent to a Life Account. (Needless to say, such figures are purely illustrative.) If we now also factor in the argument in Chapter 7 concerning citizens' primitive resource rights in relation to land (see Section 7.3), then a variant on this proposal might also include some sort of Housing Account.[44] Henceforth when I speak of the basic-capital proposal, I should be understood to be referring to a basic-capital scheme with a structure of something like this kind. In this form the proposal clearly has as much in common with the idea, currently gaining ground in continental Europe, of a plurality of 'social drawing rights', each attuned to a specific type of contingency and life-cycle need, than to the single cash grant advocated by Ackerman and Alstott.

There are, of course, costs to this sort of basic-capital scheme. Not least are the likely administrative costs involved in monitoring the use-restricted element of such a scheme. If these are prohibitive, reciprocity-based and paternalistic concerns can and should still be addressed by developing an appropriate educational dimension to the scheme. By this I mean that the state should seek to promote the kind of capacities and dispositions—virtues, to use a more old-fashioned word—that will lead citizens to make reciprocity-friendly and prudent use of their capital grants. Indeed, it is important for any basic-capital scheme to incorporate an educational element of this kind. The success of such schemes, in terms of reducing brute luck disadvantage and market vulnerability over the long term, depends in part on the capacity of citizens to plan ahead, to think about the future, and to prioritize longer-term interests over short-term advantage. Without these capacities, citizens will make poor use of their capital grants, and the extra security that these grants potentially give will be precariously held and frequently lost. Accordingly, it is important to educate all citizens in the effective management of their capital and to encourage the development of the necessary virtues of forward planning and self-discipline.[45]

There are many other design questions that arise in thinking about the structure of a basic-capital scheme. For example, if we do allow citizens a modest lifetime accessions quota, as I have argued we should, should those who have received some wealth from others receive somewhat less from the state? There is at present much interest in the United States in so-called Individual Development Accounts (IDAs). Under IDA schemes, eligible individuals (those with incomes at or below some proportion of the poverty line) agree to save for specified purposes (e.g. a training course), and for every dollar they save the government provides a matching contribution in the ratio of 1 : 1 or higher (typically 2 : 1, with some schemes going as high as 7 : 1).[46] Should some of the resources necessary for a generous scheme of universal capital grants instead be used for schemes, such as IDAs, that encourage the independent accumulation of capital by the relatively asset-poor? Not least: What level of capital grant is, in general or on average, appropriate? I cannot consider all of these design issues here, but the latter question is obviously of great importance. I have given some indication of what I take to be the appropriate scale of ambition above, though it is not my purpose here to suggest any specific sum. We will get a better idea of why a generous basic-capital scheme is the appropriate objective, however, if we first get a clearer sense of the purpose of the basic-capital scheme, that is, of the justice-related and other desirable ends that we can expect to advance by means of such a scheme. I have already alluded to some of these ends in this section, but I will explore them more fully below.

8.4   *Arguments for Basic Capital*

In Section 8.2 we saw how the conventional institution of inheritance appears to be unjust both because it produces brute luck inequalities in wealth and because it enables people to enjoy income in violation of the claims of reciprocity. A right to basic capital of the kind described above, financed (at least in part) from the hefty taxation of wealth transfers, offers an alternative model of inheritance that is at once egalitarian, serving to help reduce class inequality to a reasonable minimum, and reciprocity-friendly. These are, however, by no means the only considerations that favour the introduction of a generous basic-capital scheme along the lines sketched out above. Further, interrelated, considerations, which I shall briefly review below, concern: (i) its potential to help prevent brute luck inequalities in earnings; (ii) its potential to help secure real opportunity for self-realization in work; (iii) its potential, already alluded to in the previous section, to reduce directly market vulnerability and the associated risks of exploitation and abuse; (iv) its potential, also noted above, to help nurture important personal capacities for forward-thinking and long-term planning; and (v) its potential to improve various aspects of economic performance. Let us take each of these considerations in turn.

A basic-capital scheme like that proposed above will help guarantee each citizen access to a high minimum of higher education and/or vocational training. This, in turn, will help to ensure a substantial degree of equality of opportunity for people to convert their natural endowments into actual marketable skills. In this way, it can be expected to help contain the overall degree of brute luck inequality in earned incomes. Obviously the basic-capital scheme will not compensate for residual brute luck inequalities in earnings potential attributable to differences in natural ability. But it will help reduce the inequalities in earnings potential that would otherwise result from differences in social background and educational opportunity. The significance of this should not be underestimated: some recent research suggests that these latter, sociological differences in fact account for a very substantial proportion of actual variation in earnings capacities.[47]

What is perhaps worth particular emphasis is the way in which basic capital functions as a *preventative* social policy in this regard. Rather than trying to correct for earnings inequality after it has emerged, it seeks to remove one of the underlying causes of this inequality. It is better to try to limit brute luck inequality in earnings as far as possible in this way, rather than relying solely on redistribution of earnings, because, in practice, such redistribution is likely to be a rather blunt policy instrument, one that fails to distinguish between unjust inequalities attributable to differential brute luck and just inequalities attributable to different income–leisure preferences. Moreover, the evidence of the past century indicates that the preventative policy of the human capital-building or -spreading kind has been of critical importance in reducing economic inequalities. The economic historian Robert Fogel points out, for example, that a large proportion of the reduction in income inequality in the United States since the nineteenth century can be explained by the spread of universal public education and the expansion of higher education.[48] Basic-capital schemes offer a way of consolidating and building on this achievement.

Secondly, basic capital can help ensure that citizens have real opportunity for self-realization in work—that is, to treat their working life as a site of meaningful challenge, rather than as a mere burden to be carried in the search for income. In part, this effect would also likely work through the access to education and training that the scheme provides. But such a scheme would also make it more feasible for citizens to establish new businesses, and this might also promote opportunity for self-realization in work. Self-realization is often connected with the ideal of the worker-managed enterprise.[49] But enterprises owned and run by their workers are relatively rare, in part perhaps because of the credit market constraints faced by asset-poor workers which militate against their formation.[50] Basic capital would provide otherwise asset-poor individuals with greater access to credit markets and, in this way, could increase the formation of worker-owned and -managed enterprises and, thereby, opportunities for self-realization in work. (There may be an important advisory role for the state in aiding the formation of sustainable enterprises of this kind, e.g. in helping potential co-workers to coordinate and helping them to form feasible business plans. Release of capital for enterprise formation might be made conditional on drawing up an approved plan.) In addition, if citizens are on average more highly and broadly skilled as a result of basic capital, and also have some realistic option to form their own enterprises, then employers might have to work harder to attract people to jobs at the lower end of the labour market. This might not only exert upward pressure on the wage rates in these jobs, but might also encourage employers to improve the quality of these jobs and of the working environment, further promoting opportunity for self-realization in work. Finally, if basic capital incorporates a time-limited basic income, as suggested above, this could have a similar effect: even a time-limited basic income would give citizens crucial additional power to refuse employment in poor-quality jobs, and would thereby increase the pressure on employers to make the jobs they offer more inherently rewarding.[51]

Thirdly, as intimated above, basic capital should help prevent the market vulnerability and dependent exchange that would otherwise result from initial asset poverty. To the extent that the capital grant is connected to productive activity, it can be expected to do this by promoting individual employability and making it easier to establish one's own business. But also important here, as I have emphasized above, is the contribution of the time-limited basic income, or Life Account, component of the grant which, if prudently managed, would give individuals a degree of independence from the labour market in circumstances of personal crisis and transition that might otherwise render them vulnerable and open to exploitation and abuse. Basic capital could help protect people from vulnerability and its consequences not only in the context of the labour market, moreover, but also in the domestic context.[52]

A related and important point concerns the potential educative impact of basic capital. As intimated in the previous section, if a basic-capital scheme is to work effectively towards the ends just described, such a scheme must almost certainly have a strong educational element to ensure that citizens have the necessary skills of capital management. At the same time, however, it can be argued that, precisely by ensuring every citizen some minimum endowment of wealth on maturity, basic-capital schemes make it that much easier for educators to nurture capacities for forward-thinking and long-term planning. Imagine, for example, an initiative to teach children the basics of financial literacy in schools. It seems likely that children will be more receptive to such initiatives if they know that there is a capital 'stake' there, in their name, waiting for them on maturity, than if they expect to inherit nothing. More generally, there is evidence that children's effort in school is affected by their perceptions of post-school opportunities: perception of limited opportunity results in less effort—which, in turn, confirms the perception of limited post-school opportunity.[53] To the extent that basic-capital schemes improve children's perceptions of post-school opportunity, as they presumably would for those children from otherwise asset-poor backgrounds, they might help to break this vicious cycle of low expectation and limited opportunity. Rather than workfare or benefit cuts, it may well be basic capital that offers the most effective response to the so-called 'culture of poverty'. And this, in turn, will contribute to the ends already described above: reduction of brute luck earnings inequality, opportunity for self-realization in work, and market security.

Finally, basic capital may achieve these justice-related ends while at the same time having a positive net effect on economic performance. In part, this might work through the effect of a basic-capital scheme on the level and breadth of workforce skills. A highly, broadly skilled workforce would make it easier for manufacturing enterprises in advanced capitalist countries to adopt quality-oriented product market strategies at a time when cost-oriented strategies are under increasing pressure from external competition. And it could reduce the likelihood of skill shortages in economic upswings, thereby dampening inflationary pressures when the economy is close to full employment. Basic capital might also improve economic performance through its aforementioned implications for the establishment of new businesses. Where credit markets are characterized by imperfect information (specifically, where borrowers have more accurate information about the likely success of their projects than lenders), credit agencies look to collateral requirements as a way of protecting themselves against bad risks. In view of their inability to offer sufficient collateral, asset-poor individuals will generally be excluded from receiving credit. They will therefore be unable to act on their good business ideas, a loss not only for them but potentially for the wider community. A basic-capital scheme, however, will help provide otherwise asset-poor individuals with the collateral they need to break into credit markets and enact these ideas. The community's latent entrepreneurial talent will have greater opportunity to manifest and develop itself.[54] We should not forget the possible detrimental effects on economic performance that a basic-capital scheme might bring, e.g. from the taxes necessary to finance it. But, in view of its potential effects on skills and entrepreneurship, it is by no means implausible that the 'global net steady-state effect'[55] of a generous basic-capital scheme on economic performance will be positive.[56]

8.5   *Financing Basic Capital: The Role of a Community Fund*

Having identified the numerous considerations that support the basic-capital proposal, I want now to turn back to the question of how a generous basic-capital scheme might be financed. As argued above, one source of funds is the taxation of wealth transfers. However, we cannot be certain that the funds raised from such taxation will be sufficient, after making due allowance for liberty-related exemptions, possible disincentive effects, and residual problems of tax avoidance, to finance a basic capital grant that is generous enough to have the effects described in the previous section. So where else might the community look to find the necessary funds? To some extent, the funds might come by folding into the basic-capital scheme some existing expenditures, such as public subsidies to those in higher education. But we are still talking at this point of a scheme that is wholly tax-financed. Are there perhaps other ways of financing such a scheme that might help to raise and stabilize its level of generosity?

One proposal that may be worth further consideration in this connection is the proposal to establish a 'community fund' based on collective asset-holding, e.g. collective share ownership. Imagine that the state owns some proportion of the shares that are traded on the stock market. The state does not own and manage particular firms or industries. It simply has its own portfolio of shares spread across various companies. Each year the state receives a return on its various shareholdings. The combined returns on these holdings are then merged and used to help finance a range of public projects, including, centrally, a generous basic-capital scheme.

The community fund idea is by no means a new one. In a sense, it is a contemporary rediscovery of the old republican idea of the 'public demesne': publicly owned lands and other assets that provide the state with revenues for the promotion of the common liberty.[57] The economist James Meade argued over many years for the creation of such a fund as one element in his model of a 'partnership economy'.[58] Meade may have picked up the idea from Hugh Dalton, Chancellor of the Exchequer in Britain's post-war Labour government, who discussed the community fund idea sympathetically in a number of books in the 1920s and 1930s.[59] More recently, Gerald Holtham has argued that a community fund offers a way to 'save social democracy' from the fiscal constraints associated with taxes on labour incomes: 'imagine the consequences of having a national patrimony of, say, £50 billion invested in equities. A rate of return of 6 per cent would allow 3 per cent each year to be devoted to [public] expenditure, some £1.5 billion initially, while the fund continued to grow at 3 per cent. This would relieve the pressure on taxation of labour income.'[60] Similar ideas surfaced recently in the United States in discussion of what the federal government should do with the large budget surplus it enjoyed. Some proposed that the government should invest a portion of the surplus in the stock market, i.e. create a community fund.[61] (The state of Alaska has already gone down this route to some extent, establishing a community fund from the sale of mineral rights which pays out an annual dividend to every citizen of the state.[62]) Other advanced capitalist countries, such as Sweden, have also already instituted collective share ownership schemes (in the Swedish case, to help finance the public pensions system).[63] In this supposedly post-socialist age the community fund idea represents a form of genuine collectivism. But it has the potential to be collectivism in the service of individualism: collective asset ownership can help to provide a secure financial base for individual-level economic entitlements, including, potentially, basic capital entitlements that give the citizen the power and dignity of an independent asset-holder. The socialist commitment to public ownership is harnessed to the liberal vision of a 'property-owning democracy',[64] rather than displacing it.

But where might the state get the funds to establish a community fund? One possibility is what we might call socialist privatization: selling assets to the private sector and using the revenues so raised to build up such a fund. For example, the British government could have used the receipts from the many privatizations of the 1980s and 1990s in this way (as some commentators and politicians in Britain argued at the time).[65] Another possibility is to employ compulsory new share issues or 'capital dilution' as a way of developing a community fund. The famous Meidner Plan provides one model of how to do this. Under the original version of this plan, drafted by the social democrat economist Rudolf Meidner in the mid-1970s, each Swedish company would have been required annually to issue new shares equal to the value of 20 per cent of its annual profits to special wage-earner funds controlled by the trade unions.[66] In this way the unions would have gradually acquired an increasing percentage of company shares over time and would eventually have become, in effect, the majority owners of Sweden's corporate sector. In principle, the state could use the same method to establish a community fund. The compulsory new share issues would be made not to the unions but to share ownership accounts owned by the state.[67] A variation on this idea is provided by Stuart Speiser's universal share ownership plan.[68] Under this plan, major firms are required from a certain date to finance all new investment projects using loans from the state. In return, the relevant firms are required to issue new shares, at current market value, equal to the cost of their new investment projects. These new shares are placed in state share ownership accounts. Dividends on the shares are used to pay off the loans, after which the dividends may be distributed to individual citizens directly, as Speiser proposes, or, say, to help finance a basic-capital scheme. Some other possibilities for getting a community fund started include taxes on inheritance, on capital gains, a wealth tax, or a one-off capital levy.[69] In the short run the establishment of a community fund may detract from spending on basic-capital schemes because scarce revenues will have to be used to get the fund started. But if the fund is established and allowed to accumulate, it could in time provide the state with a significant stream of revenue in addition to that from taxation. And this is why it is arguably desirable to establish such a scheme: not for its immediate pay-off in the promotion of justice-related objectives, but because of its potential to open up new possibilities for public spending in pursuit of these objectives over the long term.

Aside from cost, the most familiar objection to the community fund idea is that it would unduly expose capital markets to political influence and manipulation. Critics do not trust the state to manage its holdings in a way that will not compromise the efficiency of capital markets. But the idea is not necessarily that the fund would be directly managed by elected politicians or civil servants. As Holtham suggests, it should be possible to establish a board of trustees 'from outside politics to supervise the fund' and to insist that they delegate its day-to-day management to the private sector. Politicians would then be placed 'at two removes from investment decisions' and the state would function, as Dalton and Meade envisaged, simply as a 'passive rentier'.[70] It is not obvious, then, that community funds could not be managed in a responsible fashion, without impairing the workings of capital markets.[71]

8.6 *Summary*

This has been a long chapter, so it may help if I recap the main points. I began by stressing how the conventional institution of inheritance produces injustice. This establishes a strong prima facie case for the abolition of inheritance. Concerns for personal liberty and economic performance warrant a modest retreat from this policy, but not too much of a retreat: heavy taxation of wealth transfers, preferably in the form of an accessions tax, can accommodate these concerns while limiting the injustices to which the conventional institution of inheritance otherwise leads. Rather than simply abolishing or limiting inheritance in its conventional form, however, we should seek to restructure it along collectivist lines by linking such taxation to the introduction of a generous scheme of basic capital grants: sizeable capital endowments paid to all citizens on maturity from public funds. I have argued that the basic capital grant should be linked, at least in part, to the support of productive participation in the community, i.e. that the relevant funds should be available specifically for purposes like education, training, setting up a new business, moving to a new job, and, perhaps, to help subsidize parental leave from paid employment. However, there is also a strong case for allowing a portion of such a grant to be used as a simple income supplement, or as what I have called a time-limited basic income. The introduction of a generous basic-capital scheme, with something like this structure, would advance a number of justice-related objectives, and could conceivably also have a positive net effect on economic performance. The revenue for such a scheme need not be confined to wealth transfer taxation. One possibility worth considera-tion for the long term is a community fund: in essence, a portfolio of publicly owned assets, e.g. shares, that would provide an additional revenue stream to the state for public spending.

In short, basic capital, supported by wealth transfer taxation, is likely to be an essential complement to the practice of welfare contractualism discussed in Chapter 6. In the absence of basic capital, it is much more likely that welfare contractualism will burden less fortunate citizens in ways that violate some of fair reciprocity's most urgent demands.

CHAPTER 9

Conclusion: The Politics of Fair Reciprocity

In the Introduction to this volume I identified three philosophies of economic citizenship that presently frame the debate over citizens' social rights: libertarian, communitarian, and real libertarian. I said I would outline and defend a fourth philosophy, and examine its implications for these rights. That task is now done. But someone who is convinced by the argument thus far might still wonder whether a politics of fair reciprocity, aimed at enacting the civic minimum, is a feasible politics in the circumstances of capitalist societies like Britain and the United States. This chapter is intended to establish reasonable doubt as regards this feasibility scepticism.

As a first step in evaluating the feasibility of a politics aimed at enacting the civic minimum we must clarify the sort of reform programme that it implies. This is the task of Section 9.1. Sections 9.2 and 9.3 then discuss two notable versions of feasibility scepticism. Section 9.2 discusses what we may call globalization scepticism, the view that the globalization of economic activities makes ambitious egalitarian reform programmes, such as that associated with the civic minimum, unfeasible. I contest this view, arguing that the real challenge is that of building a wide and credible domestic coalition in favour of reform. This response immediately invites a second type of scepticism, however: populist scepticism, the view that fair reciprocity, and the reform programme it supports, have no plausible prospect of winning widespread support among the citizenries of real-world capitalist democracies. Section 9.3 considers and contests this populist scepticism. I argue that the reform programme associated with the civic minimum, and the philosophy of fair reciprocity that underpins it, have clear material relevance, speaking to genuine problems and

needs in the economic life of citizens in these societies, and a resonance with popular values, and that together these provide a possible
basis for winning popular support. Section 9.4 concludes.

9.1   *The Civic Minimum: A Reform Programme*

What sort of policies should we look to enact in order to establish the
civic minimum in the circumstances of capitalist societies like Britain
and the United States? At the outset of Part II, I emphasized that
we should be wary of trying to draw overly specific and determinate
policy conclusions from general principles of economic justice. Very
often the policy implications of specific, justice-related commitments
will depend on the state of the world, and there may be reasonable
disagreement among analysts and other citizens over what the true
state of the world is. Moreover, in the case of justice as fair reciprocity,
there are a plurality of commitments that citizens are asked to attend
to: commitments to prevent certain kinds of brute luck disadvantage,
to protect citizens from market vulnerability, to see that contributive
obligations are met, and so on. In some situations the commitments
may conflict, and citizens may then disagree about which commitments
should get priority. This too can lead to reasonable disagreement about
the policy implications of this conception of justice. Keeping these
cautionary remarks in mind, let us now clarify the picture of the civic
minimum that emerges from the discussion in Part II.

'Making work pay'. All those who are expected to satisfy a minimum
work expectation must receive a decent minimum income in return for
doing so. This includes not only a level of post-tax earnings sufficient
to cover a standard set of basic needs, but also a decent minimum of
health-care and disability coverage, set in accordance with the conception of appropriate compensation for handicaps outlined in Chapter 2.
The model of a minimum wage combined with in-work benefits for
the low-paid, including child-care subsidies for low earners, is certainly
one credible approach to this task.[1]

From a work-test to a participation-test. Work-tests within the welfare system are, according to the argument of Chapter 6, legitimate
in principle. But in order that different forms of productive contribution be treated equitably, social policy must be structured in a way
that acknowledges the contributive status of care work. This implies
a need to offer some public support for care workers, relieving their
need to do paid work to maintain access to the generous basic-needs

package described above. Relevant policies here might include payment of a decent social wage to those engaged in looking after the elderly or handicapped on a full-time basis and publicly subsidized parental leave from paid employment. In other words, access to the generous basic-needs package should be conditional not on satisfying a work-test, narrowly construed in terms of paid employment, but on satisfying a broader participation-test, where participation is understood to include paid employment and (at least in addition) specified forms and amounts of care work. Acknowledging the contributive status of care work in this way may help alleviate problems of work–family life balance that presently afflict many households in Britain and the United States. While it is arguably inappropriate for the state to promote any particular conception of family life, and thus any particular vision of how paid employment and care work should be divided within a family, it is worth noting that such support need not necessarily serve to reinforce traditional, gendered divisions of labour within the family. One possibility, for example, is to endow citizens with individual, non-transferable parental leave accounts, as part of a broader basic capital or social drawing rights strategy (see below). If the funds are non-transferable to partners or to other uses, and are simply forgone if not used, then men, as well as women, will have an incentive to take parental leave.[2] Thought also needs to be given to ensuring the quality of publicly subsidized care work. One possibility might be to require, or at least encourage, full-time carers to join local carers' groups and networks that could reduce the isolation of individual carers and help carers pool knowledge and resources.[3]

Towards a two-tiered income support system. As I noted in Chapter 7, the debate over 'welfare reform' is often polarized between supporters of an unconditional basic income that is not subject to any work- or participation-test, nor to any time limit, and supporters of time-limited workfare. An alternative approach, suggested in Chapter 7, looks to establish a two-tiered system of income support. The first tier, which we may call conventional welfare, would be contractualist in kind. It would offer support through a mix of income-related and universal benefits, but support that is also linked to, and conditional on, productive contribution. While work- or participation-tested, support at this level would not be time-limited. Provided citizens meet the relevant contribution requirements, they would remain eligible for the relevant support. The second tier might then consist of something like the time-limited basic income discussed in Chapters 7 and 8. This would be an additional income grant, not subject to any work- or participation-test, but which would be time-limited. Citizens could trigger the entitlement for a fixed amount of time over the full course of their working lives, but would not enjoy it indefinitely.

Universal capital-grant or social drawing rights. Chapter 8 set out the case for instituting a generous capital endowment as a basic right of economic citizenship. I suggested there that a scheme of universal capital grants might in part incorporate the time-limited basic income mentioned above (functioning as what I termed a Life Account). Otherwise, the grants could be linked to activities that are related to productive contribution in the community, such as education, training, setting up a business, and, perhaps, care work (functioning as what I termed a Participation Account). As suggested above, an individual right to paid or subsidized parental leave might be incorporated into a grant of this kind. (Another possibility, drawing on the argument set out in Section 7.3, would be to include something like a Housing Account in the basic capital endowment as an approximation of the citizen's primitive resource right in relation to land.)

Accessions tax. Chapter 8 set out the case for heavy taxation of wealth transfers (inheritances, bequests, *inter vivos* gifts). Such taxation is important to help prevent class inequality and violation of reciprocity. There is a strong case for hypothecating the funds from taxation of wealth transfers to the funding of a universal capital-grant scheme.

These would seem to be some of the key policy ideas and policy areas that reformers in countries like Britain and the United States would need to focus on if they were to reform the terms of economic citizenship so as to meet the demands of fair reciprocity (in its non-ideal form). But this short list is not, by any means, exhaustive of the policies and institutions that might be necessary, or helpful, in this regard. Throughout the discussion in Part II, I assumed that the state should act to guarantee citizens *equal opportunity for high-quality primary and secondary education.* Exactly how the state can best meet this guarantee, and how it should handle possible trade-offs in its implementation, are highly controversial questions that I cannot enter into here. But justice as fair reciprocity, even in its non-ideal form, most certainly requires that the state structure the education system so as to meet this principle of equal opportunity for quality education.[4] The discussion in Part II also uncovered a number of other policy ideas, not mentioned in the foregoing list, which might also feature as part of the civic minimum, or in support of it. One such idea, discussed briefly in Section 7.5.2 is the proposal for a *privilege tax–subsidy scheme*: a system of taxes and subsidies based on degree of childhood privilege, along the lines recently proposed by Bruce Ackerman and Anne Alstott.[5] Another idea, also floated in Section 8.5, is the proposal to establish a *community fund*, based on public-asset ownership, to help put the financing of the civic minimum on a more secure footing over the long term. Further discussion would doubtless reveal many other policies as potentially helpful in meeting the demands of fair reciprocity (in its non-ideal form). For example, in order to ensure that all citizens are able to satisfy their reciprocity-based contributive obligations with self-respect, it may be necessary in some contexts for the state to act as an employer of last resort, directly employing citizens who would otherwise enter long-term unemployment or subsidizing their temporary employment with another employer.[6] A more complete analysis would also have to give consideration to how a system of public pensions provision might be integrated into a policy programme of the kind described above.[7]

Further thought also needs to be given to the kind of governance structures that could assist the enactment and operation of the civic minimum. I have given some attention to this issue in the preceding discussion, emphasizing the role that deliberative bodies such as citizens' juries might have in elaborating the content of specific social rights (e.g. in helping to develop a bill of rights for welfare recipients as suggested in Section 6.4). But there is perhaps also a critically important role for structures that can coordinate the reform of social-rights provisions with decision-making in other areas which could impact significantly on the credibility and efficacy of new social-rights provisions. There has been much interest of late in the 'new social pacts' that have exemplified this kind of policy coordination in some European countries, most successfully in the Netherlands.[8] In this case, the pacts have brought key social interests together, on an ongoing basis, to negotiate what is in effect a new social contract, in which wage moderation and the flexibilization of employment (flexibility in working patterns, wages, and working time), and reform of taxation, are exchanged for the development of social-rights provisions that make the new, flexibilized labour market consistent, not only with higher employment, but with decent incomes for all those in the workforce, greater income security, and opportunity for family life (so-called 'flexicurity'). The pacts represent a form of corporatist governance, but are by no means a replication of the corporatism classically associated with the Nordic social democracies. For instance, while they do involve some centralization of wage determination, they also permit a degree of autonomy to local negotiators in determining pay and conditions. In some cases, notably the Republic of Ireland, there has also been innovation with regard to the groups that are formally represented in the relevant negotiations: not only employers, trade unions, and the state, but also representatives of the unemployed and the poor, helping to defuse the risk that corporatist bargaining will advance the interests of employers and unionized 'insiders' at the expense of unemployed or non-employed 'outsiders'. As I shall explain further below, such structures may have a critical role to play in the introduction and operation of policies like those set out here, and to this extent can be seen as an important supplement to, and support for, the civic minimum.

9.2   *Against Globalization Scepticism*

Is the civic minimum feasible? Even if one is more or less persuaded by the foregoing account of fair reciprocity, and of the policies it supports, one might wonder whether reforms of the envisaged kind are feasible in advanced capitalist countries. It is sometimes argued that the internationalization of production, trade and capital movements— in common parlance, 'globalization'—has tightened the constraints faced by policy-makers, ruling out the pursuit of ambitious egalitarian aims. For egalitarian initiatives imply high levels of public spending and, therefore, either large public deficits or high taxation (or both). Large, ongoing deficits will create fears of inflation and exchange rate depreciation, prompting swift and unsustainable capital flight. High taxes will reduce the competitiveness of local firms, and will act as a strong incentive to firms (and, to a lesser extent, workers) to migrate elsewhere. Economic stability and competitiveness, so the argument runs, thus require a regime of low taxation and public spending, and therefore the abandonment of egalitarian ambitions. Far from being on the side of fair reciprocity, history is in fact on the side of the libertarians and near-libertarians who wish to reduce the welfare state to a minimum.

What are we to make of this argument? Note first that even if this story is substantially true, it does not necessarily have the implication that libertarians and near-libertarians are eager to draw. Were the story true, it would indeed spell trouble for egalitarianism conceived as a wholly *national* political project. But then perhaps the appropriate conclusion to draw is that egalitarians should seek to realize their aims, in part, through the creation of new transnational or supranational structures of governance. Through such institutions, egalitarians could seek to harmonize national standards of social protection, and so prevent the downward pressure on such standards that trade and tax competition are supposed to create.[9] Admittedly, this reply to the globalization sceptic would then have to confront the argument that egalitarian policies depend on the solidarity born of a common national identity, something that would be lacking at the level of transnational institutions.[10] But some such argument now has to be made, in addition to the simple economic argument, and it may be that decisive replies to such additional arguments are to be had.[11]

The simple form of globalization scepticism described above is, however, far from being clearly correct. Pointing this out has become something of an industry among students of political economy.[12] The critics argue that in some respects the degree of economic globalization in recent years has been exaggerated.[13] They also argue that the implications of globalization, in particular for the feasibility of egalitarian social policy, have been misunderstood.[14] As one popular commentator, Adair Turner, points out, when we look around the world we see different advanced capitalist countries with very different levels of taxation and public spending as a proportion of national product. Moreover, there is little sign that the higher-tax and higher-spending nations are under pressure to bring their overall tax and spending levels down to the level of the low-tax and low-spending nations.[15] An obvious flaw in the globalization argument against egalitarianism presented above is that it focuses only on one side of the tax and spend equation. Taxation and resultant public spending can produce goods that enhance trade competitiveness and/or make the nation attractive to capital: efficient transport infrastructures; well-educated and healthy workforces; an environment in which citizens may be more flexible in work and business precisely because they are better cushioned against possible failure; an environment of social cohesion that results in reduced threat of crime and disorder, and, in turn, reduced costs of monitoring and protecting property. Moreover, taxes on labour incomes do not necessarily imply higher labour costs, and so damage competitiveness, if workers are collectively willing to receive a corresponding portion of their wages in the form of social spending and public services.

In fact it is this issue, the willingness of citizens to accept the taxes necessary to sustain public spending for social justice, rather than globalization per se, that is of fundamental importance to the feasibility of egalitarian policy (as, of course, it always has been).[16] If taxes are increased to finance spending for social justice, and there is no popular support for this, citizens will respond by pressing for compensatory wage increases. Unless these increases are matched by corresponding productivity growth (and, in a post-industrial economy in which services account for the bulk of output and employment, productivity growth tends to be sluggish[17]) this would threaten to create a situation of accelerating inflation as capital-holders try to claw back their share of the social product through unanticipated price increases. As inflation picks up, the exchange rate comes under pressure to fall to maintain trade competitiveness. This creates new inflationary pressures. Rational investors would foresee this chain of events, however, and, fearing depreciation of the exchange rate, would respond to any announcements of increased taxation and spending by withdrawing capital straight away. It is in this respect that one aspect of globalization, the growth in international financial flows, is important. Given how mobile financial capital has become, a fall in the exchange rate would happen sooner rather than later, immediately creating the very inflationary pressures that investors fear. To regain the confidence of the markets, the government would quickly have to retrench, following a classic pattern of egalitarian governments capitulating to the *mur d'argent*. It was a dynamic of this sort that underlay the failure of the infamous Mitterrand expansion in France in the early 1980s.[18]

It is essential to understand, however, that what 'the markets' would be responding to in such a case is not the increase in taxation and spending as such, but the fear that, because the increase lacks sufficiently wide and deep domestic support, it will generate higher, accelerating inflation. In itself it is not necessarily of concern to international investors if the citizens of a given country wish to share a relatively large proportion of their earned income with each other through redistributive taxation, or to enjoy a relatively large portion of their earnings as tax-financed public services rather than as cash in hand. What will definitely concern them, when taxation and public spending programmes are announced, is whether the citizens of a given nation do genuinely support the level of redistribution and public provision these programmes imply, because this is what determines whether or not these programmes will be inflationary. If this analysis is correct, then it suggests that a government committed to increasing taxation and public spending, in order to better realize social-justice commitments, would have to concern itself with two things: firstly, with ensuring that there is indeed a wide and deep consensus for the taxation and spending plans they have in mind; and secondly, with ensuring that this consensus is effectively signalled to decision-makers in capital markets. The second requirement is just as important as the first. For, following the logic of the argument laid out above, what matters in determining the reaction of investors is their perception of what domestic citizens feel about these plans. To prevent destabilizing shifts in capital markets, and subsequent retrenchment, domestic consensus on the desirability of increased social-justice expenditures must be there and it must be made appropriately *manifest*. I will return to the issue of how support for such expenditures might be cultivated below, but for the moment let us assume that such support is there. How might it then be communicated to 'the markets'?

It might be argued that democratic elections provide such a communication mechanism. To some extent they do. But even where an election does provide a fairly clear mandate for a policy of increasing social-justice expenditures, investors might always wonder about whether citizens really accept the overall distributive implications of these expenditures. Corporatist arrangements of the kind described above may be one way of overcoming this residual credibility gap. For these arrangements force the relevant social groups to recognize the distributive implications of their public spending and tax preferences, and offer them the opportunity to make agreements on things like pay and working practices that take due account of these implications. Provided that these agreements are generally respected by the parties to them, they should represent a credible signal of citizens' commitment to absorb the cost of the social-justice expenditures they have voted for. (Of course, sensible agreements on pay and the like may not be made unless the state itself has made a credible commitment to fiscal probity and to monetary discipline, which itself may have implications for the institutions of economic governance.[19]) Establishing such arrangements implies that the state will act to reshape the associational environment within which pay, social policy, and other related policies are made. Does the state have the right to do this? Does it have the capacity? I have examined the first question elsewhere, concluding that, subject to certain limitations, the state does indeed have such a right.[20] The second question is largely an empirical one. On the one hand, students of the new corporatism emphasize the high degree of contingency involved in its emergence, and caution against too readily assuming that such arrangements can be exported to nations that do not have them.[21] On the other hand, they point out that such structures have emerged, and operated with some success, in nations, such as the Republic of Ireland, that have previously had little tradition of corporatism. And this suggests that such structures can be developed where they are presently lacking.[22]

With or without the aid of such arrangements, it seems likely that the need to prevent destabilizing movements in exchange markets will push egalitarian governments towards a gradualist strategy. A sudden large increase in social-justice expenditures is, I suspect, more likely to excite fear than a series of modest increases. A danger with gradualism, of course, is that it can easily lose momentum. For this reason it is essential that gradualism be principled. By this I mean that it must be rooted in a clear conception of justice and linked to a concrete vision of the kind of policies and institutions that are ultimately necessary to achieve justice, so understood. And this is obviously where the enterprise of political theory, and volumes like this, can be of help.

9.3   *Against Populist Scepticism*

Assume now that we do have an effective method of communicating support for egalitarian initiatives. This still leaves the question of whether such support can indeed be mustered. The populist sceptic questions whether a politics of fair reciprocity, aimed at enacting the civic minimum, can win wide support. Populist scepticism is sometimes bolstered by claims that changes in the social structure of advanced capitalist societies, specifically the decline of the industrial working class, have deprived egalitarians of a clear, majority constituency. Politicians of the left must now construct coalitions that bridge the economically marginal, remnants of the traditional working class, and new middle-class groups (such as 'wired workers' of the 'information age'). Since the last are the most easy for politicians of the right to detach, coalition-builders of the left must give their interests and preferences special attention, and this, so the argument runs, precludes an ambitious egalitarian politics.[23]

If a philosophy of economic citizenship, and an associated reform programme, are to win wide popular support, they must be attractive on two levels.[24] Firstly, they must be *materially relevant*. They must address genuine economic problems and needs that are of concern to citizens. Secondly, they must be *value-resonant*. They must address these problems and needs in a way that runs with the grain of widely shared values. This is not to say that a philosophy of economic citizenship should simply reflect a pre-existing consensus about social justice (assuming for the moment that such a thing exists). It should be clear from the discussion above that in some important respects the philosophy of economic citizenship developed in this book, based on the conception of justice as fair reciprocity, almost certainly challenges some prevalent, majority assumptions about what justice requires. But if a philosophy of economic citizenship akin to that of fair reciprocity is to develop wider support, it must have some significant points of contact with values that are at present widely and deeply held among the real-world citizenries of capitalist democracies. In the short run these points of contact provide a vital resource for winning support for modest reform programmes. Looking to the longer term, they provide a starting point for a democratic conversation that may lead, in time, to a shift in the way social justice is popularly conceived, a shift that opens the way for further and more fundamental reforms. I shall argue that fair reciprocity, and the reform programme associated with the civic minimum, pass these two tests of material relevance and value-resonance, and that the civic minimum is therefore within the bounds of a plausible democratic politics.

Let us turn first to the issue of material relevance. To assess material relevance we first need to make clear the material challenges that presently confront the citizenries of advanced capitalist countries. One major challenge confronting advanced capitalist countries is that of how to reconcile high employment with tolerable levels of income inequality. In their respective ways, high levels of non-employment and high levels of income inequality are both threats to social cohesion. High rates of non-employment leave some citizens feeling excluded from mainstream social participation and, where the population is ageing, increase the burden of support for the elderly on those left working. High levels of income inequality may be associated with increased criminality[25] and with an increased risk of poor health for the population as a whole.[26] However, it is widely believed today that high levels of employment can only be sustained through employment growth in the service sector, and that employment growth in the service sector has as its corollary (in the short term, at least) an increase in wage inequality.[27] As Torben Iversen and Anne Wren point out, efforts to break out of this trade-off by expanding public-sector employment at moderately high wages will run into insurmountable fiscal problems.[28] There is, then, a need for policies that can improve the trade-off between employment and income inequality. A second, related challenge concerns the quality of jobs in the new service economy. Many of the new jobs created in this economy are of poor quality, not only in that they are low-paid, but in that they offer little opportunity for self-realization at work, and little prospect for future advancement to better-paying, and more challenging, jobs. Policy analysts, such as Gosta Esping-Andersen, emphasize the need for a 'mobility guarantee' that will help ensure that some citizens are not trapped in poorer-quality jobs, but will have a real prospect of moving out of them into better jobs over their working lives.[29] A third challenge concerns the balance between employment and family life. In the past, balance was achieved simply by a convention that women 'do family' and men 'do employment'. Aside from its economic and cultural difficulty, restoring this convention is morally indefensible. It denies women equal economic opportunity with men and, in the process, increases women's economic dependency on, and thus their risk of exploitation and abuse by, men. But, as things stand in countries like Britain and the United States, citizens, and particularly women citizens, are finding it difficult to combine participation as equals in the labour market with the demands of family life.[30]

The reform programme associated with the civic minimum addresses all three of these challenges. Consider first the problem of reconciling high employment with a limitation of income inequality. The reform programme outlined above includes a commitment ('make work pay') that directly addresses this problem. It demands that the earnings of low-paid workers be supplemented by generous in-work benefits (perhaps, but not necessarily, on the model of the United States' Earned Income Tax Credit). Fair reciprocity supports making these benefits generous enough both to ensure a decent standard of living for those meeting their basic work expectation, and to maintain work incentives for the low-paid.[31] This directly redistributive response aims to dampen the effects of increased wage inequality on inequality in final incomes. But policy might also constructively address the dynamics that lead to increased wage inequality in the first place, without necessarily sacrificing the goal of high employment. Specifically, if the supply of educated, skilled labour can be increased rapidly enough, this should tend to reduce the existing inequalities between the wages of skilled and unskilled workers.[32] In this context, it is easy to see why so many policy analysts and policy-makers have recently become concerned both with the quality of primary and secondary education systems, and with ensuring that adult citizens have ongoing access to quality education and training ('lifelong learning').[33] The reform programme associated with the civic minimum speaks to this concern in at least two ways. Firstly, it sanctions forms of welfare contractualism that link income support with educational and training initiatives designed to enhance the skills and employability of the unemployed. Secondly, and perhaps more significantly, it would endow every citizen with a generous capital grant that she can then use to develop marketable skills; universal basic capital would assure every citizen access to a high level of education and training.

The basic-capital proposal can also be seen as offering a response to the second of the two problems identified above, the problem of entrapment in poor-quality employment. As I explained in Section 8.4, provision of generous basic capital grants offers a way of promoting real opportunity for self-realization in work. At the individual level, the capital grants provide a way for citizens to access credit, education, and training, and use these resources to escape poor-quality employment. And, in the aggregate, the effect of many citizens having this opportunity could be to increase pressure on employers to improve the content of relatively poor-quality jobs.

Turning, finally, to the third problem identified above, the relevance of the reform programme associated with the civic minimum again seems evident. This reform programme includes a commitment to pay to give financial support to full-time carers, and to offer public subsidy for those seeking to take time out of employment to meet parental responsibilities. In addition to these policy commitments, however, one must take into account the possible contribution of the underlying philosophy of fair reciprocity to the resolution of this problem. Arguably, one of the main obstacles to increased public support for parents and other carers, perhaps especially in the United States, is ideological: specifically, the idea that having a child, or deciding to care for an elderly or sick relative, is, as noted in Section 5.2, simply a personal lifestyle choice on a par with a decision to pursue an interest in collecting stamps or bungee-jumping, and, as such, cannot ground a legitimate claim to public aid.[34] The philosophy of fair reciprocity, at least as elaborated in Part I, provides a way of challenging this ideology. Care work, according to my elaboration of fair reciprocity, is not properly seen as akin to a hobby. It represents (or, at least, can represent) a form of contribution in satisfaction of the demands of reciprocity and, as such, warrants public recognition and a measure of public support. Fair reciprocity empowers parents and other carers to make the case that their care work is a form of active citizenship, of labour for the common good, which should be supported as such.[35]

So in at least these three ways, the civic minimum does address real problems and needs in contemporary capitalist societies. The problems do impact on the lives of most citizens, directly or indirectly, making it easier for them to see the point and value of policies that address these problems. This provides a basis for winning popular support for these policies. To be sure, some of the problems certainly impact much more directly on some groups of citizens than on others. The second problem of entrapment in poor-quality employment, for example, is less likely to affect more educated workers directly. For this reason, a politics of fair reciprocity, aimed at enacting the civic minimum, will have to make an appeal that goes beyond mere self-interest. To bridge inequalities in citizens' experience, and to help persuade citizens to prioritize policies that offer solutions to these problems, it will almost certainly also have to excite and appeal to a sense of civic idealism.

This brings us to a second pertinent feature of the civic minimum, and its supporting philosophy of fair reciprocity, its value-resonance.

There are, I suggest, three potentially important ways in which fair reciprocity, and the reform programme it supports, resonate with popular values (that is, the values held by real-world citizenries of capitalist democracies like Britain and the United States). Firstly, key elements of the civic minimum can be readily defended in terms of the value of equal opportunity. Of course, the majority understanding of this value in capitalist societies like Britain and the United States is at present far removed from the kind of egalitarianism that fair reciprocity, in its ideal form, demands. The majority commitment is probably towards some form of meritocracy, qualified by a commitment to prevent brute luck immiseration.[36] However, it is important to recognize that there is considerable room for debate about what this commitment concretely demands. The non-ideal form of fair reciprocity offers one interpretation of what a qualified meritocracy is. Key elements of the civic minimum, such as the proposed combination of universal capital grants and wealth transfer taxation, can be readily defended in meritocratic terms, as policies that serve to reduce class-based obstacles to meritocratic equal opportunity.

Some elements of the civic minimum, such as the basic-capital scheme, can also be defended in terms of the values of freedom, personal independence, and individual self-development, that play such a large part in the culture of many contemporary capitalist democracies. Such values are routinely appealed to by libertarian and near-libertarian critics who seek to reduce social-justice expenditures. But the foregoing account of justice as fair reciprocity indicates how these values can also be used to make the case for social rights, such as the proposed right to basic capital. The essential idea, which has been articulated by a long line of republican thinkers on political economy at least as far back as Rousseau, and more recently by real libertarians such as Bruce Ackerman and Philippe Van Parijs, is that freedom and independence have a material basis, and that if citizens have a right to freedom and independence, they must have, by right, meaningful access to a decent share of their society's resources. Thus, in making a popular case for the civic minimum, one need not appeal to the claims of 'equality' in opposition to those of 'liberty'. One can appeal to both values, and to the further thought that, in certain important respects, the two values are mutually dependent.

Thirdly, the civic minimum is readily defensible in terms of widely shared norms of reciprocity and responsible citizenship. The concern for substantive economic reciprocity is, of course, a central concern of justice as fair reciprocity, and this concern is reflected in the content of the civic minimum and the associated reform programme described above. Fair reciprocity, even in its non-ideal form, does demand a high level of redistribution towards the less advantaged. But it does not call on citizens to solidarize with others regardless of their willingness to do their bit by way of productive contribution to the community. In this way, it affirms the dignity, by honouring the effort, of hard-working, tax-paying citizens.

Some political scientists in the United States have recently discussed the prospects for a 'new progressive politics' there, and a striking feature of their work is the emphasis some give to the importance of attending to reciprocity in the design of reform programmes, and in the underlying public philosophy of progressive politics. Consider, for example, Theda Skocpol's discussion of what makes for successful innovations in American social provision. Skocpol reviews a number of relatively successful initiatives, dating back to the nineteenth century (including public schools, benefits for Civil War veterans, Social Security, and the GI Bill of 1944), and asks what features of these initiatives explain their success. She argues that one key feature is their consistency with a norm of substantive reciprocity. As Skocpol puts it,

The most enduring and popularly accepted social benefits in the United States have never been understood as poor relief or as mere individual entitlements. From public schools to Social Security, they have been morally justified as recognitions of or as prospective supports for individual service to the community. The rationale of *social support in return for service* has been a characteristic way for Americans to combine deep respect for individual freedom and initiative with support for families and due regard for the obligations that all members of the national community owe to one another.[37]

If 'liberal Democrats' in the United States have lately confronted a 'political impasse' in developing social rights, this, Skocpol claims, is because after the 1944 GI Bill they abandoned 'the long-standing formula for successful American social provision—giving support to people who are seen as contributors to the community, whatever their social class'.[38]

Skocpol's argument is consistent with that developed by Ruy Teixeira and Joel Rogers in their recent examination of the prospects for a popular progressive politics in the United States.[39] Teixeira and Rogers are specifically concerned to refute the claim, floated at the beginning of this section, that progressive advance has been stymied by social change that has diminished the importance of the working class in favour of relatively high-income, high-skilled workers. They point out that in the United States the white working class (defined as ethnically white workers with little or no higher education) still constitutes a majority of the electorate, and they show how its preferences have been crucial in deciding the outcomes of recent presidential and congressional elections. The main reason for the defeat of progressive politics in recent decades lies in the failure of the Democrats to hold and win back the support of the white working class. On the one hand, members of this group have suffered stagnation or decline in living standards since the early 1970s, an experience that has conflicted with 'deeply held and broadly shared' values such as 'opportunity, fair reward for effort, the centrality of hard work and individual achievement, and social commitment'.[40] But Democrats have not sufficiently addressed the problems of this group or respected their values. Republicans have instead succeeded in presenting 'big government' and taxation as the source of their problems, particularly by emphasizing Democratic support for assistance programmes ('welfare') that seem to violate the aforementioned working-class values.[41] Accordingly, Teixeira and Rogers argue that to win back the white working class, progressives in the United States must adopt a policy programme that explicitly addresses the economic problems of this group in a way that affirms their values. This implies, I think, a policy agenda, and a supporting public philosophy, that focuses on spreading opportunity and assets while at the same time emphasizing the citizen's obligation to work hard and display 'social commitment'. Fair reciprocity and the civic minimum would seem to fit the bill.[42]

What applies in the United States does not necessarily apply elsewhere, of course. But to the extent that these values are shared by the citizenry in other countries, fair reciprocity, and reform programmes like that associated with the civic minimum, will have a popular resonance. And given this resonance, it does not seem wholly unrealistic to think that a politics of fair reciprocity could excite a supporting sense of civic idealism. As suggested above, these points of contact between fair reciprocity and popular values provide the opening for a democratic conversation in which those committed to fair reciprocity seek to alter popular perceptions of how these values are best understood, and of what these values demand. Such a conversation would be difficult to start, however, if fair reciprocity did not have some direct and significant resonance with popular values to begin with.

Thus far my discussion of feasibility scepticism has assumed that we are talking primarily about the feasibility of simply *expanding* the overall level of social-justice expenditures by the state to cover various new policy initiatives (such as universal capital grants). This makes sense, I think, in Britain and the United States, nations with relatively 'liberal' welfare states, where public spending and taxation levels are relatively low by international standards. It may make less sense, however, in other countries, such as Germany, France, or Sweden, where levels of expenditure and taxation are somewhat higher. In these countries it seems likely that new expensive commitments, like universal basic capital, may not be feasible except in the context of a general *restructuring* of social-justice expenditures. Some existing welfare state commitments would have to be curtailed in order to make way for new programmes of the kind associated with the civic minimum. Such a restructuring process will of course produce winners and losers, and the populist sceptic might leap on this point to throw doubt on the likelihood of reform: surely powerfully placed potential losers will simply veto restructuring. However, two facts suggest that this scepticism may be misplaced.

Firstly, there is a widespread view that existing patterns of welfare spending in some of these countries, such as Germany, are undesirable, and perhaps unsustainable. There is consequently a growing interest in restructuring welfare spending, shifting spending towards programmes that are in some respects similar to those associated with the reform programme set out above. Specifically, a number of policy analysts envisage a shift away from heavy subsidization of early withdrawal from the labour market, matched by a shift of spending towards things like in-work benefits for the low-paid, greater 'activation' of the unemployed within the welfare system, subsidies for parental leave, and 'social drawing rights' (saving accounts that individuals would be able to access to support education, training, and temporary sabbaticals from employment).[43] Typically, they envisage this restructuring of welfare spending as occurring in conjunction with a reform of labour market structures and the tax code to foster employment growth (particularly in the service sector). The overall aim is that described above: to increase levels of employment while at the same time protecting citizens from low incomes and income insecurity, entrapment in poor-quality jobs, and the erosion of family life. The Netherlands has already moved some way in this direction, for example, and some argue that countries like France and Germany ought to move in a similar direction.[44]

Secondly, the record thus far suggests that political coalitions in support of such restructuring can be put together.[45] Here again commentators stress the contribution of the 'new social pacts' that have provided an institutional context for the negotiation of the restructuring process. Research suggests that successful negotiation of change has depended on convincing affected parties that existing policies are indeed unsustainable; on assuring parties that the aim is to restructure, rather than merely retrench, social spending; and, not least, on the willingness of some parties, notably organized labour, to conceive of their constituency of interest in broad rather than narrow terms, e.g. as including the unemployed and non-employed. Change is far from inevitable; but it has proved possible in some countries, and this suffices to cast reasonable doubt on populist scepticism concerning the feasibility of restructuring social-welfare expenditures so as to enact a reform programme of the kind associated with the civic minimum.

My argument against populist scepticism in this section has stressed the resonance of fair reciprocity, and the reform programme it supports, with popular values. However, an egalitarian critic might find some of these resonances a cause for concern. In his recent survey of contemporary liberal egalitarian theorizing about economic justice, Will Kymlicka comments that 'a scheme of justice that encourages everyone to view their co-citizens as putative cheats is not a promising basis for developing trust and solidarity'.[46] It might be argued that this criticism applies especially to 'a scheme of justice' based on fair reciprocity given the emphasis that fair reciprocity places on the duty of every citizen to make a productive contribution and the injustice of subsidizing free-riders. However, I would question whether in any even modestly sized community 'trust and solidarity' can be built and maintained around egalitarian policies and institutions without explicit, official adherence to a norm of substantive economic reciprocity. This, I think, is the insight implicit in analyses like Skocpol's, an insight that is drawn out more explicitly in work such as that of Bowles and Gintis, to which I referred in Chapter 3.[47] Where reciprocity is not officially demanded and expected of citizens, trust and solidarity may, for that reason, be harder to build and maintain. Certainly, the opponents of egalitarian policies and institutions will not hesitate to exploit uncertainties about the extent of substantive economic reciprocity to generate distrust and undermine solidarity.

One further consideration may be advanced against the egalitarian critic. It is sometimes argued that efforts at egalitarian reform will be undermined by the ability of high-skilled workers to migrate to low-tax nations. (This is, of course, another line of argument behind globalization scepticism.[48]) Now perhaps one response to this argument is to make the point that relatively high-tax, egalitarian economies might provide some benefits to high-skilled workers, such as higher-quality public services, that partly offset the higher taxes they pay. But we cannot be sure how strong this offsetting factor will be. A more fundamental response focuses on the social ethos surrounding work and economic life in general. If high-skilled workers see their working lives as connected with good citizenship, with being a contributor to a common project in which all should do their bit, then they will probably be less likely to abandon their country for lower taxes elsewhere. Thus, it is important that the public philosophy underpinning efforts at egalitarian reform be supportive of such an ethos. Fair reciprocity is I suggest supportive of this ethos. The resonance it has with popular concerns over reciprocity can and should be used to stimulate a more wide-ranging discussion about the relationship between work and citizenship. And one aim of this conversation should be to encourage high-skilled workers to see their working lives as implicated in their civic responsibilities; to see their jobs not merely as instruments for personal satisfaction, but as opportunities for contributions to a common good. As Leonard Hobhouse put it, 'We want a new spirit in economics—the spirit of mutual help, the sense of a common good. We want each man to feel that his daily work is a service to his kind . . .'.[49] An egalitarian politics which does not place the same emphasis as fair reciprocity does on the centrality of work to responsible economic citizenship may find it harder to encourage this social ethos, and for this reason may be less successful in achieving its goals.

9.4 *Concluding Caveats*

I have argued that a philosophy of economic citizenship based on justice as fair reciprocity, committed to a reform programme akin to that outlined in Section 9.1, does have potential political relevance. Globalization does not rule fair reciprocity out as economically unfeasible. The reform programme it supports speaks to genuine needs and problems in advanced capitalist societies. It does so, moreover, in a language that resonates with popular values. At the same time, a politics of fair reciprocity need not, and ought not, uncritically to echo these values. It can and should use its points of contact with popular values to initiate conversations about economic citizenship with a view to radicalizing popular understanding of these values, thereby opening possibilities of deeper, more far-reaching reform. In closing, however, I want to make explicit some remaining problems and areas of reasonable disagreement; and, not least, to recall an important caveat to the main argument of this book.

One problem has to do with intergenerational equity in the transition to a society that realizes the civic minimum. Consider the proposal for a scheme of universal basic capital grants. Such proposals typically envisage that the grant will first be paid at some future date to a birth cohort of citizens just entering the labour market. All citizens who enter the labour market after this date will also receive the basic capital grant. But what about those citizens who entered the labour market before this date? Do they get nothing? Of course, some people (such as the author) may have received roughly equivalent benefits to the basic capital grant, such as tuition-free higher education at internationally prestigious universities, and so it may indeed be reasonable for them to get nothing. Others, however, will not have received such benefits, and it seems unfair to discount their interests. Surely the community is obliged to do something to alleviate their position, especially if they are relatively disadvantaged in the labour market and no discrimination is made between them and younger citizens in enforcing the demands of reciprocity through the welfare system. One obvious possibility is a policy on the model of the Individual Development Accounts (IDAs) recently pioneered in parts of the United States: schemes of generously subsidized saving for those on low incomes.[50] But these policies will obviously cost something, and this will tend in practice to depress the level at which universal basic capital grants for younger cohorts can be introduced. There is, then, a major issue as to how we ought to trade off the interests of younger and older generations in the transition to a society that realizes the civic minimum. I have not considered this important issue in this volume, but it is, alas, one that real-world policy-makers would have to confront.[51]

A second problem, or set of problems, concerns international equity. The focus of this book has been on justice within a given community, and the implicit assumption throughout most of the discussion has been that this community is something like a modern nation state. Further thought needs to be given, firstly, to how a reform programme like that described above might be pursued in a coordinated way within transnational political communities such as the European Union. Throughout the book I have also assumed that membership within a given political community is an unproblematic given. In the real world, however, it clearly isn't. Many millions of people from poorer and politically unstable parts of the world are desperate to achieve membership of richer, stabler political communities, and increasing amounts of state resources in richer, stabler countries are devoted to the task of denying them a presence.[52] So further thought needs to be given, secondly, to the question of how membership of a given political community is justly determined. Egalitarian commitments suggest a presumption against immigration controls. On the other hand, rapid large-scale immigration may destabilize efforts to make a given political community internally more just. How these (and doubtless many other) considerations are appropriately balanced, and what kind of policies would reflect this balance, are vitally important questions that I have bracketed here. But, again, a real-world politics of fair reciprocity would have to formulate a response to them as a matter of some urgency.

Moving from the theory to the political practice of fair reciprocity is in other ways a complicated and controversial task. Take one apparently simple question: Should a proponent of fair reciprocity support recent reforms in, say, Britain, that have tightened the link between welfare and work? Given that the appropriate background conditions for fair reciprocity are not in place, she might quite reasonably oppose such reforms. But what if, as Lawrence Mead argues the shift to welfare contractualism makes it easier to get issues concerning the wider structure of opportunity and the distribution of wealth onto the political agenda? If there is good reason to think this will indeed happen, then a proponent of fair reciprocity might cautiously support the shift to contractualism. The huge risk involved in such a strategy is evident, and in the case of the United States it has thus far produced only a modest pay-off for those most disadvantaged in the labour market.[53] But the plausibility of such a strategy is not something we can assess outside the particular political context in which the shift to contractualism is taking place. In short, even if the theory of justice as fair reciprocity gives us a clear picture of where we should be headed, exactly how we might get there, or closer to there, given where we start from, is a highly context-specific question, and one on which the citizens of real-world capitalist democracies might reasonably, and quite passionately, disagree.

Finally, it is important that we keep the civic minimum itself in perspective. We should keep in mind that a society which enacts the civic minimum would satisfy justice as fair reciprocity only in its non-ideal form. Some degree of significant brute luck disadvantage would almost certainly remain in this society, and so, following the argument set out in Chapter 4, we cannot regard such a society as fully just. But the civic minimum should be judged from a number of perspectives. We should certainly judge it from the perspective of fair reciprocity in its ideal, comprehensively egalitarian form, from which perspective it is wanting. But we should also judge it from the perspective of where we are today, and by reference to the broader aims of the modern egalitarian movement. Viewed from this perspective creating a society that has enacted the civic minimum, and thereby satisfied the demands of fair reciprocity in its non-ideal form, would be a great achievement. It would be a market society, with some unjust inequality in incomes and wealth. But nevertheless it would be a society of a kind that generations of economic democrats, from Paine onwards, have aspired to: a society of citizens, equal in that they are all free of the proletarian condition, and active in a common labour that is an expression of their mutual respect.

NOTES

Preface

1. See Bernard Crick, 'The Decline of Political Thinking in British Public Life', in Crick, *Essays on Citizenship* (London: Continuum, 2001), 169–89, specifically 189.
2. Jane Lewis, *Pictures of Welfare: An Inaugural Lecture Delivered Before the University of Oxford on 7 June 2001* (Oxford: Oxford University Press, 2001), 4.
3. Andrew Vincent, 'The New Liberalism and Citizenship', in Avital Simhony and David Weinstein (eds.), *The New Liberalism: Reconciling Liberty and Community* (Cambridge: Cambridge University Press, 2001), 205–27, specifically 217. Lewis perceives a similar shift, though she stresses how a conception of individual obligations was built into the operation of post-war social insurance systems. See Lewis, *Pictures of Welfare*, 8–13.

Chapter 1

1. Thomas Paine, 'Agrarian Justice' (1797), in Michael Foot and Isaac D. Kramnick (eds.), *The Thomas Paine Reader* (Harmondsworth: Penguin, 1987), 471–89, specifically 482.
2. Lisa A. Keister, *Wealth in America: Trends in Wealth Inequality* (Cambridge: Cambridge University Press, 2000), 109.
3. See T. H. Marshall, 'Citizenship and Social Class', in Marshall, *Citizenship and Social Class* (Cambridge: Cambridge University Press, 1950), 1–85.
4. Gosta Esping-Andersen, *The Three Worlds of Welfare Capitalism* (Princeton: Princeton University Press, 1990) provides the classic discussion of institutional variation in welfare capitalism.
5. See Ralf Dahrendorf, *Life Chances: Approaches to Social and Political Theory* (Chicago: University of Chicago Press, 1979), esp. 106–21.
6. See, in particular, Michael Harrington, *The Other America: Poverty in the United States* (Baltimore: Penguin, 1962), Anthony Atkinson, *Poverty in Britain and the Reform of Social Security* (Cambridge: Cambridge University Press, 1969), and Peter Townsend, *Poverty in the United Kingdom: A Survey of Household Resources* (Harmondsworth: Penguin, 1979).
7. For an excellent discussion of the forces behind the slowdown and growing distributional conflict, see Philip Armstrong, Andrew Glyn, and John Harrison, *Capitalism since 1945* (Oxford: Blackwell, 1992).

8. See Paul Pierson, *Dismantling the Welfare State* (Cambridge: Cambridge University Press, 1994).

9. See Alissa Goodman, Paul Johnson, and Steven Webb, *Inequality in the UK* (Oxford: Oxford University Press, 1997), 91–4; *Joseph Rowntree Inquiry into Income and Wealth*, vols. i and ii (York: Joseph Rowntree Foundation, 1995), specifically i. 14, fig. 2.

10. See Goodman *et al.*, *Inequality*, 114–34.

11. *Rowntree*, i. 14, fig. 2.

12. For a helpful review, see Richard B. Freeman and Lawrence F. Katz, 'Rising Wage Inequality: The United States vs. Other Advanced Countries', in Richard B. Freeman (ed.), *Working under Different Rules* (New York: Russell Sage Foundation, 1994), 29–62.

13. *Rowntree*, ii. 43, fig. 23.

14. See Freeman and Katz, 'Rising Wage Inequality', 32–3.

15. Keister, *Wealth in America*, p. 64, table 3.2.

16. See *Rowntree*, i. 31, fig. 15; ii. 102–3.

17. See Carey Oppenheim, 'The Growth of Poverty and Inequality', in Alan Walker and Carol Walker (eds.), *Britain Divided: The Growth of Social Exclusion in the 1980s and 1990s* (London: Child Poverty Action Group, 1997), 17–31, specifically 19–21; and *Rowntree*, ii. 32.

18. *Poverty in the United States 1999* (Washington: US Census Bureau, 2000), p. vii, fig. 2.

19. Comparable figures for Germany and France are roughly eleven and six people per thousand. In other EU countries the figures are much lower. See Robert Walker, 'Poverty and Social Exclusion in Europe', in Walker and Walker (eds.), *Britain Divided*, 48–74, specifically 68–9.

20. Someone is judged to be unemployed if they are in the labour force but not in a job; someone is judged to be in non-employment if they are unemployed or out of the labour force.

21. *Rowntree*, i. 14, fig. 2.

22. See Richard Layard, Steve Nickell, and Richard Jackman, *The Unemployment Crisis* (Oxford: Oxford University Press, 1994), specifically 1–10.

23. Edward Balls and Paul Gregg, *Work and Welfare: Tackling the Jobs Deficit* (London: Institute for Public Policy Research, 1993), 7–8.

24. See Christopher Jencks and Paul E. Peterson (eds.), *The Urban Underclass* (Washington: Brookings Institution, 1991), David J. Smith (ed.), *Understanding the Underclass* (London: Policy Studies Institute, 1992), and William Julius Wilson (ed.), *The Ghetto Underclass: Social Science Perspectives* (Newbury Park, Calif.: Sage, 1989).

25. See William Julius Wilson, *The Truly Disadvantaged: The Inner City, the Underclass, and Public Policy* (Chicago: University of Chicago Press, 1987), and *When Work Disappears: The World of the New Urban Poor* (New York: Knopf, 1996). Wilson's analysis is concerned specifically with the black ghetto poor in the urban United States, but his basic theory of isolation and concentration effects producing behavioural

pathology may also have some relevance in understanding the dynamics of disadvantaged communities in Europe.

26. For a helpful account of the emergence of the language of social exclusion and inclusion in Britain in the 1990s, see Ruth Levitas, *The Inclusive Society* (Basingstoke: Macmillan, 1998), esp. 7–28, 128–58.

27. For cogent explanation, see David Miller, 'Why Markets?', in Julian LeGrand and Saul Estrin (eds.), *Market Socialism* (Oxford: Oxford University Press, 1989), 25–49, and John Roemer, *A Future for Socialism* (Cambridge, Mass.: Harvard University Press, 1994), 37–45.

28. Though some qualifications should be made for specific individuals, this seems to me to be the main trajectory of the work of those who have sought to develop and explore an 'analytical Marxism'. For an instructive discussion of where Marxism stands in the wake of the analytical turn, see Erik Olin Wright, 'Marxism after Communism', in Wright, *Interrogating Inequality: Essays on Class Analysis, Socialism and Marxism* (London: Verso, 1994), 234–55.

29. The need for Marxists to pay more explicit attention to the values underpinning socialism is given a materialist explanation in G. A. Cohen, 'Equality: From Fact to Norm', in Cohen, *If You're an Egalitarian, How Come You're So Rich?* (Cambridge, Mass.: Harvard University Press, 2000), 101–15.

30. Exports as a share of gross domestic product (GDP) have steadily increased in the advanced capitalist countries. For example, the share of exports in GDP grew in the United States from 5.8% in 1973 to 6.3% in 1987 and stood at 11.4% in 1997 (as compared with 4.1% in 1913). Comparable figures for the United Kingdom are 11.5%, 15.3%, and 21% (compared with 14.7%); for France, 11.2%, 14.3%, and 21.1% (compared with 6%); and for Germany, 17.2%, 23.7%, and 23.7% (compared with 12.2%). See David Held, Anthony McGrew, David Goldblatt, and Jonathan Perraton, *Global Transformations* (Oxford: Polity Press, 1999), p. 180, table 3.11.

31. For example, the estimated annual turnover of foreign exchange markets increased from US$17.5 trillion in 1979 to around US$300 trillion in 1995. Put another way, the value of such transactions was twelve times the total value of exported goods in the world in 1979, and was sixty times this value in 1995. See Held *et al.*, *Global Transformations*, p. 209, table 4.9.

32. See Paul Pierson, 'Post-Industrial Pressures on the Mature Welfare States', in Pierson (ed.), *The New Politics of the Welfare State* (Oxford: Oxford University Press, 2001), 80–104.

33. Deindustrialization matters, firstly, because it implies a reduction in the rate of productivity growth, and thus in the growth dividend available to fund welfare programmes. It is also widely thought to make increased inequality in wages the price of high employment. See ibid. 83–7.

34. See ibid. 93–4. Pierson also stresses the importance of changes in house-hold structure, such as the growth in single-parent families, which place new demands on the welfare state. Of course, the pattern and pace of demographic change differs across countries.
35. See ibid. 88–92.
36. See Tom Clark and Jayne Taylor, 'Income Inequality in the 1990s: A Tale of Two Cycles?', *Fiscal Studies*, 20/4 (1999), 387–408.
37. *Households below Average Income: 1994/95–1998/9* (London: Government Statistical Service, 2000).
38. The official poverty rate rose in the early years of the decade, but has fallen steadily since then and by 1999 had reached its lowest level for twenty years at 11.8%. See Joseph Dalaker and Bernadette D. Proctor, *Poverty in the United States 1999* (Washington: US Census Bureau, 2000), p. vii, fig. 1.
39. Estimates for the year 1999 put the proportion of people under the age of 18 living below the official poverty line at 16.9%. See ibid., p. vi, table A.
40. See Erik Olin Wright and Rachel Dwyer, 'The American Jobs Machine', *Boston Review*, 25/6 (Dec. 2000–Jan. 2001), 21–6. Wright and Dwyer classify jobs by occupation and sector and take hourly earnings as their measure of job quality. They then group jobs by occupation and sector into ten job-quality deciles and investigate how each has grown from 1992 to 1999. They find that the highest job-quality decile contributed most to overall employment growth, accounting for just over 20% of this growth, but that the second-biggest contributor was the lowest job-quality decile, accounting for 17% of overall employment growth. This pattern contrasts with that of the 1960s (1963–70), when employment growth was concentrated at the top and middle of the job-quality deciles.
41. According to one recent commentary, 'between 1979 and 1999, the average real hourly wage for those with a college degree went up 14 percent. . . . In contrast, average wages for those with only some college fell 4 percent; for those with a high school diploma, 10 percent; and for high school drop-outs, a stunning 24 percent.' See Ruy Teixeira and Joel Rogers, *America's Forgotten Majority: Why the White Working Class Still Matters* (New York: Basic Books, 2000), 12–13.
42. Keister, *Wealth in America*, 65–6.
43. On the distinct role of efficiency, justice, and liberty arguments in defence of laissez-faire capitalism, see G. A. Cohen, 'Freedom, Justice, and Capitalism', in Cohen, *History, Labour, and Freedom: Themes from Marx* (Oxford: Oxford University Press, 1988), 286–304.
44. Robert Nozick, *Anarchy, State, and Utopia* (Oxford: Blackwell, 1974).
45. See ibid. 174–82. What Nozick says is in fact somewhat more ambiguous than this, but the account given here seems the most plausible interpretation of what he means. On this point of interpretation, and for a generally helpful analysis of Nozick's theory of justice in acquisition, see Jonathan

Wolff, *Robert Nozick: Property, Justice and the Minimal State* (Oxford: Polity Press, 1991), 100–15, esp. 112.

46. One must say 'in principle' because, as Nozick recognizes, in real-world capitalist societies the pattern of entitlements is shaped to a great extent by historic acts of theft and expropriation that violate Nozick's own principles of justice in acquisition and transfer. Nozick adds that there should be rectification for these historic violations of people's entitlements, though he does not develop this aspect of his entitlement theory in any detail.

47. It should be noted that Nozick's theory of justice does admit of a very modest welfare right: as said above, the system of property rights as a whole must give each person access to the welfare level he or she would have been able to attain in the baseline world in which all external resources remain unowned. The modesty of this right is worth emphasizing, however: if someone with very limited self-owned powers would likely starve if left to herself in the baseline world, then she has no claim to assistance or compensation if, consistent with justice in acquisition and transfer, she happens to be starving in a private-ownership world. As for those who would likely attain a modest level of welfare in the baseline world, Nozick argues that the efficiency-enhancing effects of private ownership will generally suffice to ensure their access to at least this level of welfare.

48. See Charles Murray, *What it Means to be a Libertarian* (New York: Basic Books, 1996).

49. For an influential recent statement of this view, see Charles Murray, *Losing Ground* (New York: Basic Books, 1984). The classic statement of the dependency critique is Alexis de Tocqueville, *Memoir on Pauperism* (1835), trans. Seymour Drescher (London: Institute for Economic Affairs, 1997).

50. See Friedrich Hayek, *The Constitution of Liberty* (1964; London: Routledge, 1996), esp. 285–305, and Milton Friedman, *Capitalism and Freedom* (Chicago: University of Chicago Press, 1963), esp. 177–95.

51. See Friedman, *Capitalism and Freedom*, 191.

52. See ibid. 196.

53. Friedman, I should add, tends much more towards the former than the latter. In *Capitalism and Freedom* (pp. 191–4) he advocates a modest negative income tax as the best way to alleviate poverty, but makes no mention of conditioning the tax on any kind of work-test.

54. For a detailed and comprehensive critique of Nozick's entitlement theory, see in particular G. A. Cohen, *Self-Ownership, Freedom, and Equality* (Cambridge: Cambridge University Press, 1995).

55. Thus, in the British case, it has been argued that monetarist policy experiments, inspired by the economic theory of the New Right, helped produce mass unemployment in the early 1980s; that deregulation of the labour

market helped produce the growth in earnings inequality; and that a principled hostility to redistribution helps explain why widening earnings inequality was not offset during the 1980s by appropriate changes in tax-benefits policy (but, if anything, was exacerbated by changes intended to make the tax-benefits system less redistributive).

56. In using this term in this context I echo Peter Dwyer. See his *Welfare Rights and Responsibilities: Contesting Social Citizenship* (Bristol: Policy Press, 2000), 72–90. The term 'communitarian' is unfortunate, however, in so far as it naturally suggests a link, which I do not intend, with those philosophers who became associated in the 1980s with the so-called 'communitarian critique of liberalism' such as Alasdair MacIntyre, Michael Sandel, Charles Taylor, and Michael Walzer. While there are some links between this 'philosophical communitarianism' and the 'political communitarianism' with which I am here concerned, the links are quite diffuse and complex and nothing I say here regarding communitarianism should be taken as necessarily applying to the work of the aforementioned philosophers.

57. The key statement of civic conservative thinking on economic citizenship is Lawrence Mead, *Beyond Entitlement: The Social Obligations of Citizenship* (New York: Free Press, 1987).

58. See Tony Blair, *New Britain: My Vision of a Young Country* (London: Fourth Estate, 1996), 236–43.

59. *New Ambitions for our Country: A New Contract for Welfare* (London: HMSO, 1998), Cm. 3805. See esp. p. 80, which offers a summary list of the parallel duties of government and citizen in the welfare sphere.

60. See Mead, *Beyond Entitlement*, and *The New Politics of Poverty: The Nonworking Poor in America* (New York: Basic Books, 1992).

61. See Amitai Etzioni, *The Spirit of Community* (New York: Touchstone Books, 1993), and William Galston, *Liberal Purposes* (Cambridge: Cambridge University Press, 1991). Neither author discusses welfare policy in any depth in these works, but they both defend the general theme of 'balancing rights and responsibilities'.

62. See e.g. Frank Field MP, *Stakeholder Welfare* (London: Institute for Economic Affairs, 1997), and Anthony Giddens, *The Third Way: The Renewal of Social Democracy* (London: Polity Press, 1998), esp. 99–128.

63. See Pierre Rosanvallon, *The New Social Question: Rethinking the Welfare State* (1995), trans. Barbara Harshav (Princeton: Princeton University Press, 2000).

64. These examples are taken from Mead, *The New Politics of Poverty*, 181.

65. See R. H. Tawney, *Equality* (1931; London: Allen & Unwin, 1965), 112–14.

66. John Rawls, *A Theory of Justice* (1971), rev. edn. (Oxford: Oxford University Press, 1999), esp. 65–73. See also John Rawls, *Justice as Fairness: A Restatement* (Cambridge, Mass.: Harvard University Press, 2001), 61–6.

67. See Rawls, *A Theory of Justice*, 64.
68. See Anthony Crosland, 'Socialism Now', in Crosland, *Socialism Now* (London: Jonathan Chapman, 1974), 15–58, specifically 15; Raymond Plant, 'Democratic Socialism and Equality', in David Lipsey and Dick Leonard (eds.), *The Socialist Agenda: Crosland's Legacy* (London: Jonathan Cape, 1981), 135–55; and David Reisland, *Crosland's Future* (Basingstoke: Macmillan, 1997), 103–4. For a view that expresses some reservations about the possible *in*egalitarian implications of Rawls's theory, see Roy Hattersley, *Choose Freedom: The Future of Democratic Socialism* (London: Michael Joseph, 1987), 51–4.
69. Commission on Social Justice, *The Justice Gap* (London: Institute for Public Policy Research, 1993).
70. See ibid. 11–16.
71. See John Gray, 'Goodbye to Rawls', *Prospect*, 24 (Nov. 1997), 8–9. I regard Gray's contrast between Rawls and Hobhouse to be exaggerated, if not altogether misplaced. The meritocratic philosophy described by Gray was certainly one current within the New Liberalism, but there was also an egalitarian current, of which Hobhouse was a representative thinker, and which exerted considerable influence on later socialist thinkers like R. H. Tawney. For an analysis of the differences between meritocratic and egalitarian New Liberalisms, see Marc Stears and Stuart White, 'New Liberalism Revisited', in Henry Tam (ed.), *Progressive Politics in the Global Age* (Oxford: Polity Press, 2001), 36–53.
72. Winston Churchill, 'Liberalism and Socialism', in Churchill, *Liberalism and the Social Problem* (London: Hodder & Stoughton, 1909), 67–84, specifically 82.
73. In the philosophical literature this view is explicitly defended by William Galston in his *Liberal Purposes*, 191–212. As noted above, such a view was also endorsed by the Commission on Social Justice in the early 1990s. It is arguably also implicit in Tony Blair's comments that the left has 'in the past too readily downplayed its duty to promote a wide range of opportunities for individuals to advance themselves and their families', and that 'Talent and effort should be encouraged to flourish in all quarters.' See Tony Blair, *The Third Way: New Politics for a New Century* (London: Fabian Society, 1998), 3.
74. This claim warrants some qualification in so far as some of the writers I have here associated with the communitarian perspective, such as Anthony Giddens, also express concern about the threat to community from the rich effectively opting out of mainstream public services. Communitarians like Giddens seem to want a meritocracy that is constrained both at the bottom and at the very top, though still permitting much talent-based inequality in between. See Anthony Giddens, *The Third Way and its Critics* (Oxford: Polity Press, 2000), esp. 116–20.
75. For criticisms of this kind, see G. A. Cohen, 'Back to Socialist Basics', and Brian Barry, 'The Attractions of Basic Income', in Jane Franklin (ed.),

Equality (London: Institute for Public Policy Research, 1997), 29–48, 157–71.

76. For a general theory of public assistance in capitalist societies as a device for ensuring social order, see Richard Cloward and Frances Fox Piven, *Regulating the Poor: The Functions of Public Welfare*, 2nd edn. (New York: Vintage, 1993).

77. See Dwyer, *Welfare Rights and Responsibilities*, 79–90. Dwyer examines 'communitarian' and 'New Labour' approaches to social policy under different headings, but argues that both have commonalities with the theories of the New Right.

78. See Selma L. Sevenhuijsen, 'Caring in the Third Way: The Relation between Obligation, Responsibility and Care in Third Way Discourse', MS, University of Utrecht, Sept. 1999.

79. For an excellent introduction to the idea of UBI and philosophical issues surrounding the UBI proposal, see Philippe Van Parijs (ed.), *Arguing for Basic Income* (London: Verso, 1992).

80. Philippe Van Parijs, *Real Freedom for All: What (if Anything) Can Justify Capitalism?* (Oxford: Oxford University Press, 1995).

81. See ibid. I shall discuss Van Parijs's main argument for the UBI proposal in Ch. 7.

82. The term 'fair reciprocity' was suggested to me by Joshua Cohen. The term is also used to refer to a conception of justice by Alan Gibbard in 'Constructing Justice', *Philosophy and Public Affairs*, 20 (1991), 264–79. However, while there are some similarities, the conception of justice outlined in this volume under the heading of fair reciprocity is not the same as the conception of justice that Gibbard describes using this term.

83. See Van Parijs, *Real Freedom for All*.

Chapter 2

1. These institutions correspond roughly to what Rawls calls the 'basic structure', and thus include the structure of political authority, the system of criminal law and personal liberties, and rules concerning the acquisition of income and wealth. I have not used Rawls's term here because I believe that these institutions should also be understood to include informal social norms that exert a strong influence on distributive outcomes, but I do not wish here to be drawn into the debate as to whether this is or is not consistent with Rawls's definition of the 'basic structure'. For helpful discussions, see John Rawls, 'The Idea of Public Reason Revisited', in Rawls, *The Law of Peoples* (Cambridge, Mass.: Harvard University Press, 1999), 129–80, esp. 156–64, and G. A. Cohen, 'Where the Action Is: On the Site of Distributive Justice', in Cohen, *If You're an Egalitarian, How Come You're So Rich?* (Cambridge, Mass.: Harvard University Press, 2000), 134–47, esp. 136–42.

2. For a fine literary evocation of this sensibility, see Kazuo Ishiguro, *The Remains of the Day* (London: Faber, 1989).

3. As Rousseau puts it: 'Man is the same in every station in life.... All distinctions of rank fade away before the eyes of a thoughtful person; he sees the same passions, the same feelings in the noble and the guttersnipe...'. See Jean-Jacques Rousseau, *Émile* (1762; London: Everyman, 1993), 223.

4. For a good discussion of the concept of dignity in modern political argument, see Robert E. Goodin, *Political Theory and Public Policy* (Chicago: University of Chicago Press, 1982), 73–94. I do not say, note, that the ideal of democratic mutual regard represents the only elaboration and application of the concept of human dignity.

5. The desire for eminence is perhaps not, on Hobbes's view, inherent in the nature of all human beings, but it is certainly inherent in the nature of enough of them to make the scramble for 'Glory' and 'Reputation' a major source of war in the state of nature. See Thomas Hobbes, *Leviathan* (1651; Harmondsworth: Penguin, 1984), ch. 13, pp. 183–8, esp. 185.

6. For a helpful discussion of the need for status and the ethos of what I have called democratic mutual regard, in the context of an analysis of Rousseau's political philosophy, see Joshua Cohen, 'The Natural Goodness of Humanity', in Andrew Reath, Barbara Herman, and Christine Korsgaard (eds.), *Reclaiming the History of Ethics: Essays for John Rawls* (Cambridge, Mass.: Harvard University Press, 1997), 102–39.

7. Cohen, *If You're an Egalitarian*, 117–47.

8. See John Rawls, *Political Liberalism* (New York: Columbia University Press, 1993), 13, 175.

9. See Michael Walzer, 'Philosophy and Democracy', *Political Theory*, 9 (1981), 379–99.

10. In Rousseau's terms, the aim is to raise democracy from the level of a mere majority will to that of a general will (roughly speaking, a will shared by all and oriented towards the good of all, acknowledged as equals). The statement in the main text also offers one interpretation of the notion of deliberative democracy. For helpful discussion, see Joshua Cohen, 'Deliberation and Democratic Legitimacy', in James Bohman and William Rehg (eds.), *Deliberative Democracy: Essays on Reason and Politics* (Cambridge, Mass.: MIT Press, 1997), 67–91, and Ronald Dworkin, 'Political Equality', in Dworkin, *Sovereign Virtue: The Theory and Practice of Equality* (Cambridge, Mass.: Harvard University Press, 2000), 184–210.

11. It is, in Rousseau's terms, a matter of showing how particular and corporate wills have obscured the content of the general will.

12. For Rawls's understanding of reasonable pluralism, see Rawls, *Political Liberalism*, 36–7. Reasonable pluralism is a pluralism of reasonable comprehensive ethical doctrines, and one feature of a reasonable comprehensive doctrine, as I understand it, is that its proponents, in affirming the doctrine, also affirm the need to find terms of cooperation that

other citizens, conceived as 'free and equal', and similarly reasonable can agree to.

13. In Rawls's terms, they share an interest in being able to frame, revise, and pursue a conception of the good. See Rawls, *Political Liberalism*, 30. The idea that the shared needs of ethical agency can provide the basis for civic morality in a pluralist society is sympathetically discussed in a number of works by Raymond Plant. See, for example, Plant, *Modern Political Thought* (Oxford: Blackwell, 1991), 265–7. See also Alan Gewith, *Human Rights* (Chicago: University of Chicago, 1982), and Len Doyal and Ian Gough, *A Theory of Human Need* (Basingstoke: Macmillan, 1991).

14. For discussion of this issue, see Philip Pettit, *Republicanism: A Theory of Freedom and Government* (Oxford: Oxford University Press, 1997), and Quentin Skinner, *Liberty before Liberalism* (Cambridge: Cambridge University Press, 1998).

15. This is close to what Ronald Dworkin means by 'ethical integrity'. See esp. Dworkin, *Sovereign Virtue*, 270–4. See also Joshua Cohen, 'Freedom of Expression', in David Heyd, *Toleration: An Elusive Virtue* (Princeton: Princeton University Press, 1996), 173–225. The conception of integrity interests I present here owes a good deal to Cohen's account of the expressive and deliberative interests which are protected by the right to freedom of expression. However, Cohen uses the term 'expressive interest' strictly to refer to the citizen's interest in articulating viewpoints and the like, whereas I am using the term to encompass a way that encompasses a broader range of activities.

16. Here I follow Cohen, 'Freedom of Expression', 188, quite closely.

17. In addition to Cohen, ibid., see, Will Kymlicka, *Multicultural Citizenship* (Oxford: Oxford University Press, 1995), 80–2.

18. I am sure this is true, as regards the comprehensive truth about the good life. Perhaps there are specific truths that are beyond reasonable doubt, e.g. that a good life cannot be centred on drug addiction. But any effort to present a list of such truths will very quickly run into reasonable disagreement reflecting what Rawls calls the 'burdens of judgement' ('the many hazards involved in the correct (and conscientious) exercise of our powers of reason and judgement'). See Rawls, *Political Liberalism*, 54–8.

19. The concern to protect deliberative integrity can have controversial implications, e.g. as regards the freedom of parents to raise their children in isolation from exposure to alternative religious and philosophical viewpoints. However, as long as we take the individual as the fundamental unit of concern and respect, some restrictions on this freedom seem justified in order to secure children's interest in developing a competence for deliberation.

20. See Cohen, 'Freedom of Expression', and also my 'Freedom of Association and the Right to Exclude', *Journal of Political Philosophy*, 4 (1997), 373–91.

21. See Amartya Sen, *On Ethics and Economics* (Oxford: Blackwell, 1987), 41.

22. I have warned here against agency-focused reductionism, but we should also be on guard against well-being or welfare reductionisms. For a striking argument against a form of welfare reductionism, see Robert Nozick, *Anarchy, State, and Utopia* (Oxford: Blackwell, 1974), 42–5. The independent importance of agency-based and well-being interests is also discussed, if not in exactly these terms, in G. A. Cohen, 'On the Currency of Egalitarian Justice', *Ethics*, 99 (1989), 906–44, specifically 917–21.

23. See Amartya Sen, *Inequality Reexamined* (Oxford: Oxford University Press, 1992).

24. See my 'Freedom of Association and the Right to Exclude', and my 'Religious Association and Employment Discrimination', available on request from the author.

25. See Ronald Dworkin, 'Equality of Resources', in Dworkin, *Sovereign Virtue*, 65–119, specifically 73–4, and Cohen, 'Currency of Egalitarian Justice'.

26. I do not think that all forms of brute luck disadvantage have the significance necessary to make them proper objects of concern for a theory of justice. See e.g. my comments on brute luck inequalities in esteem in n. 40 below. The foregoing is nevertheless only a provisional list of some types of significant brute luck disadvantage. I will introduce others in the course of the discussion, though these will remain central to much of the analysis.

27. On popular attitudes towards desert and equality, see David Miller, *Principles of Social Justice* (Cambridge, Mass.: Harvard University Press, 2000), 63–73. The evidence presented by Miller suggests that people generally support some mitigation of this kind of inequality, but not anything like full correction for it.

28. For further relevant discussion, see Rawls, *Political Liberalism*, 262–5, Brian Barry, *Justice as Impartiality* (Oxford: Oxford University Press, 1995), 124–5, and Joshua Cohen, 'Structure, Choice, and Legitimacy: Locke's Theory of the State', *Philosophy and Public Affairs*, 15 (1986), 301–24. Rawls and Barry discuss how libertarian theorists tend to take certain institutional commitments as valid and binding prior to any social contract. Cohen discusses how this same feature is exhibited in John Locke's theory of the state, drawing out a contrast with Rousseau's theory, which sees all institutional design, as I do here, as a matter for the collective body of the citizenry animated by an egalitarian conception of the common good.

29. I owe this formulation to G. A. Cohen, *Self-Ownership, Freedom, and Equality* (Cambridge: Cambridge University Press, 1995), 68: 'According to the thesis of self-ownership, each possesses over himself, as a matter of moral right, all those rights that a slaveholder has over a complete chattel slave as a matter of legal right, and he is entitled, morally speaking, to

dispose over himself in the way such a slaveholder is entitled, legally speaking, to dispose over his slave.'

30. See Sect. 4.2 for a discussion of the form such redistribution might take.
31. Nozick, *Anarchy, State, and Utopia*, 169.
32. See in particular Michael Otsuka, 'Self-Ownership and Equality: A Lockean Reconciliation', *Philosophy and Public Affairs*, 27 (1998), 65–92. The gist of this approach is also described, though not endorsed, in G. A. Cohen, 'Are Freedom and Equality Compatible?', in Cohen, *Self-Ownership, Freedom, and Equality*, 92–115.
33. The fullest discussion is Cohen, *Self-Ownership, Freedom, and Equality*. See esp. pp. 209–44.
34. The key article to read on this subject remains Anthony Honoré, 'Ownership', in Honoré, *Making Law Bind* (Oxford: Oxford University Press, 1987), 161–92.
35. See, in particular, John Christman, 'Self-Ownership, Equality, and the Structure of Property Rights', *Political Theory*, 19 (1991), 28–46.
36. See in particular my discussion of wealth transfer taxation in Sect. 8.2.
37. See Miller, *Principles of Social Justice*, 63–73.
38. At least this is the form the desert-based defence of inequality usually takes. For discussion, and attempted rebuttal, of a somewhat different version of this defence, see Dworkin, *Sovereign Virtue*, 325–7.
39. See Miller, *Principles of Social Justice*, 147–8.
40. If, however, it is wrong to distribute income on the basis of talent-based performance, why is it acceptable that certain kinds of social esteem, such as that enjoyed by superior pianists and athletes, be distributed on this basis? This question is posed as a challenge to egalitarian critics of talent-based inequalities by David Miller. (See Miller, *Principles of Social Justice*, 304 n. 32.) Here it is important to emphasize that the egalitarian concern is not to suppress reward for differential talent-based performance for its own sake, but to prevent or correct for significant brute luck disadvantage, and that not all the inequalities in talent-based reward necessarily constitute, or result in, significant brute luck disadvantage. For example, the fact that I have lost out to another citizen every time in an athletic competition, and that my rival has the greater esteem accorded to one who wins gold, rather than silver, medals, need not threaten my essential self-respect, or our sense of equality as citizens, and so arguably does not constitute a brute luck disadvantage of the kind that should be of concern to a theory of justice. Moreover, the esteem some receive as victorious athletes may be balanced by the esteem that others receive as winners in other kinds of contests, and/or by the esteem they receive for social service, political participation, religious activity, conscientious parenting, and so on. (For helpful discussion, see Nozick, *Anarchy, State, and Utopia*, 245–6, and also David Miller, 'Complex Equality', in David Miller and Michael Walzer, *Pluralism, Justice, and Equality* (Oxford: Oxford University Press, 1995), 197–225.) Allowing some spheres of social life to be

characterized by talent-based reward need not result in a worrying overall inequality of social esteem.

41. Another possible response to the objection might be to drop the idea of *compensating* for handicaps in favour of the idea of *preventing* them. But prevention may not be feasible in all cases. Moreover, the idea has ominous eugenic implications that could invite major invasions of individual liberty and/or undermine the civic equality of handicapped and non-handicapped citizens. As explained below, however, my use of the term 'compensation' should be understood to include the provision of therapies and treatments that remove handicaps or directly mitigate their effects.

42. See Ronald Dworkin, 'Equality of Resources', 73–83, 92–104, and, for an extension of the theory to cover justice in health care, see also Dworkin, 'Justice and the High Cost of Health-Care', in *Sovereign Virtue*, 307–19.

43. Note that equality of access to land and capital need not entail giving citizens equal tradeable shares of these assets. See Sects. 7.1 and 7.3 for a discussion of alternative forms of securing access to external assets.

44. Dworkin, 'Equality of Resources', 78–9.

45. For further relevant discussion, see Dworkin, 'Equality of Resources', 100–3.

46. See Robert E. Goodin, 'Exploiting a Person and Exploiting a Situation', in Andrew Reeves (ed.), *Modern Theories of Exploitation* (London: Sage, 1987), 166–200.

47. For relevant discussion, see David Purdy, *Social Power and the Labour Market* (London: Macmillan, 1987), 36–58.

48. See Dilip Hiro, *Black British, White British: A History of Race Relations in Britain* (London: HarperCollins, 1992), 28–9.

49. It is an interesting question whether it is always and necessarily wrong to take advantage of market-based power in this way. An intuition of this sort certainly seems to lie at the heart of the traditional theory of the 'just price', according to which transactors should seek to agree on a price that covers costs of production with a reasonable profit and not take maximum advantage of circumstantial bargaining power. Nevertheless, the injustice of exploitative exchange is surely greater when, as discussed above, the extraction of vulnerability rents exacerbates existing inequality of opportunity. On the just-price doctrine, see William Temple, *Christianity and Social Order* (1942; New York: Seabury Press, 1977), specifically 53.

50. See Thomas Pogge, *Realizing Rawls* (Ithaca, NY: Cornell University Press, 1989), 49.

51. See G. A. Cohen, 'Are Disadvantaged Workers who Take Hazardous Jobs, Forced to Take Hazardous Jobs?', in Cohen, *History, Labour, and Freedom: Themes from Marx* (Oxford: Oxford University Press, 1988), 239–54, esp. 245–9.

52. Exactly where we set this threshold is not something I shall try to specify exactly here, but if we are to stay true to the underlying idea that

an unacceptable alternative is thoroughly bad in an absolute sense, the relevant threshold should be set fairly low.

53. The question of whether you genuinely consent to take the job and of whether you are forced to take it are in my view two different questions. In the situation described here you are, I think, forced to take the shirt-ironing job in view of the absence of an acceptable alternative. This shows, I think, that we can sometimes genuinely consent to do things that we are forced to do.

54. On this point, I am indebted to Pettit, *Republicanism*, esp. 85–7, and Skinner, *Liberty before Liberalism*.

55. John Rawls, *Justice as Fairness: A Restatement* (Cambridge, Mass.: Harvard University Press, 2001), 44–5. I have not explicitly considered what Rawls calls the 'political liberties' here, such as the rights to vote and to run for political office. But I assume throughout that citizens have such liberties, and that the value of such liberties must be protected.

Chapter 3

1. See also Paul Warren, 'Self-Ownership, Reciprocity, and Exploitation; or, Why Marxists shouldn't be Afraid of Robert Nozick', *Canadian Journal of Philosophy*, 24 (1994), 33–56, specifically 50–1. The other conception of reciprocity I discuss below, the fair-dues conception, can be seen as a form of what Warren calls 'asymmetrical reciprocity' (an addition, I think, to the two forms he identifies) in contrast to the 'perfect reciprocity' embodied in the strict-proportionality conception.

2. See Gregory Claeys, *Machinery, Money and the Millennium* (Princeton: Princeton University Press, 1987), and G. D. H. Cole, *Socialist Thought: The Forerunners 1789–1850* (New York: St Martin's Press, 1953), 102–19, 132–9.

3. Karl Marx, *Critique of the Gotha Program* (Peking: Foreign Languages Press, 1976).

4. Ibid. 16.

5. See John Bates Clark, *The Philosophy of Wealth* (1887; New York: Augustus M. Kelley, 1967), and *The Distribution of Wealth* (1899; New York: Augustus M. Kelley, 1965).

6. See Milton Friedman, *Capitalism and Freedom* (Chicago: University of Chicago Press, 1961), 161–76. Friedman believes this principle is ultimately justified, however, only because, so he thinks, it promotes social utility and respects individual liberty.

7. Marx, *Critique of the Gotha Program*, 16.

8. Thomas More, *Utopia* (1516), trans. John Sheehan and John P. Donnelly (Milwaukee: Marquette University Press, 1995), 21, 50.

9. Gerrard Winstanley, *The Law of Freedom and Other Writings* (1653; Harmondsworth: Penguin, 1973).

10. Ibid. 381.

11. I outline and defend this interpretation of Marx in 'Needs, Labour, and Marx's Conception of Justice', *Political Studies*, 44 (1996), 88–101. See also Warren, 'Self-Ownership, Reciprocity, and Exploitation'.

12. See Karl Marx, 'The Civil War in France' (1871), in *Karl Marx: Selected Writings*, ed. David MacLellan (Oxford: Oxford University Press, 1994), 544.

13. See my 'Needs, Labour, and Marx's Conception of Justice', 99–101.

14. See Rosa Luxemburg, 'The Socialisation of Society' (1918), trans. Dave Hollis, <www.marxists.org>, 1999. Lenin and Trotsky strongly emphasized the duty to work, though, of course, they did so in a context of economic emergency during and following civil war. For discussion of Trotsky's work ethic, see Baruch Knei-Paz, *The Social and Political Thought of Leon Trotsky* (Oxford: Oxford University Press, 1978), 262–9. (However, I think I am right in saying that even Paul Lafargue accepted that there would be some basic labour requirement that all citizens would be expected to meet in post-capitalist society. What distinguished his Marxism was his extreme emphasis on, and optimism about, the capacity of public ownership and productivity growth to reduce, dramatically, the length of the working day. For a good discussion of Lafargue, see Leszek Kolakowski, *Main Currents of Marxism*, ii: *The Golden Age* (Oxford: Oxford University Press, 1978), 141–50.)

15. Robert Tressell, *The Ragged Trousered Philanthropists* (1914; London: Flamingo/HarperCollins, 1993).

16. See ibid. 250–85, and, for the quoted passage, specifically p. 275.

17. John Stuart Mill, *Autobiography* (1873; Harmondsworth: Penguin, 1989), 175.

18. For example, in his influential book *Liberalism* (1911), Hobhouse writes that 'The central point of Liberal economics . . . is the equation of social service and reward. This is the principle that every function of social value requires such remuneration as serves to stimulate and maintain its effective performance; that every one who performs such a function has the right, in the strict ethical sense of that term, to such remuneration and to no more . . . Further, it is the right, in the same sense, of every person capable of performing some useful social function that he should have the opportunity of so doing . . .'. See *Liberalism and Other Writings*, ed. James Meadowcroft (Cambridge: Cambridge University Press, 1993), 100. For a fuller discussion of this functionalist theory of distributive justice in the writings of Hobhouse and Hobson, see Marc Stears and Stuart White, 'New Liberalism Revisited', in Henry Tam (ed.), *Progressive Politics in the Global Age* (Oxford: Polity Press, 2001), 36–53.

19. See R. H. Tawney, *The Acquisitive Society* (1920; New York: Harcourt Brace Jovanovich, 1948), 52–83. For a discussion of similar ideas about social justice in guild socialist circles, see Marc Stears, 'Guild Socialism and

Ideological Diversity on the British Left, 1914–1926', *Journal of Political Ideologies*, 3 (1998), 289–306.

20. See Henry George, *Poverty and Progress* (1885; New York: Robert Schackenbach Foundation, 1962). Mill was chair of the Land Tenure Reform Association, which sought in the 1870s to prevent the privatization of common land and to impose a tax on the 'unearned increment' to land values caused by economic development. See John Stuart Mill, 'The Right of Property in Land' (1873), in *The Collected Works of John Stuart Mill.*, ed. Ann P. Robson and John M. Robson, xxv: *Newspaper Writings* (Toronto: University of Toronto Press, 1987), 1235–43.

21. See Harold Laski, *The Grammar of Politics* (London: Allen & Unwin, 1925), 184.

22. C. A. R. Crosland, *The Future of Socialism* (New York: Macmillan, 1957), 208.

23. John Rawls, *A Theory of Justice* (1971), rev. edn. (Oxford: Oxford University Press, 1999).

24. Ibid. 65–73.

25. See Richard Musgrave, 'Maximin, Uncertainty, and the Leisure Trade-Off', *Quarterly Journal of Economics*, 88 (1974), 625–32.

26. See John Rawls, *Justice as Fairness: A Restatement* (Cambridge, Mass.: Harvard University Press, 2001), 179. See also John Rawls, 'Reply to Alexander and Musgrave', *Quarterly Journal of Economics*, 88 (1974), 633–55.

27. Rawls, *Justice as Fairness*, 179.

28. See John Rawls, *Political Liberalism* (New York: Columbia University Press, 1993), 181–2 n. 9.

29. If we say, with Rawls, that Malibu surfers enjoying the full sixteen hours' leisure are as well off as those in work enjoying the level of income of the worst-off group, then we have to conclude that the surfers are also made better off should the income of those in work increase owing, say, to some technological breakthrough. But it is odd to say this given that the Malibu surfers will be entitled to no more income, and will have only the same amount of leisure, as before. See Philippe Van Parijs, *Real Freedom for All: What (if Anything) Can Justify Capitalism?* (Oxford: Oxford University Press, 1995), 98, also 131–2.

30. Rawls, *Justice as Fairness*, 179.

31. J. A. Hobson, *The Social Problem* (1902; Bristol: Thoemmes Press, 1996), 112–21, specifically 118, 121. The same basic idea can also be found in the work of John Locke, according to whom we ought 'to look upon it is as a mark of goodness in God that he has put us in this life under a necessity of labour', for it is 'a benefit even to the good and the virtuous, which are thereby preserved from the ills and idleness or the diseases that attend constant study in a sedentary life'. See John Locke, 'Labour', in *John Locke: Political Writings*, ed. David Wootton (Harmondsworth: Penguin, 1993), 440–2, specifically 440.

32. See Lawrence Becker, *Reciprocity* (London: Routledge & Kegan Paul, 1986), 83–4, 354–5, for discussion of this link.

33. Rawls, *A Theory of Justice*, 386–91.

34. See esp. Lawrence Mead, *The New Politics of Poverty: The Nonworking Poor in America* (New York: Basic Books, 1992).

35. This is, of course, only one of the two characteristics of a pure public good. The other is non-rivalry: roughly, that one person's consumption of the good does not reduce the opportunity of others to consume it.

36. And, one should add, on one's capacity to contribute *without threat to core well-being*. For one might be strictly capable of working, say, and yet afflicted so that one is filled with acute pain the moment one starts to work.

37. It has been suggested that individuals need not make a productive contribution, i.e. produce goods or services, in return for a share of the social product because simple non-interference with producers, mere respect for their right to deploy their property productively, warrants reciprocation in the form of a share of their product. This is, however, an unpromising line of argument. To see why, consider the following case. Edward and Freda are the sole inhabitants of a territory of which each has been allotted an equal share. Unworked, each allotment of land generates a weekly output of *l* leeks. Edward is happy to live off *l*, doing no work. Freda works her allotment, producing an additional leek output of *s*. According to the proposal, Freda owes Edward some fraction of *s* in view of Edward's non-interference with her property rights. But if this is so, then surely Edward also owes Freda an equivalent in reciprocation for *her* respect for his property rights (for she did not interfere when he chose to lie down and listen to the breeze in the grass, any more than he interfered when she chose to cultivate her allotment). So no net transfer of product from Freda to Edward is justified, even if we were to accept the premiss that non-interference warrants reciprocation in the form of resources. More fundamentally, however, I do not see why non-interference is something that Freda (or Edward) should have to pay for out of their respective resource bundles. Fitting and proportionate reciprocation for others' non-interference with you and yours is, I suggest, simply non-interference with them and theirs. I am grateful to Joshua Cohen for discussion of this point.

38. As van Donselaar puts it, 'a parasitic . . . relation exists between two persons A and B if in virtue of that relation A is worse off than she would have been had B not existed or if she would have nothing to do with him, while B is better off than he would have been without A, or having nothing to do with her—or vice versa'. See Gijs van Donselaar, *The Benefit of Another's Pains: Parasitism, Scarcity, Basic Income* (Amsterdam: University of Amsterdam, 1997), 3; see also pp. 15–66 for an extended analysis of parasitism so defined. A revised version of this book is forthcoming with Oxford University Press. As will become clear in later chapters—see esp.

Ch. 7—I have learned a great deal from van Donselaar's work (though perhaps still not enough). See also David Gauthier, *Morals by Agreement* (Oxford: Oxford University Press, 1986) especially pp. 96–7.

39. Becker, *Reciprocity*.
40. Ibid. 89, 82.
41. Ibid. 105–6.
42. Ibid. 133.
43. Ibid. 163–72.
44. See Lawrence Becker, 'The Obligation to Work', *Ethics*, 91 (1980), 35–49. Becker here argues against the view that there ought to be an enforceable obligation to work for all citizens, but that it is legitimate to enforce work specifically in return for what he characterizes (problematically in my view) as 'special benefits', which include welfare payments. I shall return to some of the arguments of this interesting article in Ch. 5.
45. Because reciprocity's 'purpose is to sustain mutually advantageous exchanges ... Balanced *benefits* ... must be the leading concern' (Becker, *Reciprocity*, 112).
46. Ibid. 112–13.
47. Ibid. 106.
48. Ibid.
49. Ibid. 107.
50. See ibid. 346–54, 355–9.
51. See ibid. 81.
52. I am much indebted here to Rawls's discussion of stability in *A Theory of Justice*. According to Rawls, 'A conception of justice is stable when the public recognition of its realization by the social system tends to bring about the corresponding sense of justice' (ibid. 154). According to Rawls, a key requirement for stability is that, under the relevant conception of justice, we can see clearly that others are committed to our good: that they are required to make an effort to benefit us, as we are called upon to do things which promote their good. Utilitarianism fails this test, and so on grounds of stability, Rawls argues, must be rejected in favour of his alternative conception of justice.
53. Karl Widerquist, for example, floats this idea in his fine essay on the exploitation objection to unconditional basic income. 'If one defines exploitation as one person taking advantage of privileges that are unavailable to another,' he writes, 'we cannot say that the person who lives solely off a basic income [an unconditional income grant available as of right to all] exploits anyone. ... An unconditional guaranteed income applies the same rules to everyone, thereby conforming to reciprocity. ...'. See Karl Widerquist, 'Reciprocity and the Guaranteed Income', *Politics and Society*, 27 (1999), 387–402, specifically 395, 400.
54. See Garrett Cullity, 'Moral Free-Riding', *Philosophy and Public Affairs*, 24 (1995), 3–34, esp. 22–3.

55. In Gijs van Donselaar's words, '*Equalizing* the opportunities for foul play is not the same thing as *removing* them. Perhaps it makes the game somewhat fairer but it doesn't make the game as it ought to be.' See van Donselaar, *Benefit of Another's Pains*, 187.

56. See John Roemer, *A General Theory of Exploitation and Class* (Cambridge, Mass.: Harvard University Press, 1982), 'Should Marxists be Interested in Exploitation?', in Roemer (ed.), *Analytical Marxism* (Cambridge: Cambridge University Press, 1986), 260–82, and *Free to Lose: An Introduction to Marxist Economic Philosophy* (London: Radius/Century Hutchinson, 1988).

57. One might hold that unequal asset endowments is itself of ultimate significance, from the standpoint of justice, or that the welfare inequality produced by asset inequality is in fact what fundamentally matters. Roemer's view is the latter, but his work nevertheless helps us assess the alternative, resourcist view that asset inequality per se is what fundamentally matters. I briefly consider the relationship between reciprocity and welfare egalitarianism below.

58. See John Roemer, 'Second Thoughts on Property Relations and Exploitation', in Roemer, *Egalitarian Perspectives* (Cambridge: Cambridge University Press, 1994), 104–11, esp. 108–10.

59. For helpful discussion, see also van Donselaar, *Benefit of Another's Pains*, 134–6.

60. On equal opportunity for welfare, see Richard Arneson, 'Equality and Equal Opportunity for Welfare', *Philosophical Studies*, 54 (1988), 79–95.

61. A cautious welfare-egalitarian argument for a qualified form of the reciprocity principle is made by Richard Arneson in 'Is Work Special? Justice and the Distribution of Employment', *American Political Science Review*, 84 (1990), 1121–41. But Arneson takes a more critical view of the demand for reciprocity in his 'Egalitarianism and the Undeserving Poor', *Journal of Political Philosophy*, 5 (1997), 327–50.

62. This case also suggests to me that the concern with reciprocity is not fundamentally reducible to a concern to maximize aggregate utility. Imagine, for example, that the effect of Jim's cooking the meal for Joanne is to reduce his welfare level to twenty-six utils (from thirty), while raising Joanne's to thirty-three and a half utils (from thirty). In this variant of the example, aggregate social utility falls as a result of the reciprocation since the cost to Jim outweighs the gain to Joanne. Nevertheless, I think Jim is still obliged to cook the meal: the fact that the benefit he can produce for Joanne is less than the modest cost to himself does not, in my view, necessarily mean that he is no longer under an obligation to provide this benefit. This is not to imply, of course, that in practice, and on the whole, societies with strong reciprocity ethics, and institutions that respect and reinforce these ethics, will not enjoy higher levels of aggregate utility than those that do not.

63. A subtle welfare egalitarian might argue that if such unhappiness is felt, and is factored into the analysis, reciprocity will serve to push welfare levels closer to equality. But this of course raises the question why someone in Jim's position should feel unhappy at non-reciprocation in the first place. If he is simply and reductively a thoroughgoing welfare egalitarian, he should not feel, in the circumstances as originally described, any unhappiness about living off Joanne's labours.

64. Utilitarians sometimes argue that we should always keep our promises because, while we can always identify specific situations in which promise-breaking will generate greater utility than promise-keeping, a world in which promises are kept will nevertheless enjoy higher long-term utility than a world in which people decide to keep or break promises based on which they think, in their situation, will produce the most utility. Could a welfare egalitarian argue, on similar lines, for a general practice of reciprocation? While in some instances reciprocation is welfare-disequalizing, perhaps a world in which reciprocation is generally practised will produce greater long-term welfare equality than one in which people decide in each instance whether reciprocation or non-reciprocation most conduces to welfare equality. Developing an argument along these lines is one way a welfare egalitarian might try to accommodate 'common-sense' ideas about reciprocity that, at first sight, do not seem consistent with strict welfare egalitarianism. But such an argument does stand in need of further development, for it is far from self-evident that a world in which people generally practise reciprocation will generate more welfare equality than one in which people reciprocate only when, in the given situation, they think it likely to be welfare-equalizing.

65. See Elizabeth Anderson, 'What is the Point of Equality?', *Ethics*, 109 (1999), 297–8. Anderson refers us in particular to Erik Rakowski, *Equal Justice* (New York: Oxford University Press, 1991), 109.

66. I also think that some of the ideas generated in the 'luck-egalitarian' literature, in particular Dworkin's model of the hypothetical insurance market, have a key role to play in helping us decide what kinds of care work should be regarded as contributions satisfying the demands of reciprocity. See Sect. 5.2.

67. In using the term 'pure gamble', I mean to refer to games of pure chance, as opposed, say, to productive endeavours that carry an element of risk. Buying a lottery ticket exemplifies what I mean by a pure gamble; setting up a new bike shop on the Cowley Road in Oxford, though a risky undertaking, does not.

68. Admittedly, the lottery millionaire may be objectionable not *only* from the standpoint of reciprocity. Someone who thinks that justice demands equality of outcomes, where outcomes are measured in terms of income or wealth, will also regard lottery millionairedom as unjust. But then presumably she would also have to regard the income inequality between

the lazy and the hard-working, for example, as unjust. The reciprocity-based objection to lottery millionairedom does not have this questionable implication, and is, therefore, perhaps a better explanation of what is wrong with such millionairedom.

69. Though perhaps there could be law requiring lottery millionaires to go on working even if they are rich enough not to feel the need to.

70. On the idea of a fair slavery gamble, see G. A. Cohen, *Self-Ownership, Freedom, and Equality* (Oxford: Oxford University Press, 1995), 21, 241–2.

71. Here I follow Anderson, 'What is the Point of Equality?', 287–337, specifically 319: 'Kant would put the point as follows: every individual has a worth or dignity that is not conditional upon anyone's desires or preferences, not even the individual's own desires. This implies that there are some things one may never do to other people, such as enslave them, even if one has their permission or consent.'

72. It does not necessarily follow from this claim that gambling should be banned. In some cases, it is on balance advisable to permit activities even though the results of these activities are unjust, and this may be one such case. Perhaps the main justice-related concerns over gambling would anyway be satisfied merely by putting legal restrictions on the size of winnings. Or perhaps, as intimated in n. 69, lottery winners could be required by law to continue to make a productive contribution even though they are rich enough not to need to work.

73. See Ronald Dworkin, *Sovereign Virtue: The Theory and Practice of Equality* (Cambridge, Mass.: Harvard University Press, 2000), 291–6.

74. Of course, many people who play the lottery in societies like our own are people who have not received a fair deal to start with from their society. It is perfectly understandable that people wish to elevate themselves above the nexus of reciprocation if reciprocity means, for them, a life of drudgery in return for a meagre income. Nevertheless, what they should be doing is struggling to make the terms of reciprocation fairer for all, not seeking to elevate themselves into a position in which they get to lord it over the drudges.

75. A critic might object: 'But this begs the question. Perhaps we only want people to have reciprocity-respecting preferences because we want them to act so as to preserve equal opportunity for welfare.' This, however, does not explain what is objectionable about the desire to be a lottery millionaire. Having and acting on such a desire is quite compatible with a concern to see that all have equal opportunity for welfare.

76. Other instrumental arguments, not explored here, might focus on how reciprocity-friendly policies and institutions increase efficiency or produce higher social utility in the long term. For example, such policies may be better in some way for creating 'social capital', e.g. in the form of stronger bonds of trust between citizens, which, in turn, may

help solve other coordination problems in economic and wider social life.

77. See Samuel Bowles and Herbert Gintis, 'Is Egalitarianism Passé? Homo Reciprocans and the Future of Egalitarian Politics', *Boston Review*, 23 (Dec.–Jan. 1998–9), 4–10.

78. As Bowles and Gintis put it (ibid. 8), 'Strong reciprocity . . . allows groups to engage in common practices without resort to costly and often ineffective hierarchical authority, and thereby vastly increases the repertoire of social experiments capable of diffusing through cultural and genetic competition. The relevant traits may be transmitted genetically and proliferate under the influence of natural selection, or they may be transmitted culturally through learning from elders and age-mates and proliferate because successful groups tend to absorb failing groups or be emulated by them.'

79. See Bo Rothstein, *Just Institutions Matter: The Moral and Political Logic of the Universal Welfare State* (Cambridge: Cambridge University Press, 1998), 136–43, 163–70.

80. Becker refers us to some of the relevant literature, in particular to Lila Krishnan and David W. Carment, 'Reactions to Help: Reciprocity, Responsibility and Reactance', *European Journal of Psychology*, 9 (1979), 435–9. See Becker, *Reciprocity*, 359. For an overview of the relevant literature, see also C. Daniel Batson, 'Altruism and Prosocial Behavior', *The Handbook of Social Psychology*, 4th edn. (New York: McGraw-Hill, 1998), 282–316, esp. 288–9, 298.

Chapter 4

1. (London: Modern Press, 1885.)

2. In answering this question here I draw on a lengthier discussion of the question in 'The Egalitarian Earnings Subsidy Scheme', *British Journal of Political Science*, 29 (1999), 601–22.

3. More exactly, one might express s_i as the difference between the societally average peak-ability wage rate and the individual's peak-ability wage rate, divided by the individual's peak-ability wage rate.

4. The ethical properties of ESS are also helpfully discussed in depth in Frank Vandenbroucke, *Social Justice and Individual Ethics in an Open Society* (Berlin: Springer, 2001), 49–56, 127–9, and in Loek Groot and Robert van der Veen, 'Basic Income versus Working Subsidies: An Assessment of the Vandenbroucke Model', paper presented at the conference 'Are Jobs Goods or Bads? Ethical Problems and Employment', University of Ghent, 16 Feb. 2001.

5. See Ronald Dworkin, 'Equality of Resources', in Dworkin, *Sovereign Virtue: The Theory and Practice of Equality* (Cambridge, Mass.: Harvard University Press, 2000), 65–119, specifically 89–90, and Philippe Van Parijs, *Real Freedom for All* (Oxford: Oxford University Press, 1995),

60–5. See also John Rawls's argument that 'head taxes' (taxes based on earnings potential) would violate the 'priority of liberty' in Rawls, *Justice as Fairness: A Restatement* (Cambridge, Mass.: Harvard University Press, 2001), 157–8. As with the slavery of the talented objection I think Rawls's argument on this point fails to take account of the distinction between ESS and lump-sum tax–subsidy arrangements.

6. For example, returning once more to the case depicted in Fig. 4.1, Alf could choose under the lump-sum scheme to take an intrinsically challenging job at 50% of his peak-ability wage rate and still end up with an after-tax income of £27,500 per year. But if Betty took a similarly challenging job at 50% of her peak-ability wage rate, she would end up with an after-tax income of exactly £0—she would only just pay off her lump-sum tax liability of £40,000 per year. To attain the same level of after-tax income as Alf attains over a full working year when he works at 50% of his peak-ability wage rate, she cannot in fact afford to take a job below 84% of her peak-ability wage rate. Thus, Betty's opportunity to trade off income for self-realization, by working in more challenging jobs below her peak-ability wage rate, is much more limited than Alf's.

7. The talented and the untalented are thus both free to take jobs below their peak-ability wage rates if they find lower-paid jobs more satisfying, but, for any given level of voluntary underemployment (employment at a given percentage below their respective peak-ability wage rates), they can expect the same reduction in final income. To go back to the example in the previous note, if Alf takes a really satisfying job at 50% of his peak-ability wage rate under ESS, he will end up with £20,000 if he works a full year in that job. If Betty takes a similarly satisfying job at 50% of her peak-ability wage rate, then under ESS she too will end up with this level of after-tax income if she works the same length of time.

8. See Vandenbroucke, *Social Justice and Individual Ethics*, 60–88. Vandenbroucke acknowledges also that even if the state could in principle access relevant information, other considerations of justice may rule out actually gathering and making use of it in the design of a system of egalitarian redistribution.

9. This point is emphasized by Vandenbroucke, ibid. 51–2, and is acknowledged in White, 'Egalitarian Earnings Subsidy Scheme', 617–18.

10. See John Stuart Mill, 'Chapters on Socialism', in Stefan Collini (ed.), *On Liberty and Other Writings* (Cambridge: Cambridge University Press, 1989), 221–79, specifically 271.

11. See esp. Joseph Carens, *Equality, Moral Incentives, and the Market* (Chicago: University of Chicago Press, 1981), and T. Martin Wilkinson, *Freedom, Efficiency and Equality* (Basingstoke: Palgrave, 2000). Carens envisages a social order in which individuals act on a social duty to maximize pre-tax earnings, while the state taxes market incomes at 100% and distributes the funds back to individuals on an egalitarian basis. Wilkinson argues this will result in an inefficient level of work. He proposes an

alternative duty: to respond to market options as one thinks one would if one could keep all the income concerned—though the income will in fact be redistributed. If not informationally demanding in the way ESS is, this is *imaginatively* demanding. Can people who are not actually going to receive the income attached to specific jobs make sufficiently vivid in their minds the question of how desirable a given job would be if they could keep this income?

12. One must say 'roughly corresponds' because few socialist thinkers have tried to elaborate in any detail just what the principle of distribution according to need entails. But the idea of distributive arrangements that correct for brute luck inequality in wealth and talent and offer appropriate compensation for handicaps, i.e. arrangements that are comprehensively egalitarian, arguably offers the best interpretation of this needs principle.

13. See e.g. the 1851 programme of the British Chartist movement. Among other things the programme called for the 'nationalization of the land', 'national, secular, gratuitous compulsory education', 'the State to open a Credit Fund for advancing money to bodies of working men desirous of associating together for industrial purposes', and 'the right of the poor to substantial relief when out of employment, and to be employed where possible on the land'. See David Jones, *Chartism and the Chartists* (London: Allen Lane, 1975), 172–3.

14. Karl Marx, *Capital* (1865), vol. i (Harmondsworth: Penguin, 1990), 762–870.

15. 'Time for education, for intellectual development, for the fulfilment of social functions, for social intercourse, for the free play of the vital forces of his body and mind, even the rest time of Sunday . . . what foolishness! . . . in its blind and measureless drive, its insatiable appetite for surplus labour, capital oversteps not only the moral but even the merely physical limits of the working day. It usurps the time for growth, development and healthy maintenance of the body. It steals the time required for the consumption of fresh air and sunlight' (ibid. 375–6).

16. See e.g. Marx's indignant account of the death of Mary Anne Walkley (ibid. 364–5).

17. In Marx's words, 'these newly freed men [from serfdom] became sellers of themselves only after they had been robbed of their own means of production, and all the guarantees of existence afforded by the old feudal arrangements. And this history, the history of their expropriation, is written in the annals of mankind in letters of blood and fire' (ibid. 875). On the process of primitive accumulation, see ibid. 873–904.

18. See Philip Pettit, *Republicanism: A Theory of Freedom and Government* (Oxford: Oxford University Press, 1997), and Quentin Skinner, *Liberty before Liberalism* (Cambridge: Cambridge University Press, 1998).

19. Pettit, *Republicanism*, 85–6.

20. See Michael Sandel, *Democracy's Discontent: America in Search of a Public Philosophy* (Cambridge, Mass.: Harvard University Press, 1996), 168–200. One critic, E. L. Godkin, expressed the concern as follows: 'no man whose bread and that of his children are dependent on the will of any other man, or who has no interest in his work except to please an employer, fulfills these conditions [of self-government]; a farmer of his own land does fulfill them. He is the only man, as society is presently constituted in almost all civilized countries, who can be said to be really master of himself' (ibid. 187).

21. Two obvious points of reference here are Marx's early writings and the writings of William Morris. See Karl Marx, 'Estranged Labour', in *Economic and Philosophical Manuscripts of 1844* (London: Lawrence & Wishart, 1977), 61–74, and William Morris, 'Useful Work versus Useless Toil' (1888), in Morris, *Signs of Change* (London: Longmans, Green, 1903), 141–73.

22. See Dworkin, *Sovereign Virtue*, 237–84.

23. It is compatible with this goal that individuals spend some period of their working life on jobs that offer no opportunity for self-realization. But individuals should not be trapped in such employment. It should constitute at most a temporary stage of working life that the citizen of average effort and prudence is able to leave behind, should she wish to do so.

24. For example, a slave who escapes her master may legitimately steal food from the master class without offering a return, but she is also obliged to help her fellow slaves in a collective struggle for freedom.

25. I assume, of course, that such an ethos would be informed and appropriately constrained by an acceptance of whatever departures from strict equality are justified in the first manner described here, e.g. by the concern to preserve a limited freedom to transfer resources between family members as an expression of familial love.

26. In other words, I think the legitimacy of educational privilege and inequality in inherited wealth is more controversial in such countries than the legitimacy of differential reward to people with unequal talents. For insightful discussion of why people might regard the latter as more legitimate than the former, see Thomas Nagel, *Equality and Partiality* (Oxford: Oxford University Press, 1991), 96–119.

27. Note that maximining talent-based inequalities is much more difficult. What has to be maximined is not earnings but earnings potential and, as I explained in Sect. 4.1.2, it is very hard to make accurate assessments of people's earnings potentials.

28. This proposal corresponds to what I call semi-ideal fair reciprocity. See Sect. 5.4.

29. See my discussion of Bruce Ackerman and Anne Alstott's proposal for a childhood privilege tax in Sect. 7.5.2.

30. Or, in terms of John Roemer's theory of exploitation, fair reciprocity in its non-ideal form aspires to eliminate capitalist exploitation based

on unequal access to external wealth, but only to mitigate somewhat socialist exploitation, based on inequality of skills. See John Roemer, *Free to Lose: An Introduction to Marxist Economic Philosophy* (London: Radius/Century Hutchinson, 1988), 131–43.

31. See Jeremy Waldron, 'Homelessness and the Issue of Freedom', in Waldron, *Liberal Rights* (Cambridge: Cambridge University Press, 1993), 309–38, specifically 313–15, and 457 n. 8.

32. For helpful discussion of this issue, see Brian Barry, 'Sustainability and Intergenerational Justice', in Andrew Dobson (ed.), *Fairness and Futurity: Essays on Environmental Sustainability and Social Justice* (Oxford: Oxford University Press, 1999), 93–117.

Chapter 5

1. The purpose and import of the qualifier 'roughly speaking' will be explained in my discussion of housework at the end of Sect. 5.2.

2. Lawrence Becker, *Reciprocity* (London: Routledge & Kegan Paul, 1987), 107. I should add that Becker is sceptical of the project I undertake in this chapter. In his paper 'The Obligation to Work', *Ethics*, 91 (1980), 35–49, Becker argues that the notion of 'socially useful work' is too 'fuzzy' to ground a generally enforceable obligation to work.

3. For further discussion of this issue, see my 'The Egalitarian Earnings Subsidy Scheme', *British Journal of Political Science*, 29 (1999), 601–22, esp. 612–14. But see also the qualifications entered in Sect. 5.3 below.

4. On prostitution, see Debra Satz, 'Markets in Women's Sexual Labor', *Ethics*, 106 (1996), 63–85; on pornography, see Catherine MacKinnon, *Toward a Feminist Theory of the State* (Cambridge, Mass.: Harvard University Press, 1989), 195–214. I cite these articles because they offer arguments in support of the claims referred to in the text, but I do not necessarily endorse their conclusions.

5. For a useful overview of problems of state failure relating to bureaucratic expansionism and interest group capture, see Dennis C. Mueller, *Public Choice II* (Cambridge: Cambridge University Press, 1989), 229–73.

6. The analytical distinction, while presentationally convenient, may not map onto a complete separation in practice. For example, the provision of merit goods, such as health care and education, may also have a public-goods dimension to the extent that the supply of such goods creates positive externalities that are non-excludable and non-rival in kind.

7. David Miller, *Principles of Social Justice* (Cambridge, Mass.: Harvard University Press, 2000), 196.

8. See Sect. 2.4. For Dworkin's own, original version of the hypothetical insurance market device, see Ronald Dworkin, 'Equality of Resources', in Dworkin, *Sovereign Virtue: The Theory and Practice of Equality*

(Cambridge, Mass.: Harvard University Press, 2000), 65–119, specifically 77–83 (handicaps insurance), 92–104 (underemployment insurance).

9. Dworkin, *Sovereign Virtue*, 78.

10. See Ronald Dworkin, 'Justice and the High Cost of Health', ibid. 307–19.

11. Of course, I am assuming here that there is a high degree of unanimity *within* each community with respect to the merit goods it prefers. If there is not, then the tyranny of the majority problem reappears as a problem internal to each community.

12. For fuller accounts of the efficient level of public-goods provision, see Hal Varian, *Intermediate Microeconomics* (New York: Norton, 1987), 570–2, and Richard Cornes and Todd Sandler, *The Theory of Externalities, Public Goods, and Club Goods* (Cambridge: Cambridge University Press, 1986), 69–76.

13. Miller, *Principles of Social Justice*, 196.

14. Ibid.

15. Ibid.

16. One possible problem (certainly, a complication) with the approach I have suggested concerns the interdependency of decisions about merit and public-goods provision. It is tempting to proceed by taking each merit and public good in turn, asking for each good what level of output is implied by the choices of an averagely prudent person in a market of the imagined kind. But this would be mistaken. For the choice made in relation to one good affects the resources available in making choices over other goods. We will need to think about how the decision made by a prudent insurer in one context (say, health care) will constrain, and so influence, her decision in another context (say, police services). Taking account of this interdependency complicates the approach, however, and certainly reduces the reliability of the intuitions we might have about appropriate levels of provision when specific merit and public goods are considered in isolation. Parenthetically, I am not sure that Dworkin takes sufficient account of this problem of interdependency in his own applications of the hypothetical insurance market approach. See Dworkin, *Sovereign Virtue*, 307–50, 427–52.

17. This claim may need some qualification, for I suppose it is possible that the average member of the community might turn out to be indifferent as between two (or more) packages of provision that she prefers over all others.

18. On deliberative opinion polls, see James Fishkin, *The Voice of the People* (New Haven: Yale University Press, 1995). For an outline of another version of deliberative democratization, in which citizens wield direct control over policy, see Joshua Cohen and Charles Sabel, 'Directly-Deliberative Polyarchy', *European Law Journal*, 3 (1997), 313–42.

19. Leonard T. Hobhouse, *Liberalism and Other Writings*, ed. James Meadowcroft (Cambridge: Cambridge University Press, 1993), 87.

20. See William Beveridge, *Social Insurance and Allied Services* (London: HMSO, 1942), esp. p. 53, para. 117, where Beveridge, trying to square the payment of social insurance benefits to the wives and widows of employed men with the 'contributory principle' (the principle that benefits should follow contributions to the social insurance scheme), argues that housewives are 'contributors in kind if not in cash'. For a fascinating discussion of how Beveridge grappled with the status of women and care work under social insurance, in consultation with many feminist organizations of the time, see José Harris, *William Beveridge* (Oxford: Oxford University Press, 1997), 392–8.

21. See Gosta Esping-Andersen, *The Three Worlds of Welfare Capitalism* (Princeton: Princeton University Press, 1990), esp. 9–34, 144–61, 191–217, and *Social Foundations of Postindustrial Economies* (Oxford: Oxford University Press, 1999), esp. 170–84.

22. Unless, of course, you inherit assets that enable you to live without working. I discuss the status of such assets in Sect. 5.4.

23. See Mona Harrington, *Care and Equality* (New York: Alfred Knopf, 1999), 30.

24. Paula Casal and Andrew Williams argue that where procreation causes a public bad, by worsening resource scarcities, it may be legitimate in principle to tax, rather than subsidize, those who have children. See Paula Casal and Andrew Williams, 'Rights, Equality and Procreation', *Analyse und Kritik*, 17 (1995), 93–116.

25. For a very helpful discussion that echoes much of the argument of this section, see Linda C. McClain, 'Citizenship Begins at Home: The New Social Contract and Working Families', in Henry Tam (ed.), *Progressive Politics in the Global Age* (Oxford: Polity Press, 2001), 95–107.

26. I thus agree with Casal and Williams that reciprocity-based arguments for financial support to parents lose force unless parents have this sort of self-conscious commitment to the wider public goods generated by parenting. See Casal and Williams, 'Rights, Equality and Procreation', 103–7, esp. 106.

27. The issue of accountability has been raised by Lawrence Mead in a discussion of the contributive status of care work. Mead cites an official running a US federal welfare programme in the 1980s who, in interview with Mead, said that he regarded mothers on welfare as federal employees paid to do the job of raising their children. Mead comments that he found the description misleading because the mothers in question were not really accountable to the government, as a federal employee would be, for doing a good job. However, while acknowledging Mead's basic point, there may be ways in which the state, on behalf of the wider community, can make it more likely that parents will indeed do a good job. For example, eligibility for public support (specifically for parental labour) might be made conditional on attending parenting classes, or parents might be required to attend such classes shortly after the birth of their

first child as an extension of the community's post-natal support services. Mead's comments were made in an exchange at the panel 'Welfare Reform and Political Theory', Annual Meeting of the American Political Science Association, San Francisco, 30 Aug.–2 Sept. 2001.

28. On this point, see the discussion in Christine Delphy and Diana Leonard, *Familiar Exploitation* (Cambridge: Polity Press, 1993), 95–6.

29. Thus, if citizens pay others to do this work for them, then, in principle, we should make a corresponding deduction from our estimate of their net productive contribution to the community.

30. I take the idea of a publicly defined work expectation from David Ellwood, *Poor Support: Poverty in the American Family* (New York: Basic Books, 1988); see esp. pp. 87–9.

31. See Sect. 6.4.

32. I am grateful to Andrew Williams for suggesting this idea.

33. This can be thought of, I think, as the work expectation that citizens in a comprehensively egalitarian society have when they enjoy a per capita share of the social product, weighted to take account of handicaps. Citizens can be given the freedom, of course, to take smaller shares of the social product in return for proportionately reduced productive contributions; where redistribution occurs in a manner similar to that we see in ESS, citizens would have this freedom.

34. The classic discussion of the separation is Adolf Berle and Gardiner Means, *The Modern Corporation and Private Property* (1932; New York: Harcourt, Brace & World, 1968).

35. To a great extent, inequalities in entrepreneurial income reflect differential option luck, as opposed to brute luck, and so there is no egalitarian reason for redistributing such income. But it must be admitted that individuals do have, as a matter of brute luck, unequal entrepreneurial abilities, and this implies that some redistribution of entrepreneurial income is warranted.

36. See David Schweickart, *Against Capitalism* (Cambridge: Cambridge University Press, 1993), 1–42, esp. 10–13, 17–18.

37. One way to appreciate this point, as Schweickart notes, is to imagine that the state performs the gatekeeper function instead of private individuals, charging workers a use-tax in return for access to the means of production. As Schweickart observes, 'We wouldn't say, would we, that the government is engaging in productive activity, or that the tax is a return for the government's productive contribution?' (ibid. 11).

38. I shall in fact defend a modest amount of such socialism in Ch. 8; see esp. Sect. 8.5 on the possibility of using a community fund to help finance social benefits.

39. This is even more obvious, I think, where the asset-producer does not lease out the asset to others, but employs it herself. As J. A. Hobson put it, 'a socialism which regards all labour as productive, all capital as predatory, is confronted with the fact that even in the most capitalist community there are many workers using the tools which they themselves have made, or

bought with their earnings. . . . The spade with which the factory worker digs his own garden in his leisure time is assuredly productive capital, earning something which may be called profit.' See J. A. Hobson, *Property and Improperty* (London: Victor Gollancz, 1937), 73.

40. R. H. Tawney, *The Acquisitive Society* (1920; New York: Harcourt Brace Jovanovich, 1948), 79.

41. Imagine, for example, that Harriet has a choice whether to lease out the asset she has produced to one group of workers, group A, whom she knows to be reliable but rather unimaginative, and another group, group B, whom she knows to be more imaginative but less reliable. She is, let us imagine, guaranteed a return of £x from group A, but could get anything from £y to £z with group B, where $y < x < z$. After taking account of egalitarian concerns, we determine that she would be entitled to, say, 50% of the £x she can get from group A. In the event, she leases to group B, who, as it happens, achieve for her a return of £z. Should we allow Harriet to keep at least part of the differential between this return and the return she is entitled to in the no-risk case? I am inclined to say that we should. There is of course the consideration that any inequality that consequently results between her and some other similarly placed individual who takes the group A alternative is, in Dworkin's terms, a matter of option luck, not brute luck, and thus not the kind of inequality that should excite our concern. Admittedly, in Ch. 3 I contended that some positive returns to option luck, specifically those to 'pure gambles', are not just. In cases where the return to option luck is connected with productive contribution, however, in contrast to the case of pure gambles, some degree of differential reward for successful risky enterprises seems appropriate. For if risk-taking, linked to productive contribution, helps the economy as a whole to develop in positive ways that would otherwise be forgone, it can be seen as a particularly helpful form of productive contribution, entitling the contributor to some extra reward.

42. See Schweickart, *Against Capitalism*, 30. Schwieckart refers us to Alfred Marshall, *Principles of Economics*, 8th edn. (New York: MacMillan, 1948), 587.

43. There is a connection here, I think, with Gijs van Donselaar's original and illuminating discussion of non-parasitical exchange among those with different preferences for a given resource. See Gijs van Donselaar, *The Benefit of Another's Pains: Parasitism, Scarcity, Basic Income* (Amsterdam: University of Amsterdam, 1997), esp. 144–65.

44. In Sect. 3.3 I briefly reviewed Lawrence Becker's argument concerning the virtue of reciprocity, according to which, roughly speaking, we ought in all social interactions to return good for good. It might be argued that in order to demonstrate this virtue, someone in Billy's position should not merely compensate someone in Milly's position, which requires paying her something to cover the frustration of one more week without a bike, but should also reward her, which would require paying her some amount

in addition to that strictly necessary for simple compensation. However, firstly, even if we concede this, the justifiable level of interest will still depend to a considerable extent on Milly's actual level of frustration. Secondly, Becker's reciprocity-based analysis anyway does not in fact point unequivocally to the conclusion that there is a right on the part of lenders to a monetary return in excess of that necessary to compensate them for their immediate loss. Rather than thinking of reciprocity in this case as something that applies on a tit-for-tat basis between individual lenders and receivers, it may be more appropriate to think of it on the mutual-aid model we associate with systems of voluntary blood donation. As in the case of a blood donor system, in a financial-loan system functioning on mutual-aid system principles citizens make available some of their financial surplus to others who are in greater immediate need. Those who benefit from such a system reciprocate by making a reasonable effort to make their own contribution to the pool. At some point most citizens will probably need to draw on the resources of the pool, and that is when they get a reciprocal benefit for their contribution.

45. Hobson, *Property and Improperty*, 78. On the following page Hobson quotes John Maynard Keynes, from *The General Theory of Employment: Interest and Money* (London: Macmillan, 1936), 376, as saying: 'Interest to-day rewards no genuine sacrifice …'.

46. See J. A. Hobson, *Poverty in Plenty: The Ethics of Income* (London: Allen & Unwin, 1931), 52.

47. The basic point is that we should not confuse the subjective cost of saving to the marginal saver with that of inframarginal savers, which will be lower. The market rate of interest will more than compensate the inframarginal savers for the subjective cost of saving. See Schweickart, *Against Capitalism*, 31–2. Schweickart makes the Hobsonian point that, for some savers, saving may not be costly in subjective terms at all; it may be inconvenient to consume one's income in full at a given point in time and a relief to be able to store some of the command on the social product it represents.

48. It might be argued that if specific goods are the product not of one's fellow citizen's labours, but of past generations, then someone can surely have an entitlement to inherit and consume a share of these goods, even in the absence of any productive service on his part. In literally consuming these particular goods, he would not be claiming a share of what his fellow citizens produce. Here, however, it is important to recall the duty of intergenerational equity and how it blends with the obligations held under fair reciprocity. Inheritors share in the obligation that members of their generation have to ensure an adequate replacement of the goods they have received from past generations. Imagine, for example, that all citizens are eligible for the same uniform inheritance from the state: a bundle of goods worth, say, £50,000, on maturity, or the cash equivalent based on a tax of these goods. In choosing to take up this inheritance, each citizen

must accept an obligation to make a contribution, weighted according to ability and other relevant circumstances, to ensure that future generations of citizens are able to receive the same inheritance. Simply to inherit these goods or capital sum, and then to draw the goods or sum down steadily over the course of one's life without replacing what one has consumed, would leave one's fellow citizens with the unfair burden of replacing what you have consumed. This point is suggested by Frank Vandenbroucke in 'Responsibility, Well-Being, Information and the Design of Distributive Policies', Center for Economic Studies, Discussion Paper Series 00.03, Katholiecke Universiteit Leuven, 2000, 38–40.

49. In the words of Winston Churchill: 'Roads are made, streets are made, services are improved, electric light turns night into day, water is brought from reservoirs a hundred miles off in the mountains—and all the while the landlord sits still. *Every one of those improvements is effected by the labor and cost of other people and the taxpayers.* To not one of those improvements does the land monopolist, as a land monopolist, contribute, and yet by every one of them *the value of his land is enhanced.* He renders no service to the community, he contributes nothing to the general welfare, he contributes nothing to the process from which his own enrichment is derived.' See 'Winston Churchill on Land Monopoly', on the web site of the Banneker Center for Economic Justice, <www.progress.org/banneker/chur.html>. See also John Stuart Mill, 'The Right of Property in Land' (1873), in *The Collected Works of John Stuart Mill*, eds. Ann P. Robson and John M. Robson, xxv: *Newspaper Writings* (Toronto: University of Toronto Press, 1987), 1235–43.

50. The full sentence reads: 'But the truth is that the concept of socially useful work is not just fuzzy around the edges. It is fuzzy through and through.' See Becker, 'Obligation to Work', 47.

51. Witness the recent tendency in the United States, noted above in Sect. 5.2, to equate productive contribution almost entirely with paid employment to the exclusion of unpaid care work.

52. I do not wish to exclude the possibility that there may be other relevant considerations not identified here.

Chapter 6

1. On developments in Britain and the United States, see Desmond King, *In the Name of Liberalism: Illiberal Social Policy in Britain and the United States* (Oxford: Oxford University Press, 1999), 219–86. For an international analysis that also covers continental Europe, see Ivar Lodemel and Heather Trickey (eds.), *'An Offer You Can't Refuse': Workfare in International Perspective* (Bristol: Policy Press, 2001).

2. Some evidence for this claim is discussed in David Miller, *Principles of Social Justice* (Cambridge, Mass.: Harvard University Press, 2000), 73–8.

3. The classic article on insurance market failure is Kenneth Arrow, 'Uncertainty and the Welfare Economics of Medical Care', *American Economic Review*, 53 (1963), 941–73. For a more general discussion, see Nicholas Barr, *The Economics of the Welfare State*, 3rd edn. (Oxford: Oxford University Press, 1998), 108–28.

4. Robert Goodin argues that provision of welfare is mandated by a collective responsibility we share as citizens to 'protect the vulnerable'. See Robert E. Goodin, 'Reasons for Welfare: Economic, Sociological, and Political—but Ultimately Moral', in J. Donald Moon (ed.), *Responsibility, Rights and Welfare: The Theory of the Welfare State* (Boulder, Colo.: Westview Press, 1988), 19–54.

5. For helpful comment on this issue, see Frank Vandenbroucke, 'European Social Democracy and the Third Way: Convergence, Divisions, and Shared Questions', in Stuart White (ed.), *New Labour: The Progressive Future?* (Basingstoke: Palgrave, 2001), 161–74, specifically 163.

6. Except in the unlikely event that workfare, in the strict sense, is the only way of maintaining the long-term willingness and capability to work of those in receipt of income support.

7. Thus, on this view, a community might subject regular income support to some form of work-test, but not the basic health-care package available to all.

8. For a comprehensive survey of the impacts of these programmes, see Judith M. Gueron and Edward Pauly, *From Welfare to Work* (New York: Russell Sage Foundation, 1991).

9. For a general review of the recent research, I am indebted to Lawrence Mead, 'Welfare Reform: Meaning and Effects', paper prepared for the round table on 'Welfare Reform and Political Theory', Annual Meeting of the American Political Science Association, San Francisco, 30 Aug.– 2 Sept. 2001. According to Mead: 'In the short run, leavers' earnings usually exceed prior welfare benefits, but families also tend to have less noncash coverage than before.'

10. I have to say that I am not sure that any of the policy ideas discussed in Pt. II of this volume directly address this problem. The proposal for a childhood privilege tax made by Bruce Ackerman and Anne Alstott, and discussed in Sect. 7.5.2, may offer a very indirect and imperfect way of addressing it; but I am in no doubt that the policy implications of this particular requirement of fair work-testing require more thought.

11. This perspective has much in common with the argument for 'fair workfare' developed by Amy Gutmann and Dennis Thompson in *Democracy and Disagreement* (Cambridge, Mass.: Harvard University Press, 1996), 273–306. It also has a close affinity with the perspective developed by Amy Wax in a number of recent publications. See e.g. Amy Wax, 'Rethinking Welfare Rights: Reciprocity Norms, Reactive Attitudes, and the Political Economy of Welfare Reform', *Law and Contemporary Problems*, 63 (2000), 257–97.

12. See T. H. Marshall, 'Citizenship and Social Class', in Marshall, *Citizenship and Social Class* (Cambridge: Cambridge University Press, 1950), 1–85.

13. See Desmond King and Mark Wickham-Jones, 'From Clinton to Blair: The Democratic (Party) Origins of Welfare to Work', *Political Quarterly*, 70 (1999), 62–74, specifically 72.

14. King, *In the Name of Liberalism*, 233. I am not entirely sure whether King intends this as a criticism, or as the basis for a criticism, of contractualism. The general thrust of his argument is critical of contractualism as 'illiberal'. But at one point he also expresses criticism of the way Marshall's ideas were used by social-policy thinkers in the post-war period (p. 247): 'It was the uncritical embrace of the social *rights* argument, as the basis for the political relationship between citizens and the state, which proved damaging intellectually since its theorists de-emphasized (or entirely ignored) the responsibilities or obligations dimension of citizenship; and thereby induced a complacency in a particular form of state-based social policy.'

15. If you leave me all the ingredients for a meal, a recipe, and all necessary cooking utensils, and I have at least moderate cooking skills, then you will almost certainly have provided me with reasonable access to a specific meal, in the above sense, even though you have not actually given me the meal itself.

16. Leonard Hobhouse, *Liberalism and Other Writings*, ed. James Meadowcroft (Cambridge: Cambridge University Press, 1911), 76.

17. On the views of the New Liberals in this area, see Michael Freeden, *The New Liberalism: A Study in the Ideology of Social Reform* (Oxford: Oxford University Press, 1978), 195–244.

18. Centrally, in Marshall's words, 'the right to a modicum of economic welfare and security' and 'the right . . . to live the life of a civilized being'. See Marshall, 'Citizenship and Social Class', 11.

19. See ibid. 78.

20. Ibid. 80. Marshall argues that the problem facing post-war Britain is not so much to get citizens to do some work, which he thinks is easy enough in a context of full employment, but to get citizens to work with the right kind of motivation.

21. In Beveridge's words, '[The] correlative of the State's undertaking to ensure adequate benefit for unavoidable interruption of earnings, however long, is enforcement of the citizen's obligation to seek and accept all reasonable opportunities of work [and] to co-operate in all measures designed to save him from habituation to idleness . . .'. See William Beveridge, *Social Insurance and Allied Services* (London: HMSO, 1942), 58.

22. On distinct, incentives-related grounds, one might add that the job in question must pay sufficiently, in combination with in-work benefits, to place the individual taking the job above the minimum income level guaranteed for the unemployed through the welfare system. This is, of

course, an adjustment of policy to non-ideal circumstances in which citizens are not sufficiently motivated by considerations of justice to look energetically for jobs without this inducement.

23. Indeed, in light of the point made in Sect. 6.2 about the danger of those with high earnings potential making a relatively poor productive contribution, we might well insist that individuals refrain from taking jobs that pay well below what they should be able to earn.

24. I have not discussed privacy directly in this volume, but respect for the integrity interests described in Ch. 2 certainly requires that the state define, respect, and protect a right to privacy.

25. See Tony Lauro, 'Fair Hearing: Legacy to the Poor', in E. Joshua Rosenkranz and Bernard Schwartz (eds.), *Reason and Passion: Justice Brennan's Enduring Influence* (New York: Norton, 1997), 233–42.

26. The purchaser–provider split involves the state contracting with non-state parties to manage welfare clients on its behalf. For an excellent analysis of policy experiments of this type and their impact on welfare recipients, see Mark Considine, *Enterprising States: The Public Management of Welfare-to-Work* (Cambridge: Cambridge University Press, 2001).

27. This issue is forcefully raised by Desmond King and Mark Freedland in 'Contractual Governance and Illiberal Contracts: Some Problems of Contractualism as an Instrument of Behaviour Management by Agencies of Government', MS, St John's College, Oxford, 2001.

28. I do not mean to insist dogmatically on direct in-kind provision. In some cases, it may be preferable to use non-transferable vouchers, though vouchers have two problems: (i) the US experience with food stamps shows that secondary markets can emerge in which the vouchers exchange for cash at a fraction of their face value; (ii) where vouchers are not paid universally to all but only to subgroups of the population, they may stigmatize those who have to use them.

29. The family cap policy is inequitable because it denies newborn children welfare benefits specifically earmarked to meet their needs as a way of punishing the mothers of these children for their perceived irresponsibility in having a child while on welfare. This is as unfair, I think, as taking away one citizen's driving licence as a way of punishing another citizen, who happens to be a close relative, for drunken driving.

30. I owe this suggestion to Andrew Williams (who does not necessarily endorse it).

31. See Gutmann and Thompson, *Democracy and Disagreement*, 300–1.

32. John Stuart Mill, *On Liberty* (1859; Harmondsworth: Penguin, 1985), 167–8. Of course Mill begs the question somewhat by describing the duties of parental support as 'legal duties', for one of the points at issue is precisely whether these duties ought to be subject to legal enforcement. Mill presumably thought that non-performance of these duties is sufficiently harmful to the children concerned to justify a policy of punishing parents who fail to perform them.

33. One other suggested sanction that has surfaced in the debate over welfare reform in the United States is to remove children from the offending parents and place them in orphanages. I do not regard this proposal as worth considering, however, because I am fairly confident that the harm caused to the children by such upheaval will in general be even greater than the harm caused by financial penalties. Other possibilities would be to sanction the hard core of workshy individuals with further restrictions on their liberty, including, at the limit, imprisonment. I do not think this option is obviously inappropriate—after all, we do think it legitimate to punish some forms of child neglect in this way. But again the upheaval involved might well be worse to vulnerable parties than financial penalties.

34. See Gerald Dworkin, 'Paternalism', in Richard Wasserstrom (ed.), *Morality and the Law* (Belmont, Calif.: Wadsworth, 1971), 107–26. In Dworkin's words (pp. 120–3): 'I suggest that since we are all aware of our irrational propensities, deficiencies in cognitive and emotional capacities, and avoidable and unavoidable ignorance it is rational and prudent for us to in effect take out "social insurance policies." We may argue for and against proposed paternalistic measures in terms of what fully rational individuals would accept as forms of protection . . .. I suggest we think of the imposition of paternalistic interferences in situations of this kind as being a kind of insurance policy which we take out against making decisions which are far-reaching, potentially dangerous, and irreversible. Each of these factors is important.' I should note that Dworkin has had some second thoughts about this theory of justifiable paternalism, but I shall not pursue and respond to these doubts here.

35. An example of this purely information-regarding form of paternalism is the British Labour government's policy, introduced in 1999, of requiring all single parents coming onto welfare benefits to attend periodic interviews at which their employment and training options will be discussed. At time of writing, single parents suffer no sanction if they choose not to pursue any of these options.

36. I am not sure that all of the conditions for a fair work-test identified in the previous sections must be satisfied before we can be reasonably confident that an otherwise valid paternalistic argument for some form of work-test does indeed hold. Most important is the protection of citizens from low income and vulnerability in the marketplace. Less important in this context is, say, the concern to prevent violations of fair-dues reciprocity from inherited wealth.

37. See Lawrence Mead, *The New Politics of Poverty: The Nonworking Poor in America* (New York: Basic Books, 1992). See also Mead, *Beyond Entitlement: The Social Obligations of Citizenship* (New York: Free Press, 1987), and Mead (ed.), *The New Paternalism* (Washington: The Brookings Institution, 1997).

38. See Mead, *The New Politics of Poverty*, 210–39. See also Lawrence Mead and Frank Field MP, *From Welfare to Work* (London: Institute

for Economic Affairs, 1997). Field here expresses some reservations as to how far Mead's analysis is applicable to Britain.

39. Mead, *The New Politics of Poverty*, 19.

40. Ibid. 21.

41. The obvious rational-choice explanation of non-work is that it is a response to low real wages among low-skilled workers—as wages for this group of workers fall, other options such as welfare and crime become more attractive. At the beginning of Ch. 4 of *The New Politics of Poverty* Mead poses the question of whether non-work can be explained as a response to low wages. But the chapter goes on to address a quite different question: whether poverty is likely to result from low-paid employment. Even if, as Mead claims, the vast majority of those in low-paid work are thereby able to get incomes above the poverty line we cannot infer from this that low wages are not the main cause of non-work. The non-work decision depends on the return to work relative to the alternatives (welfare, crime), not on the return to work relative to a rather arbitrary official definition of the poverty line. For a comprehensive discussion of alternative explanations of non-work among the poor in the United States, see David Ellwood, 'Understanding Dependency', in Mary Jo Bane and David Ellwood, *Welfare Realities: From Rhetoric to Reform* (Cambridge, Mass.: Harvard University Press, 1994), 67–123.

42. Someone who is competent in Mead's second sense, i.e. geared to a life of material advance and success, will typically have this specific, reciprocity-based civic competency. But the reverse does not necessarily follow. What Mead does, I think, is to misidentify the specific civic competency with which he is really concerned with a quite distinct personal quality, materialistic ambition, which is imperfectly correlated with possession of this civic competency.

43. Mead, *The New Politics of Poverty*, 239.

Chapter 7

1. This definition follows that given by Philippe Van Parijs in 'Competing Justifications of Basic Income', in Van Parijs (ed.), *Arguing for Basic Income* (London: Verso, 1992), 3–43, specifically 3, and accords with that adopted by the Basic Income European Network (BIEN). The growth of interest in UBI is reflected in the growing number of books on, or which contain lengthy discussions of, the concept. In addition to *Arguing for Basic Income*, and other works referred to in this chapter, see Fred Block, *Postindustrial Possibilities: A Critique of Economic Discourse* (Berkeley and Los Angeles: University of California Press, 1990), esp. 204–8; Samuel Brittan and Steven Webb, *Beyond the Welfare State: An Examination of Basic Incomes in a Market Economy* (Aberdeen: University of

Aberdeen, 1990); Tony Fitzpatrick, *Freedom and Security: An Introduction to the Basic Income Debate* (London: Macmillan, 1999); Hermione Parker, *Instead of the Dole: An Inquiry into the Integration of Tax and Benefit Systems* (London: Routledge, 1989); David Purdy, *Social Power in the Labour Market: A Radical Approach to Labour Economics* (London: Macmillan, 1988); Philippe Van Parijs, *What's Wrong with a Free Lunch?*, eds. Joshua Cohen and Joel Rogers (Boston: Beacon Press, 2001); and Tony Walter, *Basic Income: Freedom from Poverty, Freedom from Work* (London: Marion Boyars, 1989). For further general information, see also the web sites of BIEN, a network of academics interested in basic income and related ideas, at <www.bien.be> or <www.basicincome.org>, and for information on the basic income issues specifically in Britain and the United States, see the web sites of the Citizen's Income Study Centre and US Basic Income Guarantee at <www.citizensincome.org> and <www.widerquist.com/usbig>.

2. Van Parijs, 'Competing Justifications', 8. For related criticism, see Eugene Torisky, Jr., 'Rawls, Van Parijs, and Unconditional Basic Income', *Analysis* 53, 1993, 289–97.

3. See Philippe Van Parijs, *Real Freedom for All: What (if Anything) Can Justify Capitalism?* (Oxford: Oxford University Press, 1995).

4. Van Parijs actually uses the criterion of leximin, rather than simple maximin. Maximin merely requires that among alternative rules of economic cooperation we choose the rules that maximize the prospects of the group that is worst off. Leximin is a form of maximin which adds the stipulation that if two sets of rules leave the worst-off group in society with the same level of prospects, then we should break the tie by asking which of these sets of rules maximizes the prospects of the next group in the distributive hierarchy, and so on as necessary up the hierarchy.

5. Indeed, Van Parijs holds that the level of the relevant income grant could conceivably be even higher than that necessary to cover a standard set of basic needs.

6. A pure natural resource is a natural resource, e.g. a plot of land, in its unimproved state. The value of a pure natural resource, therefore, is simply the value of that resource in this state, e.g. the value which a particular piece of land has in virtue of its natural fertility, deducting any value added by human improvements to its fertility. The idea of valuing natural resources in abstraction from the value of improvements has a long history, appearing, for example, in recurrent proposals for the 'site value taxation' of landholdings.

7. See Van Parijs, *Real Freedom for All*, 101.

8. Firstly, in contrast to what is assumed in the standard Walrasian model, in the real world there may often be a positive relationship between worker productivity and the real wage; higher wages may have motivation effects that increase productivity and profitability so that firms have no incentive to allow currently unemployed workers to bid wages down

to a market-clearing level. Secondly, in contrast to what is assumed in the standard Walrasian model, in the real world there are turnover costs (costs associated with the firing of existing employees and the hiring and training of new workers), the existence of which allegedly enables existing 'insider' employees to claim a wage in excess of the wage at which unemployed 'outsiders' are willing to work, without prompting their employer to hire these outsiders who are willing to work for less. The focus on motivation effects is characteristic of recent 'efficiency wage' theories of unemployment, and the focus on turnover costs, of recent 'insider–outsider' theories. For a good review, see Assar Lindbeck, 'The Microfoundations of Unemployment Theory', *Labour*, 5 (1991), 3–23.

9. See Van Parijs, *Real Freedom for All*, 106–9.
10. Once employment rents are included in the UBI tax base, 'it is then no longer ludicrous to suggest that the non-discriminatory concern with people's access to the means for the pursuit of their conceptions of the good life, the leximinning of real freedom, should demand that people be given an adequate basic income' (ibid. 108).
11. Van Parijs's rejoinder to this potential difficulty takes up Ch. 3 of *Real Freedom for All*, 58–88. I will not attempt to evaluate the adequacy of the rejoinder here. For an incisive critique, see Brian Barry, 'Real Freedom and Basic Income', *Journal of Political Philosophy*, 4 (1996), 242–76.
12. See Van Parijs, *Real Freedom for All*, 108.
13. It might be said that lifestyle non-workers *do* make a productive contribution precisely by making their share of job assets available to those who are more enthusiastic about work. But this claim rests on an implausibly stretched construal of when someone makes a productive contribution to the community. If a given lifestyle non-worker were to disappear, then the share of job assets he would have under Van Parijs's proposal would be reallocated across the populace. If workers maintained their original level of effort, then output and the original production possibilities, based on the existing supply of non-labour means of production and their willingness to work, would remain unchanged. The workers would simply have to surrender less of their social product to lifestyle non-workers because, following the reallocation of the newly available job asset share, they would not have to buy access to the means of production from lifestyle non-workers to the same extent as before. The fact that the lifestyle non-worker is a pure burden on the working population indicates that *he* is not in fact contributing anything to production. When he transfers a job asset to someone who wishes to make (more of) a productive contribution, he then *allows someone else* to make a (greater) productive contribution—at a price. But—and this question gets to the core of the objection to Van Parijs's job assets argument for UBI—why should those who wish to make a productive contribution be put in the position where they have to buy permission to make a (greater) contribution from those who wish to share in the social product without making a contribution?

14. See Gijs van Donselaar, *The Benefit of Another's Pains: Parasitism, Scarcity, Basic Income* (Amsterdam: University of Amsterdam, 1997), esp. 104–65.

15. See van Donselaar's discussion of 'equalized civic feudalism' (ibid. 185–7). Van Donselaar draws attention to the practice in the early Dutch republic whereby certain citizens owned particular jobs and the wages they commanded. Instead of doing these jobs however, the citizens concerned would often lease them to others, who then did the actual work. Part of the injustice involved in this practice derives from the unequal endowment of such jobs. But, as the analysis above suggests, even an equal division of jobs may result in unjust, parasitic transfers where citizens have different independent interests in taking up the productive opportunities society endows them with.

16. For example, imagine that we wish to design a fair system of subsidies for rail transport so as to reduce traffic congestion. The reciprocity principle presented in Pt. I of this volume provides little immediate guidance on how we might set the level of subsidy. Van Donselaar's analysis does provide guidance, suggesting that the appropriate level of subsidy for rail transport should be at a level that just compensates ex-car users for switching to rail. See ibid. 162–5. (Of course, if individuals have different degrees of preference for cars over rail, i.e. a different degree of independent interest in using roads, the analysis implies that the subsidies should be proportioned to preference, the more rail-loving getting proportionately less subsidy. This would probably be unfeasible in practice. But by helping us see what the ideal policy would be, van Donselaar's analysis may nevertheless contribute to the design of a reasonable second-best policy.)

17. On gatekeeping, see the discussion of capital and contribution in Sect. 5.5.

18. Of course, given other, background inequalities, some rent extraction of this kind might mirror transfers that seem justified on egalitarian grounds, e.g. transfers intended to compensate for disability. But the commitment to simple equal division of job assets in Van Parijs's argument is not grounded in any such consideration: compensation for handicaps is something, in his view, that justifies movement away from the baseline of equal tradeable asset shares, not something that justifies taking equality as the baseline. And it is anyway just as conceivable that the incidence of rent extraction might run counter to the pattern of transfers otherwise justified on egalitarian grounds, e.g. from a disabled work-enthusiastic person to a very able person with a strong preference for leisure.

19. See Gar Alperovitz, 'Distributing our Technological Inheritance', *Technology Review* (Oct. 1994), 31–6, specifically 33.

20. Van Parijs considers and rejects the technological inheritance argument in *Real Freedom for All*, 103–6.

21. I have discussed skill- or talent-based inequality earlier in this volume (see esp. Sect. 4.1), and it should be clear from this earlier discussion that

correction of such inequality does not necessarily call for an UBI. I shall discuss inequality in inheritances of wealth further below (see Ch. 8), and we will see that here again an UBI is not necessarily implied by the commitment to reduce this inequality.

22. In much of his discussion van Donselaar assumes that independent interests in external resources are interests in using resources productively. But he is not in fact committed to the view that independent interests in external resources are necessarily production-oriented.

23. See Jeremy Waldron, 'Homelessness and the Issue of Freedom', in Waldron, *Liberal Rights* (Cambridge: Cambridge University Press, 1993), 309–38, esp. 322–5.

24. One example is the community allotment one finds in many parts of Britain: land is held as common property by local authorities and then leased to local citizens to cultivate as they wish, the land reverting to the community if it lies unused. See George Monbiot, 'A Rights-Based Approach to Landscape Conservation', <www.oneworld.org/tlio>.

25. In an earlier paper I argued that the citizen has a right to an income grant equal to a per capita share of the current market value of land (and historic man-made wealth such as inherited housing stock). See my 'Liberal, Equality, Exploitation, and the Case for an Unconditional Basic Income', *Political Studies*, 45 (1997), 312–26. This position is well criticized by Philippe Van Parijs in 'Reciprocity and the Justification of an Unconditional Basic Income: Reply to Stuart White', *Political Studies*, 45 (1997), 327–30. The discussion in this section is an attempt to retrieve and restate what I think is the valid intuition underlying my earlier argument.

26. The consent theory of political obligation is defended by Alan J. Simmons in *Moral Principles and Political Obligations* (Princeton: Princeton University Press, 1979). For an outline and defence of the reciprocity or fairness theory, see George Klosko, *The Principle of Fairness and Political Obligation* (Lanham, Md.: Rowman & Littlefield, 1992).

27. See Philippe Van Parijs, 'The Second Marriage of Justice and Efficiency?', in Van Parijs (ed.), *Arguing for Basic Income* (London: Verso, 1992), 215–40.

28. See Bill Jordan, 'Basic Income and the Common Good', in Van Parijs (ed.), *Arguing for Basic Income*, 155–77.

29. See Carole Pateman, 'Freedom and Democratization: Why Basic Income is to be Preferred to Basic Capital', in Keith Dowding, Stuart White, and Jurgen DeWispelaere (eds.), *The Ethics of Stakeholding* (forthcoming).

30. Probably the most widely discussed revenue-sharing proposals are Martin Weitzman's proposal for profit-sharing enterprises and James Meade's proposals for 'discriminating labour–capital partnerships'. On the former, see Martin Weitzman, *The Share Economy: Conquering Stagflation* (Cambridge, Mass.: Harvard University Press, 1985), and on the latter, see James Meade, *Agathatopia: The Economics of Partnership* (Aberdeen: University of Aberdeen, 1989).

31. See Meade, *Agathatopia*, 29–30, 34–8.
32. This is the vexed issue of how far the family itself should be governed by norms of justice appropriate to the public sphere. A view that would exempt family life wholly from these norms is utterly implausible, and has in fact been the subject of trenchant criticism by liberal thinkers at least since John Stuart Mill and Harriet Taylor wrote *On the Subjection of Women*. But the view that would require the family to be a full microcosm of the liberal political order is also probably too extreme. A state that respects the expressive integrity of its citizens (see Sect. 2.2) should allow them to form households that exhibit elements of patriarchy or matriarchy, provided that the integrity interests of children in such households are adequately protected, and all adult parties are free to leave these households without suffering impoverishment. For helpful discussion of this issue, see John Rawls, 'The Idea of Public Reason Revisited', in Rawls, *The Law of Peoples* (Cambridge, Mass.: Harvard University Press, 1999), 129–80, specifically 156–64, and Brian Barry, *Culture and Equality* (Oxford: Polity Press, 2000), 130–54.
33. The limited earnings potential of one partner may make that partner financially dependent on the other, and this other can then take advantage of the dependency relationship to pressure for an exploitative household division of labour. See Susan Moller Okin, *Justice, Gender, and the Family* (New York: Basic Books, 1989), 134–69.
34. See Philippe Van Parijs and Robert van der Veen, 'A Capitalist Road to Communism', *Theory and Society*, 15 (1986), 635–55.
35. See Rick van der Ploeg and A. Lans Bovenberg, 'Against the Basic Instinct: Why Basic Income Proposals will not Do the Job', *New Economy*, 3 (1996), 235–40.
36. See Anthony Atkinson, 'The Case for a Participation Income', *Political Quarterly*, 67 (1996), 67–70.
37. See Mickey Kaus, *The End of Equality* (New York: Basic Books, 1992), esp. 81–5, and James McCormick, *Citizens' Service* (London: Institute for Public Policy Research, 1994).
38. See Van Parijs, *Real Freedom for All*, 231.
39. Dore envisages basic income being phased in for youths and carrying corresponding 'duties of unpaid community service, duties which are compulsory and universal, though widely flexible in form'. See Ronald Dore, *Taking Japan Seriously: A Confucian Perspective on Leading Economic Issues* (Stanford, Calif.: Stanford University Press, 1987), 223.
40. One response to the standard exploitation objection to UBI is to say that UBI will not itself be modified to meet reciprocity-based concerns, but that it will be accompanied by other policies which will directly address these concerns. This form of republican basic income is an example of how this response might be put into practice. I am grateful to Erik Olin Wright for conversation on this point.

41. This is one way we might develop Richard Dagger's proposal that certain rights of citizenship be conditional on participation in a citizens' service programme. See Richard Dagger, 'Republican Virtue, Liberal Freedom, and the Problem of Civic Service', paper presented to the Oxford Conference on Republicanism, Maison Française d'Oxford and Nuffield College, Oxford, 30 June–1 July 2000.

42. See André Gorz, *Paths to Paradise: On the Liberation from Work* (London: South End Press, 1985), esp. theses 17–19, 40–7.

43. See Ferdinand Kinsky, 'Federalism and the Personalist Tradition', in Henry Tam (ed.), *Progressive Politics in the Global Age* (Oxford: Polity Press, 2001), 54–65, specifically 57–8.

44. Personal communication.

45. My focus here is on targeting those disadvantaged in the labour market. But it should be noted that many capitalist countries, including Britain, already have a targeted basic income based on age in the form of universal child benefits.

46. See Bruce Ackerman and Anne Alstott, *The Stakeholder Society* (New Haven: Yale University Press, 1999), 155–77.

47. An obvious objection to the proposal is that it would give parents an incentive to limit their earnings so that their children qualify for the tax credit. Ackerman and Alstott have two main responses to this objection. Firstly, the levels of childhood privilege tax and credit can be set so that, for most earners, the present value of the costs incurred by relegating oneself to a lower earnings tranche for the required number of years to enable one's children to qualify for a lower privilege tax (or a subsidy) exceed the present value of the benefits to one's child from qualifying for this lower tax (receiving the subsidy). Secondly, if a lot of parents reduce their labour supply and depress their earnings, the thresholds defining privilege or underprivilege for their cohort of children should be correspondingly adjusted down. This method of setting the thresholds makes it more risky for parents to try to game the system: they will be imposing a definite loss on themselves and their children in return for a highly uncertain gain.

48. More exactly, the 1996 Act required that only 20% of families remain on welfare (Temporary Assistance for Needy Families, or TANF) for longer than five years from the signing of the Act, including repeat spells. States were given the option, though, of supporting families beyond five years using their own resources, and some states, such as New York, intend to do this. The TANF programme comes up for reauthorization in 2002, and at the time of writing it is unclear what new measures will be incorporated into the programme. It is unlikely, however, that the time-limit provisions introduced in 1996 will be abandoned. For basic information on the 1996 Act, I am grateful to Lawrence Mead, 'Welfare Reform: Meaning and Effects', paper prepared for the roundtable on

'Welfare Reform and Political Theory', Annual Meeting of the American Political Science Association, San Francisco, 30 Aug.–2 Sept. 2001.

49. I do not mean to imply here that suffering such an emergency should be a condition of eligibility for this time-limited basic income, merely that such a basic income would provide the citizen with a fund which they could keep in place to draw upon in such an emergency. Citizens might squander the fund, of course. But then they might squander an ordinary UBI.

50. See Anthony Atkinson, 'Beveridge, the National Minimum, and its Future in a European Context', in Atkinson, *Incomes and the Welfare State* (Cambridge: Cambridge University Press, 1996), 290–304. See also Commission on Social Justice, *Social Justice: Strategies for National Renewal* (London: Vintage, 1994), 221–65.

51. See Robert Haveman, 'Equity with Employment', *Boston Review*, 22 (Summer 1997), 3–8.

Chapter 8

1. See Lisa Keister, *Wealth in America: Trends in Wealth Inequality* (Cambridge: Cambridge University Press, 2001), 62–8. Keister's most recent figures are for 1995, and they show the top 1% owning 38.5% of net worth and 47.2% of financial wealth. The bottom 40% own 0.2% of the nation's net worth and −1.3% of its financial wealth.

2. See ibid. 65.

3. Figures for Britain are taken from John Hills, *Inquiry into Income and Wealth*, vol. ii (York: Joseph Rowntree Foundation, 1995), 95.

4. Ibid. 95–6.

5. Ibid. The Gini coefficient for the distribution of marketable wealth stood at 0.66 in 1976 and after dipping to 0.64 in 1986 was back at 0.66 by 1992. See Gavin Kelly and Rachel Lissauer, *Ownership for All* (London: Institute for Public Policy Research, 2000), 5–6, for a summary of more recent trends.

6. See John A. Brittain, *Inheritance and the Inequality of Material Wealth* (Washington: Brookings Institution, 1978), and C. D. Harbury and D. M. W. N. Hitchens, *Inheritance and Wealth Inequality in Britain* (London: Allen & Unwin, 1979), esp. 116–27.

7. Keister, *Wealth in America*, 255.

8. Ibid.

9. For a general overview, see Henry J. Aaron and Alicia H. Munnell, 'Reassessing the Role for Wealth Transfer Taxes', *National Tax Journal*, 45 (1998), 119–43, esp. 132–7. On the British case, see Paul Ryan, 'Inheritance: Symbols and Illusions', in Andrew Glyn and David Miliband (eds.), *Paying for Inequality: The Economic Cost of Social Injustice* (London: Institute for Public Policy Research/Rivers Oram, 1994), 181–204.

10. A recent British study using data from the National Child Development Study found a strong association between asset poverty and poor performance in later life in terms of earnings, employment, health, entrepreneurship, and marital stability. The association remained even after efforts were made using attitudinal variables to control for personality type. See John Bynner and Sofia Despotidou, *Effects of Assets on Life Chances* (London: Centre for Longitudinal Studies, Institute of Education, 2001), available on the British government's Department for Education and Employment web site, <www.dfee.gov.uk>.

11. Leonard Hobhouse, *The Labour Movement*, 3rd edn. (New York: Macmillan, 1912), 17.

12. R. H. Tawney, *Equality* (1931; London: Allen & Unwin, 1964), specifically 37–8.

13. Similar considerations are central to David Haslett's case against inheritance in David W. Haslett, 'Is Inheritance Justified?', *Philosophy and Public Affairs*, 15 (1986), 122–55. Haslett argues that inheritance is incompatible with the value of 'equality of opportunity', which is related to our concern with significant brute luck disadvantage and class inequality, and with the value of 'distribution according to productivity', which is related to (though certainly not identical to) the concern for reciprocity.

14. We should, however, probably draw a firm distinction here between what we ordinarily think of as charitable donations and donations to things like political campaigns. Respect for citizens' expressive and deliberative interests almost certainly requires that citizens be allowed the freedom to make transfers of the latter sort (let us call them political transfers). But the scope of this freedom is properly constrained by the need to prevent the rich from acquiring excessive influence and voice within the political process.

15. Haslett also entertains a quota of this kind as a way of handling what he calls the 'family heirlooms problem'. See ibid. 152–3. Haslett would tax away all transfers above the quota.

16. An issue which needs further attention than I can give it here is that of how to treat parental contributions to educational expenses. I assume here that, in order to meet the requirement that class inequality be reduced to a reasonable minimum, there ought to be a similar ceiling on such expenditures, with expenditures above the ceiling paying a wealth-transfer tax or counting against the child's lifetime accessions quota.

17. See ibid. 150.

18. The points in this paragraph are made by Haslett, ibid. 144–8, and by Stephen Munzer in *A Theory of Property* (Cambridge: Cambridge University Press, 1990), 414–16.

19. See Ryan, 'Inheritance: Symbols and Illusions', 200–1.

20. See Haslett, 'Is Inheritance Justified?', 147.

21. As the quotation at the head of this chapter indicates, the essential thought was well expressed by Thomas Paine in defending his own version of the basic-capital proposal in *Agrarian Justice*.

22. See Commission on Taxation and Citizenship, *Paying for Progress: A New Politics of Tax for Public Spending* (London: Fabian Society, 2000), 53–5. The Commission's focus groups expressed hostility to inheritance taxation and in the Commission's opinion poll over 50% of those asked thought that 'no inheritances should be taxed'.

23. Paul Ryan suggests a connection of this sort. See Ryan, 'Inheritance: Symbols and Illusions', 204. The connection is also called for in the report of the Fabian Society's Commission on Taxation and Citizenship. See *Paying for Progress*, 286–7.

24. The classic case for an accessions tax is set out in James Meade, *Efficiency, Equality and the Ownership of Property* (London: Allen & Unwin, 1964), 54–8. See also Munzer, *A Theory of Property*, 403–11, and Marc Fleurbaey, 'An Egalitarian Democratic Private Ownership Economy', *Politics and Society*, 21 (1993), 215–33.

25. According to Meade: 'The rich property owner would now have every incentive to pass on his property in small parcels to persons who had up to date received very little by way of gift or inheritance.' See Meade, *Efficiency, Equality and the Ownership of Property*, 57. Meade also emphasizes that an accessions tax will have a limited impact on the incentive to accumulate wealth because the individual's tax liability on wealth she receives gratuitously from others is wholly dependent on how much wealth she has already acquired in this way and not at all dependent on how much wealth she has acquired through her own efforts.

26. See Robert Haveman, *Starting Even: An Equal Opportunity Program to Combat the Nation's New Poverty* (New York: Simon & Schuster, 1988), 168–71.

27. Ibid. 169.

28. Michael White, *Against Unemployment* (London: Policy Studies Institute, 1991), 215–21, specifically 215–16.

29. A modest form of Individual Learning Accounts was introduced by the 1997–2001 Labour government. The scheme was soon withdrawn, however, because some people offered bogus educational courses to get the subsidies it provided. The episode underscores the need to implement basic-capital policies in the context of a strong regulatory framework in which funds can be accessed to buy educational or training services only from approved providers. The Learning Account scheme may be reintroduced at a later date once the regulatory issues have been addressed.

30. See Commission on Social Justice, *Social Justice: Strategies for National Renewal* (London: Vintage, 1994), 141–7.

31. Bruce Ackerman and Anne Alstott, *The Stakeholder Society* (New Haven, Conn.: Yale University Press, 1999).

32. On the idea of a childhood privilege tax, see Sect. 7.5.2.

33. David Nissan and Julian Le Grand, *A Capital Idea: Start-Up Grants for Young People* (London: Fabian Society, 2000). Nissan and Le Grand propose to give each individual the right to £50,000 by gratuitous transfers from others, with all wealth transfers (inheritances, gifts, and bequests) beyond this being subject to tax. They estimate that a £10,000 capital grant could be financed at an average tax rate on wealth transfers of 25%.
34. Ibid. 12–13.
35. Kelly and Lissauer, *Ownership for All*.
36. HM Treasury, *Saving and Assets for All* (London, HM Treasury, 2001).
37. Ibid. 17.
38. Ibid. 18.
39. See e.g. Robert Kuttner, 'Rampant Bull', *American Prospect*, 39 (July–Aug. 1998), 30–6.
40. See John Stuart Mill, *On Liberty* (1859; Harmondsworth: Penguin, 1984), 173.
41. See Philippe Van Parijs, *Real Freedom for All: What (if Anything) Can Justify Capitalism?* (Oxford: Oxford University Press, 1995), 45–8.
42. Ackerman and Alstott, *The Stakeholder Society*, 133–42.
43. I owe the term 'Life Account' to Sue Regan. See Sue Regan, 'Asset-Based Welfare: Options and Policy Design Questions', paper prepared for the seminar 'Asset-Based Welfare', Institute for Public Policy Research, London, Nov. 2000.
44. I argued in Sect. 7.3 that something like a housing allowance might serve as a way of recognizing each citizen's primitive resource right in relation to land, though the fit is clearly very approximate.
45. Considerations of this sort arguably underlie Ackerman and Alstott's insistence that eligibility for capital grants be restricted to those who lack a criminal record and who successfully complete high school: such restrictions give individuals an incentive to stay on the right side of the law and to finish school and this, in turn, will nurture dispositions towards forward-thinking and personal responsibility.
46. Thus far, IDA schemes have been administered by local organizations based in low-income communities, and offer savers training in financial literacy: indeed, participation in programmes designed to build financial literacy may be a requirement of receiving the government's matching contribution. For more details, see Larry Beeferman and Sandra Venner, *Promising State Asset Development Policies: Promoting Economic Well-Being among Low-Income Households* (Waltham, Mass.: Asset Development Institute, Center on Hunger and Poverty, Brandeis University, 2001), and Robert Friedman and Michael Sherraden, 'Asset-Based Policy in the United States', paper prepared for the 'International Assets Seminar', Center for Social Development/Institute for Public Policy Research, London, Jan. 2001. IDAs have provided the model for the so-called Saving Gateway proposed in the British government's recent consultation paper, *Saving and Assets for All* (see n. 36).

47. See Ackerman and Alstott, *The Stakeholder Society*, 162, where the authors cite recent research which estimates that only 10–15% of observed earnings inequality can be explained by genetic differences between people.
48. See Robert W. Fogel, *The Fourth Great Awakening and the Future of Egalitarianism* (Chicago: University of Chicago Press, 2000), 222–3, who refers to universal public education as 'the largest socialist enterprise in history'.
49. See Jon Elster, 'Self-Realization in Work and Politics: The Marxist Conception of the Good Life', in Jon Elster and Karl Ove Moene (eds.), *Alternatives to Capitalism* (Cambridge: Cambridge University Press, 1989), 127–58.
50. This, at least, is the argument of Samuel Bowles and Herbert Gintis. See e.g. their 'Efficient Redistribution: New Rules for Communities, States and Markets', in Erik Olin Wright (ed.), *Recasting Egalitarianism: New Rules for Communities, States and Markets* (London: Verso, 1998), 3–71, specifically 36–9.
51. Here I borrow one of the central intuitions of Robert van der Veen and Philippe Van Parijs's case for basic income in their article 'A Capitalist Road to Communism', *Theory and Society*, 15 (1986), 635–55.
52. Vulnerability and exploitation in the domestic context depend on the costs attached to the respective exit options of the partners in a household; many women are currently vulnerable and exploited in view of the relatively and absolutely high costs of the exit option. In a variety of ways, basic capital will increase the feasibility of the exit option, and can therefore also be expected to reduce the extent of domestic exploitation. For helpful analysis of the problem of domestic exploitation, on which I draw here, see Susan Moller Okin, *Justice, Gender, and the Family* (New York: Basic Books, 1989), 134–69.
53. See Stewart Wood, 'Education and Training: Tensions at the Heart of the British Third Way', in Stuart White (ed.), *New Labour: The Progressive Future?* (Basingstoke: Palgrave, 2001), 47–62, specifically 59.
54. See Karla Hoff, 'Market Failures and the Distribution of Wealth: A Perspective from the Economics of Information', in Wright (ed.), *Recasting Egalitarianism*, 332–57.
55. I take the concept of the 'global net steady-state effect' of a policy from Jon Elster. See Jon Elster and Karl Ove Moene, 'Introduction', in Elster and Moene (eds.), *Alternatives to Capitalism*, 1–38, specifically 15–21.
56. For further ideas about how asset-based redistributions might improve economic performance, see Bowles and Gintis, 'Efficient Redistribution'. See also Philippe Aghion and Peter Howitt, *Endogenous Growth Theory* (Cambridge, Mass.: MIT Press, 1998).
57. See Jean-Jacques Rousseau, 'Political Economy' (1755), in Rousseau, *The Social Contract*, ed. Christopher Betts (Oxford: Oxford University Press, 1994), 3–41, specifically 27–8.

58. James Meade, *Agathatopia: The Economics of Partnership* (Aberdeen: University of Aberdeen, 1989).

59. See e.g. Hugh Dalton, *Principles of Public Finance*, 7th edn. (London: Routledge, 1932), 173–80. Meade was one of a group of young economists whom Dalton encouraged to help advise the Labour Party and the British government in the 1930s and 1940s.

60. Gerald Holtham, 'Ownership and Social Democracy', in Andrew Gamble and Tony Wright (eds.), *The New Social Democracy* (Oxford: Blackwell, 1999), 53–68, specifically 61. Holtham envisages using the community fund to finance increments to health-care and educational spending. See also Gerald Holtham, 'A Community Fund could Save Social Democracy', *The Independent* (18 Apr. 1995). The community fund also played a central role in the thinking of Britain's Social Democratic and Liberal Parties in the 1980s and early 1990s. See e.g. Paddy Ashdown, *Citizens' Britain* (London: Fourth Estate, 1989), 128–30.

61. The idea was floated by Bill Clinton in his 1999 State of the Union Address as a way of ensuring the long-term solvency of the federal pensions scheme. Nothing came of the proposal, and it is unlikely to be revived in the near future.

62. See J. Patrick O'Brien and Dennis O. Olson, 'The Alaska Permanent Fund and Dividend Distribution Program', *Public Finance Quarterly*, 18 (1990), 139–56.

63. When it established a new public pensions system in 1959, the Swedish government channelled some of the new pensions taxes into public agencies (the APs) which were required to use these tax revenues to help finance new investments in the public and private sectors. These original agencies were not allowed to invest in shares, but in 1973 the government modified the AP system by establishing a new agency, the Fourth AP Fund, which was mandated to use its resources to purchase shares in the Swedish corporate sector. Additional collective share ownership funds, the wage-earner funds, and a Fifth AP Fund were respectively established in 1982 and 1988. By 1990 these funds together held shares equal to about 7% of the total net value of the corporate sector. The funds were managed by boards which included union, employer, and government representatives, and, operating on largely commercial criteria alone, they consistently made a good return on their investments. The wage-earner funds have since been abolished. For a detailed discussion of the politics of collective asset ownership in Sweden, see Jonas Pontusson, *The Limits of Social Democracy: Investment Politics in Sweden* (Ithaca, NY: Cornell University Press, 1992).

64. John Rawls, *A Theory of Justice* (1971), rev. edn. (Oxford: Oxford University Press, 1999), pp. xiv–xv, and, at greater length, Rawls, *Justice as Fairness: A Restatement* (Cambridge, Mass.: Harvard University Press, 2001), 135–40, 158–62.

65. In a related vein, Sam Brittan proposed to use revenues from North Sea Oil to establish universal individualized capital stakes. See Brittan, *The Role and Limits of Government: Essays in Political Economy* (Minneapolis: University of Minnesota Press, 1983), 260–1.

66. See Rudolf Meidner, *Employee Investment Funds: An Approach to Collective Capital Formation* (London: George Allen & Unwin, 1978). The politics of the wage-earner fund proposal are analysed in depth in Pontusson, *The Limits of Social Democracy.*

67. For a proposal of this sort—state-centred Meidnerism—see Ronald Dore, *Taking Japan Seriously: A Confucian Perspective on Leading Economic Issues* (Stanford: University of California Press, 1987), 222–3.

68. See Stuart M. Speiser, *The USOP Handbook: A Guide to Designing Universal Share Ownership Plans for the United States and Great Britain* (New York: Council on International and Public Affairs, 1986). Speiser's proposal also attracted some discussion in British Liberal Party circles in the 1980s.

69. For a concrete wealth tax proposal, see Edward Wolff, 'Time for a Wealth Tax?', *Boston Review*, 21 (1996), 1–4. Further possibilities are discussed in Holtham, 'Ownership and Social Democracy', specifically 61–2.

70. Holtham, 'Ownership and Social Democracy', 61.

71. I should note, however, that some proponents of community funds do see them as a device for achieving greater popular control over the flow of investable resources. Particularly noteworthy here is a recent article by Robin Blackburn in which he argues for legislation to democratize the management of existing occupational pension funds, and for the establishment of popularly managed community funds, based on collective, state-enforced saving, to provide further state pensions. Blackburn speculates that, in time, it may be possible to link management of the various funds together in such a way as to establish real popular control over investment flows: a system of 'complex socialism'. See Robin Blackburn, 'The New Collectivism: Pension Reform, Grey Capitalism, and Complex Socialism', *New Left Review*, 233 (Jan.–Feb. 1999), 3–65. Whether it is desirable to employ community funds in the way Blackburn envisages is debatable. Blackburn argues that this programme of democratization will strike a blow against the endemic 'short-termism' of Anglo-American capital markets, and so improve, rather than impair, economic performance. Others, I am sure, will see in his proposals a recipe for the undue politicization of capital markets. I adopt a strictly agnostic stance on the issue for purposes of this volume.

Chapter 9

1. For an early and excellent outline of this approach, championing the Earned Income Tax Credit, see David T. Ellwood, *Poor Support: Poverty*

in the American Family (New York: Basic Books, 1988). For a discussion of how this approach might be developed in Britain, see Carey Oppenheim, 'Enabling Participation? New Labour's Welfare-to-Work Policies', in Stuart White (ed.), *New Labour: The Progressive Future?* (Basingstoke: Palgrave, 2001), 77–92.

2. See Janet C. Gornick and Marcia K. Meyers, 'Building the Dual Earner/Dual Carer Society: Policy Developments in Europe', paper prepared for the conference 'Rethinking Social Protection', Minda de Gunzburg Center for European Studies, Harvard University, 26–8 Jan. 2001.

3. For a helpful overview of policy options in this area, see Helen Wilkinson, 'The Family Way: Navigating a Third Way in Family Policy', in Ian Hargreaves and Ian Christie (eds.), *Tomorrow's Politics: The Third Way and Beyond* (London: Demos, 1998), 111–25, esp. 122–3 on 'new parentalism'.

4. For an excellent review of the issues, see Harry Brighouse, *School Choice and Social Justice* (Oxford: Oxford University Press, 2000).

5. Bruce Ackerman and Anne Alstott, *The Stakeholder Society* (New Haven: Yale University Press, 1999), 155–77.

6. See e.g. Robert M. Solow, *Work and Welfare* (Princeton: Princeton University Press, 1998); Richard Layard, 'The Prevention of Long-Term Unemployment', in John Philpott (ed.), *Working for Full Employment* (London: Routledge, 1997), 190–203; Richard Arneson, 'Is Work Special? Justice and the Distribution of Employment', *American Political Science Review*, 84 (1990), 1121–41; and Michael Rustin, 'A Statutory Right to Work', in Rustin, *For a Pluralist Socialism* (London: Verso, 1985), 147–72.

7. One possibility that seems broadly consistent with fair reciprocity would consist of a modest unconditional citizen's pension paid out of general tax revenues, combined with a system of compulsory saving for funded pensions in which contributions of high-paid workers are used to subsidize the contributions of low-paid workers and the state meets some or all of the contributions of care workers. But one would need to think harder, for example, about how such arrangements would relate to the universal capital-grant scheme.

8. See Martin Rhodes, 'The Political Economy of Social Pacts: "Competitive Corporatism" and European Welfare Reform', in Paul Pierson (ed.), *The New Politics of the Welfare State* (Oxford: Oxford University Press, 2001), 165–94.

9. See Philippe Van Parijs, *Real Freedom for All: What (if Anything) Can Justify Capitalism?* (Oxford: Oxford University Press, 1995), 226–30.

10. For an argument to this effect, see David Miller, *On Nationality* (Oxford: Oxford University Press, 1995).

11. For an argument that nationalistic sentiment can be fully compatible with, and can indeed help inspire, transnational solidarity in support of justice,

see my 'Republicanism, Patriotism, and Global Justice', in Daniel A. Bell and Avner de Shalit (eds.), *Forms of Justice* (New York: Rowman & Littlefield, forthcoming).

12. For a recent helpful review of the literature, see Christopher Pierson, *Hard Choices: Social Democracy in the 21st Century* (Oxford: Polity Press, 2001), 64–89. On the (limited) role of tax competition in constraining options for redistribution, see also Andrew Glyn, 'Aspirations, Constraints, and Outcomes', in Andrew Glyn (ed.), *Social Democracy in Neoliberal Times* (Oxford: Oxford University Press, 2001), 1–20, specifically 11–13.

13. For example, in the early stages of this debate Andrew Glyn contended that the growth in international trade, as measured by the share of national product going to exports, had not increased very much in recent years, and that foreign direct investment, while it had increased, still accounted for a very modest share of overall investment expenditures in the advanced capitalist countries. See Andrew Glyn, 'Social Democracy and Full Employment', *New Left Review*, 211 (1995), 33–55.

14. See e.g. Geoffrey Garrett, *Partisan Politics in the Global Economy* (Cambridge: Cambridge University Press, 1998); Paul Pierson, 'Investigating the Welfare State at Century's End', in Pierson (ed.), *New Politics of the Welfare State*, 1–16.

15. See Adair Turner, *Just Capital: The Liberal Economy* (Basingstoke: Macmillan, 2001).

16. This claim, and the argument that follows, is indebted to Glyn, 'Social Democracy and Full Employment', and 'Aspirations, Constraints, and Outcomes'.

17. Robert Rowthorn and Ramana Ramaswamy, *Deindustrialization: Causes and Implications*, IMF Working Paper 97/42 (Washington: International Monetary Fund, 1997).

18. 'It was precisely the absence of a credible policy for reducing and holding down inflation, that is for containing distributional conflict, that made the turn to deflation inevitable . . .'. See Glyn, 'Social Democracy and Full Employment', 50.

19. Investors need to be assured that citizens will be constrained to accept the tax implications of their public-spending preferences, and that they will not try to escape the implications of their implicit tax preferences for take-home pay through compensatory wage increases. The first assurance is necessary because investors will reasonably view regular recourse to deficit-financing as likely to lead to higher inflation (if only because inflation is a good way to reduce the real value of debt). This assurance can be achieved if the government is able to make credible commitments to fiscal probity, i.e. to avoid recourse to large-scale deficit-financing and the accumulation of substantial public debt. The second assurance can be achieved through coordinated wage agreements, but agreements may only exhibit the requisite level of moderation where the government

makes a credible commitment to monetary discipline, i.e. refuses to allow the money supply to grow to accommodate rising inflation (which implies a willingness to allow unemployment to rise in the short run in place of inflation). Central-bank independence is one way a government might seek to make a credible commitment to monetary discipline.

20. See Stuart White, 'Trade Unionism in a Liberal State', in Amy Gutmann (ed.), *Freedom of Association* (Princeton: Princeton University Press, 1998), 330–56.

21. This is an important cautionary theme of Jelle Visser and Anton Hemerijck's account of the revival and transformation of Dutch corporatism. See Visser and Hemerijck, *'A Dutch Miracle': Job Growth, Welfare Reform and Corporatism in the Netherlands* (Amsterdam: University of Amsterdam Press, 1998).

22. See Rhodes, 'Political Economy of Social Pacts', and also Maurizio Ferrera, Anton Hemerijck, and Martin Rhodes, 'Effective Responses: Policy Mixes and Institutional Reform', in their *The Future of Social Europe: Recasting Work and Welfare in the New Economy*, report prepared for the Portuguese Presidency of the European Union, 2000, excerpted in Anthony Giddens (ed.), *The Global Third Way Debate* (Oxford: Polity Press, 2001), 114–33. Ferrera *et al.* present 'competitive corporatism' as a desirable form of governmental innovation to facilitate and coordinate the adoption of innovative employment and social policies.

23. See Ruy Teixeira and Joel Rogers, *America's Forgotten Majority: Why the White Working Class Still Matters* (New York: Basic Books, 2000), 23–31, who attribute this position to thinkers associated with the Democratic Leadership Council in the United States. For a statement of the latter's position, see William Galston and Elaine Kamarck, 'Five Realities that Will Shape 21st Century US Politics', *Blueprint: Ideas for a New Century*, 1 (1998), 6–27.

24. Here I follow Teixeira and Rogers, *America's Forgotten Majority*, 18–19, though the essential idea arguably goes back at least as far as Antonio Gramsci's discussion of hegemony.

25. If increased inequality involves a fall in the pay of low-skilled workers, and a corresponding contraction in the generosity and/or availability of welfare benefits, citizens with poor labour market prospects may find criminal activity an attractive alternative. For discussion of this dynamic in the United States, see Richard Freeman, 'The Limits of Wage Flexibility to Curing Unemployment', *Oxford Review of Economic Policy*, 11 (1995), 63–72.

26. See Richard Wilkinson, *Unhealthy Societies: The Afflictions of Inequality* (London: Routledge, 1996).

27. For powerful diagrammatic illustration of the latter claim, see Torben Iversen, 'The Dynamics of Welfare State Expansion: Trade Openness, De-industrialization, and Partisan Politics', in Pierson (ed.), *New Politics of the Welfare State*, 45–79, specifically p. 70, fig. 2.7.

28. See Torben Iversen and Anne Wren, 'Equality, Employment and Budgetary Restraint: The Trilemma of the Service Economy', *World Politics*, 50 (1998), 507–46.
29. See Gosta Esping-Andersen, 'Recasting Welfare Regimes for a Postindustrial Era', in Esping-Andersen, *Social Foundations of Postindustrial Economies* (Oxford: Oxford University Press, 1999), 170–84, esp. 180–4.
30. In the US context, see Mona Harrington, *Care and Equality* (New York: Alfred Knopf, 1999). See also Esping-Andersen, 'Recasting Welfare Regimes', for a more general analysis of the problem.
31. This implies the need to avoid severe withdrawal tapers whereby benefit is clawed back pound for pound as earnings increase.
32. A point emphasized by Adam Przeworski in 'How Many Ways Can be Third?', in Glyn (ed.), *Social Democracy in Neoliberal Times*, 312–33, specifically 332.
33. See e.g. Esping-Andersen, *Social Foundations*, 183–4. See also Stewart Wood, 'Education and Training: Tensions at the Heart of the British Third Way', in White (ed.), *New Labour*, 47–62.
34. As Mona Harrington puts it (*Care and Equality*, 30), 'The reigning idea is not at all complicated: the private family is responsible for family care and should provide it through its own resources.'
35. For an argument along these lines, addressed to a popular audience, see Stuart White and Diana Gardner, 'Juggling with Reciprocity: Towards a Better Balance', in Anna Coote (ed.), *The New Gender Agenda: Why Women Still Want More* (London: Institute for Public Policy Research, 2000), 99–108.
36. See David Miller, *Principles of Social Justice* (Cambridge, Mass.: Harvard University Press, 2000), 61–92.
37. See Theda Skocpol, 'A Partnership with American Families', in Stanley B. Greenberg and Theda Skocpol (eds.), *The New Majority: Toward a Popular Progressive Politics* (New Haven: Yale University Press, 1997), 104–29, specifically 111. Skocpol's argument in this article is based on her earlier work on the development of the welfare state in the United States, notably *Protecting Soldiers and Mothers: The Political Origins of Social Policy in the United States* (Cambridge, Mass.: Harvard University Press, 1992).
38. Skocpol, 'Partnership with American Families', 118.
39. See Teixeira and Rogers, *America's Forgotten Majority*.
40. Ibid. 19; see also pp. 62, 156–7.
41. According to Teixeira and Rogers (ibid. 62), 'government did almost nothing to relieve [their problems]. It seemed, by turns, monumentally indifferent, hopelessly feeble, and even insulting to [the] majority's core values—fair reward for effort, the centrality of hard work and individual achievement, social responsibility and order, equal opportunity for all'.
42. There is at least a broad similarity between the reform programme associated with civic minimum, as described above in Sect. 9.1, and the reform

programme outlined by Teixeira and Rogers as a basis for winning back support from the white working class. See ibid. 155–6.

43. See e.g. Ferrera *et al.*, 'The Future of Social Europe'; Esping-Andersen, *Social Foundations*, 17–184. The proposed exchange is most explicitly and fully described in the paper by Ferrera *et al.*

44. This would certainly seem to be the import of Ferrera *et al.*, 'The Future of Social Europe'. Note that in the Dutch case an important feature of the overall restructuring process has been to encourage the growth in part-time and temporary employment. Unions have agreed to a relaxation of the employment rights of full-time core workers in return for the extension of employment and generous welfare rights to more peripheral workers.

45. For a very thorough discussion, to which I am indebted, see Paul Pierson, 'Coping with Permanent Austerity: Welfare State Restructuring in Affluent Democracies', in Pierson (ed.), *New Politics of the Welfare State*, 410–56, esp. 445–54. I should emphasize that my discussion in the main text does not distinguish sufficiently between restructuring in the context of so-called 'conservative' and 'social democratic' welfare states. Pierson's paper provides a discussion that is sensitive to these differences.

46. See Will Kymlicka, *Contemporary Political Philosophy: An Introduction*, 2nd edn. (Oxford: Oxford University Press, 2001), 95.

47. See Samuel Bowles and Herbert Gintis, 'Is Egalitarianism Passé? Homo Reciprocans and the Future of Egalitarian Politics', *Boston Review*, 23 (Dec.–Jan. 1998–9), 4–10.

48. This line of argument is central to Philippe Van Parijs's helpful discussion of globalization scepticism. See Van Parijs, *Real Freedom for All*, 226–30.

49. Leonard Hobhouse, *The Labour Movement*, 3rd edn. (New York: Macmillan, 1912), 75.

50. On the form and structure of IDA schemes, see Ch. 8 n. 46.

51. This issue also arises, of course, in considering how fast the government should build up a community fund to help finance social-justice expenditures in the future.

52. For a lucid, insightful discussion of the situation, see G. M. Tamas, 'On Post-Fascism', *Boston Review* (Summer 2000), 42–6.

53. Mead's argument has recently found an echo among some US social democrats. According to David Glenn, 'There is a plausible case to be made that the 1996 welfare reform law will, perversely, strengthen the safety-net in the long run by bringing labor and other interest groups together in new alliances.... If America's poor are perceived as "fellow workers"—so this argument runs—the public will be more likely to support decent public policies, not only for the very poor but for the broader working-class.' Evidence for such a trend includes an increase in the national minimum wage since 1996, and the child-care and health-care programmes that many states have initiated to complement welfare reform. See David Glenn, 'I Thought You Said She Worked Full Time', *Dissent* (Summer 2001), 101–5, specifically 104.

INDEX